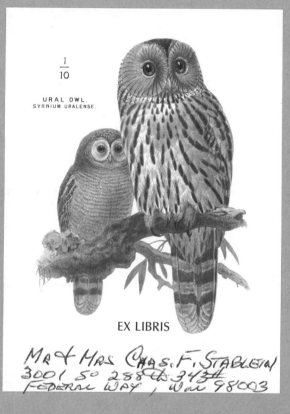

$\dfrac{1}{10}$

URAL OWL.
SYRNIUM URALENSE.

EX LIBRIS

MANY HAPPY RETURNS:
THE LIVES OF EDGAR CAYCE

Many Happy Returns

THE LIVES OF EDGAR CAYCE

W. H. CHURCH

Harper & Row, Publishers, San Francisco
Cambridge, Hagerstown, New York, Philadelphia
London, Mexico City, São Paulo, Singapore, Sydney

To protect the identity of those individuals, living or dead, who obtained psychic readings from Edgar Cayce and who appear in the pages of this narrative, the individual case numbers have been substituted for actual names in the present.

Extracts from the Edgar Cayce readings are identified by file reference number throughout, usually appearing in the notes at the rear of the book but sometimes incorporated in the body of the text itself. (The number to the left of the hyphen identifies the specific individual or subject, while the number following the hyphen denotes the sequence, where multiple readings have been given for that particular individual or subject.)

Chapters 8, 13, and 14 were previously published in abridged form in the *A.R.E. Journal,* under the titles "Edgar Cayce and the Siege of Troy," "The Two Lives of John Bainbridge," and "A Child of Love," respectively (issues of publication, as named: vol. XVIII, no. 5, Sept. 1983; vol. XIX, no. 1, Jan. 1984; and vol. XVI, no. 6, Nov. 1981).

FIRST EDITION

Library of Congress Cataloging in Publication Data
Church, W. H.
    MANY HAPPY RETURNS.
    Bibliography: p.
    1. Cayce, Edgar, 1877–1945.   2. Psychical research—
United States—Biography.   3. Reincarnation—Case Studies.
I. Title.
BF1027.C3C48   1984   133.8′092′4 [B]   84–47717
ISBN 0-06-250150-X

84 85 86 87 88 10 9 8 7 6 5 4 3 2 1

For Gladys, who knew him best

Contents

Preface

The late American psychic Edgar Cayce probably did more than any other contemporary figure to reintroduce and popularize the ancient doctrine of reincarnation, which Western civilization had arbitrarily rejected when it decided to adopt Christianity.

Yet the notion that Christianity and reincarnation are somehow incompatible is a tragic misconception. It has created a schism where one never should have existed. For one who is willing to look, there is evidence enough in passages from both the Old and the New Testaments of the Bible to support the conclusion that not only was reincarnation a respected and commonly accepted doctrine in the days of the ancient prophets but it may well have been a doctrine accepted and taught by Jesus Himself. Certainly the apostle Paul appears to have espoused a belief in reincarnation quite openly, as is attested to in certain sayings of his about the synonymity of Adam and Jesus—and in more mystical terms, Melchizedek and Jesus, as the risen Christ.

Can any other doctrine than reincarnation and its corollary, the law of karma, so readily explain or justify the seeming inequities of the human condition in which we find ourselves? Karma, which is simply the law of cause and effect carried forward from one incarnation to another, is totally in consonance with two well-known biblical precepts: "As ye sow, so shall ye reap," and, "As the tree falls, so shall it lie."

As Edgar Cayce so succinctly put it, "The entity is ever meeting self." This was the recurrent theme in more than twenty-five hundred life readings he gave, including those given on his own past lives. There can be no better introduction to the subject of reincarnation and karma, surely, than a true narrative, such as the present one, tracing the long cyclical journey of a soul in search of its Self.

And when that soul-entity is Edgar Cayce, we are bound to gain some unique perspectives: not only was he a master of the subject, when we consider his extensive trance-state counsel to the many hundreds of people who had life readings from him over a span of several decades, but his own prior lives seem to have run the gamut from saintly priest to abject sinner, thus providing us with a rich diversity of examples of soul development and soul retrogression to study and ponder.

This story concerns a soul-entity who was unusual in many ways—perhaps older than most, and probably wiser. The reader will discover, among other things, that Edgar Cayce was blessed from the beginning with a special relationship with the Master of men. It was a relationship that inevitably shaped and colored his character and often brought him back into the earth-plane with an intensity of purpose and a selfless dedication that few of us can match or even comprehend. Not too surprisingly, one of the themes repeatedly stressed in the Edgar Cayce readings was the need to stand aside and watch self pass by. Cayce, ever fearful of the cult of personality, warned repeatedly against making a "cult" of any kind of his work here in the earth, which he felt should stand on its own and speak for itself. Above all, he eschewed any attempt on the part of well-meaning individuals to elevate him to a status above his fellow mortals. He well knew what a sinner he had been in some of his prior lifetimes and what a sinner in many respects he still was. He certainly didn't want to add to his karmic load the sin of self-glorification!

In consequence, Edgar Cayce was probably one of the most genuinely humble, self-effacing men who ever lived. Although it may be hard to maintain that image of him in light of some of the unusual revelations about his past lives and accomplishments contained in this narrative, let us remember that only those souls who have tasted greatness can come to appreciate true humility. Out of his many lives, with their multitude of lessons, Cayce had finally learned that the way to God is through self-immolation; there is no other way to reach the Higher Self, or to nurture the God-seed within us.

Finally, though the underlying philosophy of the Edgar Cayce readings is inevitably and closely linked to the Christian religion in which Edgar himself grew up and which he always practiced in an exemplary manner, it is worth noting that tolerance of other religious faiths and belief systems remained paramount in his psychic readings and in his personal life. Indeed, he had an abiding respect for that governing principle found at the root of most of the world's major religions, "The Lord thy God is One!" The spirit of this teaching was eloquently captured in metaphorical language in the following excerpt from Work Reading 254-87: "Are there not trees of oak, of ash, of pine? There are the needs of these for meeting this or that experience . . . Then, all will fill their place. Find not fault with *any,* but rather show forth as to just how good a pine, or ash, or oak, or *vine,* thou art!"

Author's Note: Here and there, throughout the narrative that follows, there inevitably occur instances wherein the information provided in the Edgar Cayce readings has been too incomplete and tenuous to provide a definite conclusion. In such cases, I have endeavored to develop the most likely and logical dénouement possible. I acknowledge, however, that others looking at the same information in the readings from a different perspective might well draw different conclusions, with an equal probability of accuracy.

1. The Flight of the Egret

The date was January 3, 1945.

A lone egret, perched on the shore of Lake Holly in Virginia Beach, Virginia, suddenly flapped its lovely, snow-white wings and rose like an omen over the Cayce residence. Slowly it circled the brown-shingled house, then disappeared toward the east—a receding white dot swallowed up in the gray, wintry mist that crouched, catlike, over the broad swell of the Atlantic Ocean.

The muffled sounds of grief, coming from a corner of the house where Gertrude Cayce was sobbing softly to herself, could barely be heard in the bedroom where her husband, Edgar, sat silently in his wheelchair, watching from the window as the snowy egret took to the air. He saw in its sudden, majestic flight a symbol of the liberated soul's departure, and in his heart he felt a great surge of rejoicing.

As he neared the end of his sixty-seventh year, the famed American psychic Edgar Cayce was physically exhausted—"burnt out," quite literally, from an overexpenditure of his own psychic energies in service to others. The tall, gaunt frame hunched in the wheelchair looked suddenly smaller than it was, and exceedingly frail. Head slightly tilted, mouth small and solemn like a wing bent down, the once-mobile face now seemed drawn and expressionless. Only in the extraordinary eyes, as blue and penetrating as ever, could one still glimpse the lively image of Edgar Cayce's former self.

In these past few years, the urgent appeals for psychic readings, as they were called, had increased severalfold as his fame increased and the war introduced new concerns for which many sought psychic answers. Mr. Cayce had found himself unable to turn away anyone who sought his help or to take the necessary periods of rest and recuperation to restore his dangerously depleted energies. Finally, he had suffered a stroke that left him partly paralyzed. In his weakened condition, the end now appeared imminent—without the intervention of a miracle.

The "miracle" for which those around him all hoped and prayed was a physical rejuvenation. The readings indicated that Edgar Cayce had once before experienced just such a bodily regeneration, through the raising of spiritual energies, during a much earlier cycle in the earth. It was during an incarnation in ancient Egypt, as the high priest Ra Ta, in the second dynasty of that particular era. At that time, the aging spiritual leader and a contingent of his loyal followers had returned from a period of exile to begin a new phase of work. (Many of them, if their individual "life" readings could be accepted as true, had now reincarnated to be with him again, as Edgar Cayce, for the furtherance of that same work, which was to aid mankind in finding the way back to the divine Source.) The resuscitated priest had not only regained his youthful vigor in that early Egyptian incarnation but had lived on for another hundred years. During that period of grace, the Great Pyramid at Gizeh was built under his direction, as high priest, with Hermes—an incarnation of the evolving Christ—as the master architect. (Actually, the famous pyramid was never designed as a tomb, as is commonly supposed, but as a temple of initiation, as well as a prophetic record in stone of coming events in the earth leading up to the end of our present century. All of this revealing information, and more, had been presented in a startling series of readings on the subject of Cayce's Egyptian incarnation.)

The notion of having lived in the earth before, or having played a significant role in the shaping of history during at least one, and perhaps as many as several, of those prior lives, had initially been very disconcerting to Mr. Cayce. A genuinely humble man, he eschewed such honors for himself; besides, he didn't know what to make of such a strange doctrine as reincarnation. His religious roots were in a typically Southern, Protestant background, noted for its rigid orthodoxy. Even the unusual nature of his psychic gifts, which had accustomed his mind to a whole new set of realities since childhood, had not quite prepared Edgar Cayce to accept, at first, what most self-respecting Christians of his acquaintance, if questioned on the subject, would have rejected with genuine abhorrence as a heathen belief system. And he would have been quick to agree that the idea of earthly recurrence, or reincarnation, did seem to be totally at odds with the tenets of the Christian faith as he had learned them.

But Edgar began to wonder: What if some of those tenets reflected a misinterpretation of the original teachings of the Christ? Was it not wholly possible that reincarnation might have been a teaching acceptable to the early church fathers, as certain scholarly sources claimed? Given the proliferation of "isms," "schisms," conflicting translations of biblical texts, and such, that had evolved from the first century onward, there at least seemed to be a logical basis for exchanging an outright rejection of reincarnation for a more tolerant form of skepticism toward that very ancient doctrine. At any rate, Edgar had learned to trust the information that came to him in trance-state through his own psychic readings. Its accuracy had been proven over and over. Moreover, it appeared to meet the highest spiritual tests, as well.

The basis for the information in his readings—unlike the less reliable pronouncements of the "mediumistic" psychic, who surrenders his or her will to become the passive channel for a "control" on the spirit-plane—had been identified as a unique process of "going within," through the use of his own etheric energies, and directly contacting the Universal Forces, without the need for an intermediary. Therefore, when faced with his first real ideological conflict, it was not too surprising that Cayce finally opted in favor of the readings and reincarnation. Besides, as a man who had made it a practice to read the Bible from cover to cover once a year, throughout his life, Edgar recalled that it contained many veiled allusions to reincarnation that the more orthodox chose to ignore. In particular, he thought of Job's haunting question: "If a man die, shall he live again?" And there was that other passage from Job, wherein the prophet appears to answer himself: "Naked came I out of my mother's womb, and naked shall I return thither." Moreover, had not the Master Himself alluded more than once to that same time-honored doctrine? First, there was His startling statement, "Before Abraham was, I *am*"—the ever-existent soul! And did He not speak plainly enough in identifying John the Baptist as a reappearance in the earth of Elijah the prophet? Also, He knew there had been rumors among the people as to His own identity as one of the ancient prophets reborn, although He neither confirmed nor denied such allegations. Yet there was Paul's meaningful reference in Corinthians to the "first" Adam and the "last" Adam. In that reference, and again in Romans 5:14, the apostle seemed to be speaking in more than mere symbols: he appeared to be identifying Jesus as a perfected incarnation of the original Adam—an interpretation, in fact, that Cayce's own readings were eventually to confirm.

As the number of life readings given by Edgar Cayce began to increase, he gradually saw that there were definite karmic patterns emerging in virtually every case. Nothing, it seemed, was by chance. Each entity in the earth was ever meeting itself and reaping the fruits of its former actions. These karmic patterns, moreover, were wholly consistent with spiritual law as presented in the Bible. The "law of karma," in fact, was really nothing more nor less than the familiar law of cause and effect, carried forward from one lifetime to the next. It was supported by two oft-quoted biblical precepts: first, "Whatsoever a man soweth, that shall he also reap," and, as its inevitable corollary, "As the tree falls, so shall it lie." Thus, the doctrine of reincarnation and karma was able to explain in properly biblical, rational terms what seemed always to have eluded the theologians—namely, the puzzling inequities of the human condition in which we all find ourselves. If the good sometimes appear to suffer for naught and the evil to go unpunished, it is only because of our limited perspective of the matter. If we could see into the past lives of the sinner and the saint, as well as the lives yet to come, we would comprehend the workings of divine justice. The judgments of God are not hurried. In His own time, He exacts from each debtor the utmost farthing and bestows upon each returning prodigal son or daughter His utmost blessing.

It is even as the psalmist sang: "He that goeth forth and weepeth, bearing precious seed, shall doubtless come again with rejoicing, bringing his sheaves with him."

Each cycle of entry into earthly consciousness, as the readings made clear, is marked by a renewed opportunity to meet and overcome any sins of omission or commission from the past. This meeting of self may be accomplished through the law of grace, as found in Him, the Redeemer, or through the law of karma and suffering, as set in the lower self and its untamed desires. All depends on the will of the entity, and the choices it makes each time around, until it can free itself from the wheel of death and rebirth in the realms of material consciousness. If it slips during one incarnation, it must make up the slippage during another and another, until its failings are erased. For, the law of the Lord is perfect. Nor has He willed than any soul shall perish.

Flesh, the readings pointed out, becomes the testing portion of the universal vibration, and the earthbound souls must continue here until the human vibration accords with the divine, as in the beginning. In the case of the evolving Christ, who became our Pattern in the earth, the readings indicated that it took some thirty incarnations from His first appearance, as Adam, until His last, as Jesus, to reach a state of full attunement, or at-one-ment with the First Cause. His "resurrection" was a process of raising the fleshly vibration so that His body could resume its celestial form, or Godlike condition, as a true Son of God. (And thus are we, too, gods in the making!)

We may expect, however, that it will take each one of us a similar number of lives, perhaps many more, to repeat the example of our Elder Brother, the Christ, in our cyclical evolution out of the long entrapment in the flesh. Edgar Cayce, through his dreams and readings, experienced recall of more than a dozen prior lives, as well as precognition of at least two earthly appearances yet to come—one in 1998, he was told, when he would re-enter as a "liberator" of oppressed mankind and another as a psychically-gifted child in Nebraska in the century following. In that latter life-time, his dream-experience indicated, he would astonish his elders by recalling intimate details of his twentieth-century appearance as the historical "sleeping prophet" of Virginia Beach.

In the interims between earthly sojourns, according to the readings, a soul-entity experiences other dimensions of consciousness. These have their equivalency in what our three-dimensional consciousness here in the earth-plane perceives as the various planetary spheres within our solar system. Such heavenly bodies as Venus, Mars, and the like certainly do exist as stellar realities, of course; but to an entity in the spiritual realm, after death, they apparently manifest a very different level of reality and rate of vibration than a three-dimensional earth-being can comprehend. Thus, in such deep metaphysical waters, it was perhaps enough to be reminded, as stated in one of the readings, that we live in a relative world, a relative universe. Here we are as babes, who must take one step at a time. As we take each step, the next is revealed to us. . . .

To Edgar Cayce now, as he sat at the window of his bedroom, monitoring the egret's rapidly vanishing flight into the eastern sky, the next step was close at hand.

His long-awaited rejuvenation was about to begin, but not quite in the manner that those around him had expected. In fact, Edgar had realized for some time now that his rejuvenation during that much earlier life in Egypt had been for a definite purpose that had no corollary in the present. His work in the earth this time around was essentially finished, with the giving of more than fourteen thousand psychic readings, which would form an inexhaustible research nucleus for generations to come. Also, he had pioneered in the establishment of holistic healing—treating body, mind, and spirit as one—as a legitimate, and sometimes near-miraculous, modality for the treatment of virtually any form of illness, including those often labeled incurable. In summary, his had been a life of continuous, unselfish service to others. Yet the next phase of the work, consisting mainly of intensive research into the material in the readings and worldwide dissemination of the findings, did not require his presence. Besides, the readings had once pointed out to Edgar that his psychic and healing activities in the earth were really the work of the Lord, by whom he had been blessed to serve as a channel. Therefore, Edgar was confident that other channels, just as worthy as himself, would be appointed to carry on when he was gone. In particular, he thought of his eldest son, Hugh Lynn, now at war in Europe, who could be relied upon to play a pivotal role in the decades immediately ahead, along with Edgar's faithful long-time secretary and friend, Gladys Davis. These two, and others, had been with him from the beginning of time, when they had all emanated from the One, projecting into the earth-plane together. As for his wife, Gertrude, who was also among that early number, Edgar already knew that it would be her soul's choice to follow him shortly to the Other Side.

Death held no fear for him, of course. He knew that life is a continuous stream of experience. Thus, to die in the material plane, as the readings had once stated it, was but to be born again into the spiritual plane. Moreover, this act of passing through God's other door, as the death-experience had been termed, was akin to the journey Edgar Cayce had taken literally thousands of times before in his out-of-body travels while giving psychic readings. All that would be different this time was that he wouldn't be returning. The silver cord must be severed at last, and the flesh-form discarded, in a process of spiritual renewal. This could be regarded as the "real" rejuvenation, and it was the one Edgar had hinted at some days previously when he had cryptically remarked to several of those close to him that they could expect to witness his complete regeneration on January fifth—a date now close at hand.

The doctor arrived as Edgar was showing signs of increasing weakness, so they moved him from his wheelchair to the bed. An oxygen mask was administered; later, however, Edgar was to push it away in a gesture of impatience. Thus did he reject any life-prolonging efforts.

At seven o'clock in the evening, Gladys was on duty at his bedside. Edgar's sister Annie entered the room with a bowlful of oyster stew. Edgar took a few sips of nourishment, then indicated that he had finished. He rested briefly. Moments later, he was dead.

The soul took its exit eastward, in the wake of the egret's earlier flight. It passed, unseen, through God's other door and came to rest in the spiritual plane, beyond the bounds of time and space.

At last the rejuvenation process could begin in earnest. And on the third day—January 5, 1945—the soul-entity's transformation was complete.

That date, not by chance, marked the holding of the funeral service in the living room of the Cayce residence on Arctic Crescent in Virginia Beach. Soon thereafter, the body would be shipped to Hopkinsville, Kentucky, for burial in the place of Cayce's birth; but now the lifeless shell lay on display in its casket. Tearful friends filed by to pay their last respects. However, those who recalled the Virginia Beach psychic's final, cryptic promise, made shortly before his death, realized that the "rejuvenated" prophet they had been told to look for on this date was not to be found in the shallow casket, where their lowered eyes rested fleetingly upon a cold, waxen figure. Rather, he was right in their midst, a warm and tangible, laughing presence. They could feel his nearness in their hearts. And in their minds, there was no doubt about it at all: Edgar Cayce was still very much *alive*.

2. Unraveling the Gordian Knot

In a wily maneuver, Alexander the Great cut the legendary Gordian knot with his sword. Thus, with a single, deft blow, he easily loosed the cord that others could not.

The author who sets out to unravel the intricate and often confusing chronology of events in the prior lives of Edgar Cayce as recorded in the readings might wish for a similarly easy way out of his dilemma. However, no verbal tricks or shortcuts will do. He knows from the outset that he must employ the legitimate skills of painstaking research and rigorous logic if he hopes to present the reader with a relatively knot-free strand of psychic rope on which to thread his story. To make the sequence of events credible, their chronology must fall into place in an orderly pattern that often seems unattainable. Yet let me see if I can offer some explanations that will set aright a number of seeming inconsistencies in a disputed handful of dates (some plainly given in the readings, others implied), while acknowledging with appropriate candor the existence of a few obvious errors of dating in the readings. These latter are not of major consequence in weighing the overall accuracy of this extraordinary psychic saga; nor do they lack a logical *raison d'être*. If we explore their probable causes, I think we can lay them properly to rest.

First, however, let me make some preliminary observations. These concern the nature of the readings themselves, with particular emphasis on their unique characteristics and relative accuracy.

When Edgar Cayce wanted to give a psychic reading, he would first loosen his clothing, such as his belt, necktie, shirtcuffs, and shoelaces, to ensure a perfectly free-flowing circulation. Then, if the reading was to be a physical one—relating to the psychic diagnosis and recommended treatment of a bodily ailment, for example—he would lie down on the couch in his office with his head to the south and his feet to the north. However, if it was to be a life reading—probing the soul records of an entity from the beginning of time—just the opposite polarization was observed. This alternating position had been recommended in one of the readings, although no one had troubled to inquire why. Conceivably, it related to the directional flow of etheronic wave forces in the atmosphere, as I shall try to explain. These waves of energy, sometimes identified in occult literature as *prāna* or *akasha,* apparently permeate the entire universe and were characterized in one of the Edgar Cayce readings as being of a "mental" nature. Thus, Cayce may have utilized these same energy currents, much as one would tune in on certain radio wavelengths, to "pick up" information on the etheric plane, whether transmitted from terrestrial or cosmic sources. But why the reverse polarization—south–north, rather than north–south—when giving a life reading as opposed to a physical reading? Could it be that etheronic currents of a cosmic nature, as they enter earth's atmosphere, flow in one direction, while those of terrestrial origin flow in another? And did the two different types of readings utilize opposing streams of energy? It would appear to be a reasonable hypothesis.

One is reminded, in fact, of a nearly identical theory propounded by André Bovis, a remarkable Frenchman who, in the earlier part of this century, impressed scientific and occult circles alike with his pioneering work on geomagnetic currents as well as the strange energy fields associated with pyramid structures. Bovis believed that the earth has positive magnetic currents running north to south and attributed an east–west flow to negative magnetic currents. But of special interest, we find, was his claim that *"any* body placed in a north–south position will be more or less polarized"[1]—a statement that certainly ties in neatly with Cayce's unique orientation, at least insofar as his *physical* readings were concerned. Moreover, if we follow Bovis's theory a bit further, in respect to what purportedly takes place in a north–south polarized human body, we may unravel a mystery; for in such a body, we are told, "telluric [earthly] currents, both positive and negative, enter through one leg and go out through the opposite hand. At the same time, cosmic currrents from beyond the earth enter through the other hand and foot. The currents also go out through the open eyes."[2] If we can assume, as I think we can, a symbiotic relationship of some sort, or possibly even an esoteric synonymity, between Bovis's oppositely flowing "magnetic" currents of cosmic and terrestrial origin and Cayce's "etheronic wave forces," perhaps we not only will have discovered why Cayce had to reverse his north–south polarization depending upon the type of psychic reading he was giving but will also have laid the groundwork for a better understanding of the operation of psychic phenomena in general. At any rate, it seems reasonable to hypothesize at this juncture that the telluric currents would provide an ideal medium for the conveyance of psychic intelligence on matters of an earthly or physical nature, whereas one would presumably have to "tune in" to cosmic currents to pick up the transmission of the akashic or "soul" records of an entity. If the picture is sometimes blurred or the sound garbled, it is possibly due to local static in the form of physical tiredness on the part of the psychic, improper spiritual preparation for the reading, or mental interference from others. (Such explanations, at any rate, were among those offered by the sleeping Cayce when the subject of inaccurate information in the readings came up—a subject to which we shall return in due time. It plays a crucial role in determining the right choice to make among certain conflicting dates in our psychic saga of the lives of Edgar Cayce.)

Meanwhile, now that the question of polarization is behind us, it is time to go back to the couch in Mr. Cayce's office. We had left him there in a reclining position, relaxed and ready for a psychic session.

Actually, the so-called sleep-state into which Edgar would voluntarily place himself for the giving of a reading (following a suggestion from the conductor, who was usually his wife, Gertrude), has been improperly termed a hypnotic condition. An Indian authority on the subject, Dr. I. C. Sharma, sets us straight: "This sleep-state," he writes, "is actually what the mystics call

Turiya Avastha, or the state of transcendental sleep-consciousness. In this state, which is usually induced voluntarily through the practice of meditation and spiritual self-discipline, the human psyche makes contact with the Cosmic Consciousness and gains knowledge which is not limited by time and space." With specific reference to Edgar Cayce, Sharma adds his view that "his spontaneous mystic ability was the result of the accumulated tendencies of previous incarnations," so that it is therefore "more appropriate to call him a pragmatic mystic than a psychic or hypnotic or sleeping prophet."[3]

Yet another perspective on Cayce's unique psychic ability was volunteered in a trance session given in 1934 by the well-known English mediumistic psychic Eileen Garrett, whose "control" was identified as an Arab named Uvani, dwelling on the "fifth plane."

Uvani, speaking through Mrs. Garrett, explained that Edgar Cayce was "using his full etheric leverage," actually passing into the etheric state when giving a reading, so that he was, as it were, "outside of his body." He was also "drawing upon his own spiritual light" to assist others, "giving you something of his own life. This is what happens."[4]

Uvani acknowledged that Cayce's unusual psychic abilities also depended to a large degree upon the high level of development he had reached in previous incarnations. "Unless he had indeed understood in the past the laws of passivity, the laws of withdrawal, and the inner law of knowing," Uvani explained, "he would not be able to get this reflection through himself," for "he uses his own spirit reflection to see, to hear and to understand."[5]

Referring to the drain on Edgar Cayce's etheric energies, however, Uvani then proposed that Cayce permit him, or other "controls" on his plane of development, to use him as a channel for expression rather than going directly into the etheric plane himself for the information in his readings. As an enticement, he intimated that the language of the readings would come through more clearly with the aid of a helper on the spirit-plane. But later, in a check-reading on Uvani's counsel, not only was there a warning against asking help from those on this or that plane, but it was made clear that Cayce's established method of "turning within" for psychic guidance was to remain unchanged. In fact, on the same date as the check-reading (February 6, 1934), Work Reading 254–71 laid the whole matter unequivocally to rest. On that latter occasion, the sleeping Cayce was specifically asked whether it would be advisable for him to seek the sort of spirit-world assistance that "Uvani claims will increase the coherence and power of the readings." The answer took the form of a pointed question: "Does Uvani claim to know better than the Master who made him?"

No further comment was required.

In that same reading, moreover, the work of Edgar Cayce was defined as "the work of the *Master* of masters." Those around Cayce were all sufficiently humbled by that remark to leave the advice of any mediumistic psychics alone, after that. If Cayce's direct method of approach to the Universal Forces sometimes resulted in jumbled syntax or nebulous phrasing, for one reason or another, that occasional drawback in the readings was of far less serious consequence, surely, than even the best-articulated remarks of a spirit control would be, whose sources and motivation could not be verified or whose level of spiritual development was in all probability inferior to Cayce's.

Edgar's own explanation of his entry into the etheric plane to give a reading was contained in a subsequently published lecture. He tells us how he prepared himself spiritually, through prayer, then awaited guidance from an inward spark of light:

Once lying comfortably, I put both hands up to my forehead, on the spot where observers have told me that the third eye is located, and pray. Interestingly enough, I have unconsciously and instinctively, from the very beginning, adopted the practices used by initiates in meditation. This instinctive putting of my hands to the point midway between my two eyes on my forehead is a case of what I mean.

Then I wait for a few minutes, until I receive what might be called the 'go signal'—a flash of brilliant white light, sometimes tending towards the golden in color. This light is to me the sign that I have made contact. When I do not see it, I know I cannot give the reading.

After seeing the light I move my two hands down to the solar plexus, and—they tell me—my breathing now becomes very deep and rhythmic, from the diaphragm. This goes on for several minutes. When my eyes begin to flutter closed (up till now they have been open, but glazed) the conductor knows I am ready to receive the suggestion [for the reading].[6]

We come, now, to the question of relative accuracy in the readings.

Any impartial researcher into the voluminous body of transcripts on file with the Edgar Cayce Foundation and its affiliate organization, the Association for Research and Englightenment, at Virginia Beach, covering more than fourteen thousand psychic readings given by Edgar Cayce, will have been properly impressed by one aspect, in particular—the never-ending validation process. I refer to the innumerable written testimonials and other supportive documents, as well as pertinent news clippings and updated research notes, appended to the various readings. These appear to confirm the high degree of accuracy Cayce achieved in all those areas where verification of his psychic powers has been available to date. Most notably, this applies to the physical readings, where his psychic diagnosis and recommended treatment of all manner of physical ailments often went contrary to the prevalent views of medical science at the time or to the specific advice of the attending physician in the case. Nevertheless, if doctor and patient could be persuaded to accept his diagnosis and follow his proposed treatment along the holistic lines that were uniquely Cayce's, the results were almost invariably positive and sometimes quite dramatic indeed. Similarly, Cayce's excellent track record as a New Age prophet of distinction continues, as the number of "hits" still accumulates. It is expected that this will be the case right through the end of this century, if major earth changes and other momentous events take place as the Virginia Beach seer predicted. Also, Cayce's psychic work in dream interpretation bore confirmatory fruit on quite a number of occasions throughout his lifetime. Yet, verification of the life readings, each with its record of multiple incarnations, has obviously proved to be more difficult. Only in isolated instances could certain scraps of evidence be uncovered—a tombstone or a historical document, perhaps—to lend validation to one or more of an entity's prior incarnations in the earth. However, in suggesting how one's former-life achievements could be put to the best vocational use in the present, Cayce often hit the nail on the head with an uncanny precision. Confirmation in this area still continues to mount, as the correspondence with younger recipients of life readings is added to the files.

Mostly, however, for those who had life readings it was a matter of accepting the information pretty much "on faith," or perhaps because of the sustaining threads of consistency that seemed to run through the various prior lives reported. There was also the convincingly logical relationship of past developments or failures to unfolding opportunities or restrictions in the present incarnation. (Surely no charlatan could have been gifted with sufficient imagination and sheer inventiveness to have spun such intricate life-patterns as Cayce's life readings revealed, with their complex interplay of karmic forces from one incarnation to the next!)

At the same time, it must be acknowledged that the sleeping seer had "good days" and "bad days"—days when the clarity and detail of a reading would be truly remarkable and other times when the phrasing would be exasperatingly indistinct and ambiguous, even self-contradictory here and there. Dates, and even names, would sometimes appear to be misstated, and occasionally certain segments of the information appeared to be out of proper chronological sequence.

Why?

Cayce himself has provided us with the best answers, which usually appeared in response to questions asked of him in trance-state over the years.

In a reading given in 1919, for instance, he was asked: "Is this information always correct?"[7] He replied that it was correct insofar as the suggestion was in the proper channel. This meant that the seeker not only had to provide the conductor of the reading with the correct specifics on the information being sought, in an articulate manner, but had to be properly motivated. A "proper" motivation for a life reading could be defined as a desire to obtain greater self-knowledge for purposes of soul development. Mere curiosity, as another reading pointedly remarked, was not enough.[8] Similarly, any form of self-aggrandizement on the part of the seeker would inevitably produce unsatisfying results. A spiritual goal, by contrast (as exhibited in the Search for God series of psychic readings, for example), always seemed to produce readings of outstanding quality and general clarity. Readings in this special category, in fact, have become the pillars on which the chronological structure of my story has been made to rest, wherever conflicting dates appear.

Reading 294–197, approaching the question of accuracy in the readings from another angle, warned that "there should not be the attempts to induce or to give information for others when physical hindrances arise," thus intimating that periods of ill health or physical tiredness on Edgar Cayce's part would have a deleterious impact upon his psychic forces, affecting the clarity or accuracy of a reading given under such unfavorable circumstances.

The most complete explanation of psychic errors or lapses, however, was contained in a detailed reading on the subject given in 1933.[9] In summary, it listed several causes, one of which was the unwillingness of the body-consciousness of either Edgar Cayce or the recipient of the reading to be properly responsive at the time. Another stated cause was ill health, which we have already covered. A third was the mental attitude of those in Edgar Cayce's presence at the time the information was being sought, as well as "combative influences" in the experience of the entity seeking. In this regard, specific reference was made to "the continual warring" between the flesh and the spirit. Apparently the fleshly consciousness of the seeker, in such an instance, would be endeavoring to exert its restrictive control "through such a period of information passing from one realm to another." The akashic records of a soul-entity, said the reading, are either positive or negative—negative being "error," positive being "good." But in attuning the forces at the psychic level for "reading back" the record that has been made, how does the information come? Cayce answered that question with another: "For what purpose is the information being sought?" On that philosophical note, the matter came to rest.

Quite another dimension of the subject came to light, however, in Reading 1100-26, in which Cayce actually interrupted his account of the entity's Egyptian incarnation in the time of Ra Ta to volunteer a revealing "aside." As if to explain to his conscious-state audience the frustrations he was then encountering in his unconscious state, he told them that the interpreting of the records was not from English or from the Egyptian language but from the language that the entity's people had brought into the land of Egypt with them. This, he went on to explain, was "not Sanskrit, not the early Persian," but apparently the Carpathian dialect. (At a time in man's ancient history when there was but one language common to all, as confirmed both in Genesis and in the Cayce readings, any notable language differences would presumably have been those of dialect only.)

At any rate, we can readily imagine what a monumental task must have confronted Cayce in giving some twenty-five hundred life readings throughout his career as a psychic. Operating strictly on his own, without benefit of a "control" in the spirit realm to translate on his behalf, he was obliged to project himself into the etheric plane and personally "read" the akashic records of an entity's prior lives in whatever language might apply to each of its many cycles in the earth-plane—often dating back to Lemurian or Atlantean times—right up to the present. (The keeper of the records, though, would usually withhold from his cognizance any prior lives of a soul-entity that did not pertain to that entity's present phase of soul development in the earth. This again demonstrated an emphasis on the constructive purpose of a life reading, which was spiritual in its essence, as opposed to the mere satisfying of human curiosity in probing into one's past lives.)

When we contemplate the horrendous language hurdle alone, it seems obvious that it must have accounted for at least some of the garbled phrasing and psychic misinformation that occasionally slipped into Edgar Cayce's transliterations of the akashic records. Dates or other figures would have been particularly vulnerable to misinterpretation, one supposes. And in the final analysis, one can only marvel at the overall clarity and consistency of those twenty-five hundred or so life readings given against such overwhelming odds.

This brings us to the question of disputed chronology. It is not a simple matter to resolve. It must be viewed in the larger context of virtually all of the life readings, not those pertaining to Cayce alone.

Let me explain.

A unique aspect of the Edgar Cayce readings is the way literally hundreds of people were drawn to the Virginia Beach psychic over the years, seemingly by chance, and eventually had life readings from him. (This does not include the thousands who came for physical readings only.) In their life readings, they nearly all discovered the existence of karmic bonds—some quite ancient, others of more recent origin—linking them to Edgar Cayce, for weal or woe. Many had been with him in his early Egyptian incarnation as the high priest Ra (or Ra Ta), a cycle that was being re-enacted in many ways in the present, Cayce was told, and was to have a special influence on his current role in the earth as the forerunner of a "new order" about to unfold, with the advent of a new age and a new root race at the turn of this century. Others from that same special group in the days of Ra had also reincarnated with him in a later cycle in Persia, when Cayce had been a nomadic ruler, teacher, and healer named Uhjltd, who perhaps left his major mark on mankind with the birth of a son named Zend whose offspring was Zoroaster. Zend himself, according to the readings, had been an early incarnation of Jesus. And those soul-entities who had been with Cayce in both his Egyptian and Persian cycles now tended to form, for the most part, a natural and close-knit nucleus about him in the present. It was as if they had entered the earth with an inherent awareness of their unique opportunities for further service to mankind at this special time, and in association with that same soul-entity who had led them in the past.

Yet others had been with Cayce in Troy, in Greece, or in the Holy Land; in France, in England, or in America, through later life-cycles; some sharing in those periods that had led to soul retrogression for Cayce, rather than soul development, or in periods of wavering between the two extremes, as in his incarnation in the early Christian epoch as Lucius.

Throughout all these various life expressions, however, the threads of karma—good or bad—had woven a common tapestry of crisscrossing lives and destinies, a vast mosaic of human action and interaction played out in recurring cycles on the stage of life. Now, in the present century, the ancient drama had reached a point of climax, as all of the actors were brought on stage again, some singly, others in clusters, to reap what had been sown in the past. The time for the harvest was at hand, and all were called, but only some appeared ready.

This conglomerate of soul-entities drawn to Edgar Cayce over the years, and given life readings, could be viewed quite appropriately in one sense as a single unit, an aggregate, an inseparable "soul cluster" of disparate but related cells. Like the various cells in a body, they each have a unique role to fulfill, either in harmony with their fellow cells or not, as they choose. As our story unfolds down through the aeons, we will see some of their number entering again and again, as if in joyous preparation for the present incarnation, always responding to their opportunities for soul growth and service to others. But there are also those "rebellious cells" in the cluster. Some, like Cayce himself in more than one of his incarnations, have only temporarily fallen out of step to learn a needed lesson here and there; they will return, purged and stronger. Others stumble repeatedly, tripping on the hard rocks of their own self-interest. These form a constant cutting-edge to themselves and others. It is not our role to judge them. They move more or less flamboyantly onto the stage and take a more or less hasty exit from our view.

Throughout, we are being presented with a frequent retelling of the different life-cycles of Edgar Cayce, as viewed briefly through the lives and actions of others who, in most instances, were also present in several of those same cycles. Events often take on a quite different shading or coloration as each of these numerous actors marches across the stage of history to his or her own drumbeat. We must sift, select, and discriminate among the bits and pieces of information dropped along the way until we have reassembled the threads of the tapestry into a historical likeness as near to the original as possible. Faced with the enormity of our task and its apparent limitations, there are frustrating moments. Yet we are often helped along, unwittingly and unexpectedly, by what may first appear as hindrances, for seemingly disparate threads have a curious way of matching up or blending with the rest. As a case in point, though not directly related to our story, there was the identification of two separate individuals in their life readings as the same biblical character, Gamaliel, who will be remembered as a leader of the Sanhedrin in the days of Jesus. One of these, Mr. [1188], was told that he had lived "in the days when the Master walked the land," but so had the other, Mr. [933], been told that his existence had been "when the Master was in the earth." All of the evidence pointed to an embarrassing duplication. But in that case, which was the "real"Gamaliel? As it turned out, *both* were entitled to the name given, having existed in a father and son relationship that history has largely ignored. It took some meticulous research to locate the records on Gamaliel the Second, who was born during the Master's lifetime. Not only was Cayce vindicated, but we found that his character analysis of the two Gamaliels in their separate readings served to differentiate them unmistakably.[10]

Such luck, however, is not always with the researcher; nor is impeccable accuracy, as already pointed out in the preceding pages, always characteristic of the readings. It is important to acknowledge the flaws, whatever their cause. Yet we must be sure they are flaws, not simply misreadings on our part. This is the point I have wished to stress in telling the Gamaliel story. Superficial evidence may sometimes suggest a psychic gaffe, whereas subsequent research or historical developments can serve to reverse the earlier misjudgment. For this reason, the Cayce material must be approached with an open mind and a great deal of cautious respect by any researcher. He may be forced to eat crow if he is not careful. (I have done so myself!)

With that qualification in print, I proceed.

In Cayce's Egyptian cycle as the high priest Ra, the conflicting dates encountered are quite problematical. Some are obviously in error. Which ones? In sifting and sorting through an extremely large body of readings relating to the many participants in that major era, this researcher found it advisable to establish a particular dating or two as the most reliable and work from there. After that, any readings for the various actors in the drama that introduced dates in conflict with the established "master" dates for the period as a whole simply had to be brought into conformity. Fortunately, as with the 11,016 B.C. birthdate given for the young king, Araaraart, ruler in the second dynasty, it was possible to demonstrate its inaccuracy by cross-checking it with more than one reference point. First, there was one of our "master" dates, the one-hundred-year time frame for the construction of the Great Pyramid, from 10,490 to 10,390 B.C., as given in one of the most lucid and reliable of all the readings on the period. The pyramid's construction had begun, we knew, while Araaraart was still alive. Secondly, since Araaraart's life span had been given as only 114 years, it was obvious that he could not have been born in 11,016 B.C.—526 years before the pyramid's construction commenced. Nor could he logically have been referred to as "the young king" at the time of Ra's exile to the Libyan mount, some nine years earlier than that. Finally, we located half a dozen different references to 10,500 B.C. as the "general" time frame for the Ra Ta period, which was in conformity with that pyramid dating in Reading 5748–6.

Thus, with persistent effort, the knotty chronological threads of our story of the many lives of Edgar Cayce began slowly to unravel, leaving only an occasional unresolved kink in the total strand.

Perhaps the thorniest of the chronological conundrums encountered along the way was the establishment of a probable time frame for Cayce's Persian cycle as Uhjltd, the nomadic ruler. No specific date had been given anywhere, to our knowledge, although there were several unmistakable allusions to its relative proximity to the Egyptian cycle that had preceded it. One of these was a statement to the effect that Uhjltd was the offspring of one of the daughters of Ra (Ra Ta), in union with a son of Zu. (But both "Zu" and "Ra," in this context, may have been tribal designations only. At any rate, the mother of Ra had been identified as a daughter of Zu in one of the readings on Cayce's memorable Egyptian period.) Next, one must not discount the possibility that Uhjltd may not have been a *direct* offspring of the union mentioned but simply a lineal descendant thereof. Even so, this could hardly be expected to place Uhjltd's advent very far removed from the days of Ra, in all likelihood. A thousand years or so, say? Perhaps, but not much more. For there were other readings implying a "quick return" to the earth-plane from the Egyptian cycle to the Persian one. In the context of the times, when a life span could be several hundred years, we might reasonably allow a millennium or so from the close of one earth-cycle to the birth into the next as a relatively "quick" return; a much longer span, however, would seem to stretch the taffy of credibility rather thin, catching us in a sticky situation.

Yet, a quite contrary view of the historicity of the Uhjltd era has won some adherents among students of the Cayce readings. This dissident view, moreover, is not without its logic. How to cope with it was our question. The readings on Cayce's life as Uhjltd had disclosed, as mentioned earlier in this chapter, that he was the father of Zend, an incarnation of the Master, and Zend was named as the father of Zoroaster. Now, just when the prophet Zoroaster lived has remained an historical enigma to this day. Most authorities place his advent betweeen the seventh and sixth centuries B.C. This doesn't make them right, of course. Manly Palmer Hall, the pre-eminent scholar in such matters, says no reliable information is available. In fact, he states that Zoroaster's arrival in the earth "is variously placed from the 10th to the first millennium B.C.," adding that "this uncertainty results, in part at least, from the destruction of the libraries of the Magian philosophers by the armies of Alexander the Great."[11] Meanwhile, in an Eileen Garrett reading[12] there is an intriguing reference by Uvani to "the *first* Zoroaster" (italics added), thus clearly implying that there had been at least two—the latter a namesake who could conceivably have revived the teachings of the original Zoroaster and may even have been the same entity in a much later incarnation. (For thus does history tend to repeat itself, moving in cycles down through the ages. We shall see ample evidence of it in the chapters ahead.)

However, a monkey wrench now comes hurtling toward our chronological structure from a quite unexpected source: the readings themselves. In a couple of the Cayce readings (1097–2 and 3356–1), one finds, in the one instance, an incarnation in the Persian period seeming to occur *after* an incarnation in the days of Moses (ca. 1300 B.C.) and, in the other, judging by its given sequence in the reading, even appearing later than the Babylonian exile of the Israelites (ca. 600 B.C.). Yet it is my conclusion, based on the impressive evidence in the readings to support a far earlier time frame for the Uhjltd period, that those two disputed incarnations in Readings 1097–2 and 3356–1, respectively, were simply given out of chronological sequence. No dates appear in either reading, and it is the sequence factor alone that has led to certain historical assumptions that are at odds with more convincing evidence pointing to a time frame nearer to 8000 or 9000 B.C. for Cayce's Persian incarnation as Uhjltd.

Actually, other examples of incarnations given out of sequence may be found in the readings. One of these, contained in Reading 2892–2, originally led to a great deal of needless confusion and controversy until Edgar Cayce's secretary, Gladys Davis Turner, eventually resolved the mix-up.[13] Moreover, it will be found that the life readings do not invariably begin a review of prior lives from the last appearance in the earth to the earliest, but sometimes in reverse sequence. So one should not discount the very real possibility of an occasional sequential mix-up, accidental or otherwise, as typified, for instance, in the "reverse" run-through of prior lives in Reading 5249–1.

Finally, with specific reference to our subject, Reading 288–29 gives us a further clue as to the ancient origins of the Uhjltd epoch, predating the days of Moses, if not those of Abraham as well. Referring to the Master's appearance as Zend, a son of Uhjltd, it is plainly stated: "No Jews then! That was years later!"

How many years later is the critical question. Abraham was the forefather of the Jewish people, and his days may have been roughly contemporaneous with those of Uhjltd. He dwelt at Ur, "on the other side of the flood," and some ten generations removed from Noah. And Noah? He was the great-grandson of Enoch, whose synonymity with the legendary Hermes, master architect of the Great Pyramid, we shall explore in Chapter 5, dealing with the Ra Ta period in Egypt.

Another knotty cycle in the lives of Edgar Cayce, chronologically considered, is the dual Bainbridge incarnation. For it seems that he chose to incarnate not once, but *twice,* under the same name, with the second appearance occurring approximately one hundred years later but in much the same environs and the same sort of squandered life as the former, carrying him from England as a youth to the adventurous shores of early America. In the second appearance, however, the readings stated that he had made his entrance into the earth-plane from Saturn's forces. This told me much. Saturn, according to the readings, is that nondimensional sphere of consciousness where all memory of the immediate past is wiped out—erased—so that an entity may start over again. It is like the legendary Lethe, river of forgetfulness. The soul-entity is provided with a clean slate and an opportunity to redeem itself in its next cycle of incarnation through the application of free will and choice. This explains the second appearance of John Bainbridge.

In the chapters that follow, the reader will find numerous other examples of questionable chronology or story line with which I have had to wrestle. But, aided sometimes by logic and as often by luck, I believe I have managed to unravel the snarls in most cases. If the reader disagrees with certain of my deductions and conclusions along the way, that is a privilege of which I would not deprive him or her. But at least it will be apparent, I hope, that I have aimed at presenting the full, unvarnished facts. No dates, names, or events in disagreement with my version have been intentionally hidden from the reader's scrutiny. If they are not there, and may be said to bear more than passing significance in putting the chronology aright or nailing down other specifics of the story, it is because I have inadvertently overlooked them.

At the same time, mine does not pretend to be an epic tale of grandiose proportions. It is but a skeletal framework by comparison. Its modest objective, within that framework, is to provide the essential verities in the many lives of Edgar Cayce, but not to overburden the reader with the minutiae of detail that a full-blown, traditional epic would require. If this is disappointing to some, I am sorry. Others, no doubt, will be relieved. I have spared them a thousand pages of laborious prose, for which they should be properly thankful.

Finally, let it be noted that this tale, even when it may manage occasionally to be entertaining, is always true. And the truth, as we all know, invariably conceals a moral. The moral at the core of this story is simple: Live joyously! Though the soul's long journey through the earth may often be difficult, as illustrated by Cayce's many incarnations here (with some still to come!), its goal is eventual liberation from the lower self and the restoration of the soul's lost godhood. That is surely cause for abundant joy. And so we express our earthly hope: "Many happy returns!"

Humor, not surprisingly, was always a vital undercurrent in the Edgar Cayce readings. Cayce frequently enjoined people to laugh more, to take themselves less seriously. Even the Master, he said, joked on the way to Calvary, as He carried His own cross.

Rejoice, then! Live every moment joyously. Joy is contagious. Man first got it from the angels. The angels are constantly rejoicing. The angel in man is the joy he entertains and sheds upon others. Joy awakens the Higher Self within us. And when the Higher Self awakens, we are free.

3. In the Beginning

Following the bead of light, as he always did, Edgar Cayce found himself propelled swiftly upward. Looking neither left nor right, he passed unhindered through the lower realms of relative darkness, where hordes of lost and despairing spirit-entities sought to hamper his ascent with their loud lamentations. Instead, he rose quickly into the increasing light and beauty of ever-higher levels of the spirit-plane. Here luminous beings reached out helpfully, as if to aid his upward passage. At last he came to the familiar hall of the akashic records, which was his goal.

The ageless keeper of the records recognized him. He greeted Edgar as an old friend.

"You come again," he said, smiling. "I have been expecting you."

Edgar nodded at the white-robed, turbaned figure, returning the smile. But before he could tell the akashic guardian that this time he had come for a look at his own records rather than those of another, his friend had vanished.

Yet he reappeared just as suddenly, like a beam of celestial light. In his hands he carried an unusually large tome. This suggested that it must contain the records of a very old soul—one whose journeys into the earth-plane possibly dated from the beginning of time. Emblazoned on the book's cover were curious markings, which Edgar intuitively recognized at once as his own soul number (for every entity in the earth is thus identified).

As he opened the book, Edgar saw that certain passages had been rendered indecipherable to him. And he knew this meant that he was not to receive full knowledge, as yet, of his many prior lives. His own Higher Self, in fact, had decreed these limitations. Only those pages that would prove helpful to his present phase of soul development were to be revealed to him. It was in accord with the universal laws.

Using his inner eye, Edgar read as much as was permitted him. Then he repeated the passages aloud, translating from the akashic form, and sometimes interjecting side comments of his own, in what frequently sounded like the archaic English of the King James version of the Bible, a book whose words were always sacred to him and a part of his innermost being. This process of vocalization was necessary, of course, so that those in the earth-plane, waiting in the room where his physical body rested, would be able to pick up the message in the akashic records from his unconscious, or superconscious, self.

At last he came to the earliest entry (for he had read the record from last to first, as he usually did). And those who now listened intently in the room where his body lay were transfixed by what they heard as the moving lips and tongue of the supine figure formed these revealing words, in a poetic translation from the akashic:

We find [the entity] in the beginning, when the first of the elements were given, and the forces set in motion that brought about the sphere as we find called earth-plane, and when the morning stars sang together, and the whispering winds brought the news of the coming of man's indwelling, of the spirit of the Creator, and he, man, became the living soul. (294-8)

A living soul, yes. But not yet a mortal, with a mortal's limitations.

Those who chose to enter into the earth-plane in that first influx of souls were celestial beings. They were the as-yet-unfallen sons and daughters of God, the First Cause and Creator. Their appearance was more in the nature of thought-forms, initially, that could be projected or crystallized into a bodily manifestation, as desired. It was simply a matter of visualization. Cocreators in their own right, they could draw upon the Creative Forces to translate mental images into material shape and substance through a change, or lowering, in the vibratory rate of the thought-pattern. For they were fully conscious of the Universal Mind as the builder. This application of spiritual law not only governed their own physical projections but met all of their material wants and needs in the earth-plane. (For, verily, thoughts are *things.*)

An aspect of their androgynous God-nature was the ability to separate, like the amoeba, and create a "companion self" at will. In this manner, they retained their spiritual purity, at first, holding to the celestial form but in a translated, visible state suited to an earthly experience, with its lower vibratory rate. They did not yet choose to engage in the tempting delights of fleshly copulation, as they witnessed all around them in the lustful antics of the multifarious creatures of the animal kingdom, whose appearance in the earth-plane had preceded their own.

Although now separated partially from their divine Source, they retained close psychic contact and continued to manifest the power of gods. Their deeds in the earth were to become the stuff of legends among later arrivals. And while they were indeed the true progenitors of Adamic man, who was to follow them in a later epoch, with the second influx of souls (including many of their own number, returning), man's lowly estate had not yet befallen these early, Olympian-like extraterrestrials. Their pristine forms were still essentially etheric, projected into material shape or withdrawn at will. Innocence illumined their brows with an innate nobility. Not yet were they wholly trapped in hardened, material encasements, as would be their fate later on. Not yet had the temptations of the flesh corrupted them or the ways of selfishness begun to lead them astray. For they knew not sin. Not yet, not yet . . .

Edgar Cayce was among that early number.

All souls emanate from the One, and they return to the One.

The soul's purpose in the earth, then, is to find its way back from whence it came, exercising the divine gift of free will to grow heavenward—or to separate itself further from its Maker.

And who is its Maker?

The first-begotten Son of God is identified in ancient tradition as the Upper Adam, or archetypal man, who preceded the earthly Adam and the material creation. In fact, it was He, as a god in His own right (for was He not made a full companion and heir of the Ineffable One?), who later became the Maker, the Creator, of the manifest universe. He is also identified as Mind, Light, the Word. The readings call Him Amilius, the name under which He first entered the earth-plane as a thought-form in the beginning, and through whom all the other souls were projected in that first influx, as well as in the second. Yet in the first cycle they came as gods, or celestial beings, whereas in the second they entered as flesh-form souls, or earthly man.

Surprisingly, the readings indicate that this same Amilius was led astray, so that He ultimately had to work out His own salvation in the earth, as well as preparing the Way for ours. For "this first-begotten of the Father," as the matter is explained in Reading 364–8, "allowed himself to be led in the ways of selfishness." In fact, although the soul's well-intentioned purpose here originally, as stated in Reading 341–8, was to "make manifest Heaven and Heaven's forces" in the material creation, actually the whole manifest universe and the physical entry into same marked an apparent act of disobedience.

It is a subject hard to comprehend. In fact, the sleeping Cayce readily admitted that it might even involve "too much knowledge for some"; yet I quote this question-and-answer explanation from one of the Search for God readings for the benefit of those who must have a logical interpretation of the matter. After all, it is a question that epitomizes the human dilemma, and its answer serves to clarify what reincarnation and soul development are all about:

Q–2. *Please explain the following from [Reading 262–96], May 24, 1936: "For the soul had understanding before he partook of the flesh in which the choice was to be made." Why (if the soul had understanding) the necessity to take [on] flesh in order to make the choice?*

A–2. Considereth thou that Spirit hath its manifestations, or does it use manifestations for its activity? The Spirit of God is aware through activity, and we see it in those things celestial, terrestrial, of the air, of all forms. And *all* of these are merely manifestations! The knowledge, the understanding, the comprehending, then *necessitated* the entering in because it partook of that which *was* in manifestation; and thus the *perfect* body, the celestial body, became an earthly body and thus put on flesh. (The explanation to some becomes worse than the first!) This, then: (This has nothing to do with Knowledge, or it is too much knowledge for some of you, for you'll stumble over it; but you asked for it and here it is!)

When the earth became a dwelling place for matter, when gases formed into those things than man sees in nature and in activity about him, then matter began its ascent in the various forms of physical evolution . . . in the *mind* [and Mind, remember, is a synonym for the first-begotten Son] of God! The spirit [as Amilius, the Son] chose to enter (celestial, not an earth spirit—he [Adam] hadn't come into the earth yet!), chose to put on, to become a part of, that which was as a command *not* to be done!

Then those so entering *must* continue through the earth until the body-mind is made perfect for the soul, or the body-celestial again. (262–99)

It is hard to imagine a more explicit, a more beautifully instructive, summary of the origins of the present human condition and its ultimate solution than is contained in those few paragraphs. They embrace a whole philosophy that some might spend a lifetime seeking, and never find. For herein we learn a marvelous secret: we learn from whence we came, and whither we must go. And it is in words such as these that one comes to realize what a remarkable contribution to mankind, albeit little recognized as yet, was made by the late Edgar Cayce. A man of relatively little formal education, and seemingly beset with as many human frailties as the rest of us, his psychic genius set him apart—this, and a great singleness of purpose. His sole objective in life was service to man and God. There have not been many who could match his selfless contribution.

But back to our story . . .

Unfortunately, there are not many substantive clues in the readings from which we can sniff out a reliable approximation as to just when the first influx of souls occurred, back in the ancient annals of prehistoric time. Yet there is at least one—and, happily, it is a rather good one. It is to be found in Reading 2665-2. In that life reading, a very early incarnation is given, preceding [2665]'s Atlantean appearance during the first of the eruptions that ultimately destroyed that fabled continent. We are told that she was among the first peoples to separate into groups, or families. The reading tells of a cave in the ancient and arid plateau region of the American Southwest—once a portion of the now-sunken continent of Lemuria, according to legend, and one of the few early landscapes of the planet that has somehow survived innumerable cataclysmic changes down through the aeons. In that cave, said the reading, drawings then made by the entity may still be seen. And it then added, in startling fashion: "Some ten million years ago"!

No earlier date, to my knowledge, can be found anywhere in the readings on which to pin our ancient origins.[1] Moreover, lest some might be tempted to conclude that a cave-dwelling entity could not have been one of the original thought-form projections of soul-beings in that initial influx with Amilius but must have been one of the "daughters of men" resulting from the later entanglements of the sons and daughters of God in the ways of the flesh, we find such understandable skepticism refuted in Reading 364-12. Therein it states that those from the first influx of souls "became dwellers in the rock, in the caves," or made their homes, "or nests, as it were, in the trees."

Let us move on.

Our next "fix " on the anthropological clock happens to pertain to a former thought-form entity, now know as Mr. [877], who was told that his earliest relationships with his friend Edgar Cayce had occurred during an earthly sojourn that "was nearer to fifty or five hundred thousand years before we even have the beginning of the LAW *as* the Law of One [in Atlantis] manifested!" (877-26).

That's going back pretty far, admittedly, despite the extremely wide latitude in the two given dates. But how far is "pretty far"? For we simply don't know when the teaching of the Law of One had its beginnings in Atlantis. But probably this occurred during the rule of Amilius. And there is this revealing reference, in yet another reading, to that rule:

As to the highest point of civilization, this would first have to be determined according to the standard as to which it would be judged—as to whether the highest point was when Amilius ruled with those understandings, as the one that understood the variations, or whether they become man-made, would depend upon whether we are viewing from a spiritual standpoint or upon that as a purely material or commercial standpoint; for the variations, as we find, extend over a period of some two hundred thousand years. (364-4)

The reading adds that this is a reference to "light years," and elsewhere it is explained that this should not be confused with the current scientific term, in the lexicon of astronomy, that applies to the speed at which light travels through the universe but to "the sun goes down and the sun goes down" years—a phrase, quite frankly, that implies synonymity with our present measurement of the solar year. But we need to consider the possibility—nay, the probability—that the passage of the aeons has seen an appreciable slowdown in the earth's rotation, both axial and orbital.

Finally, from a more esoteric perspective, I think we can justifiably posit that, though the earth may be slowing down, thus lengthening our modern-age year in relation to prehistoric times, man himself has experienced just the reverse: in short, his life span has shrunk in relation to the millennial-like life span of Adam and his early progeny as recorded in Genesis; the life span of the early Atlanteans and their progenitors may well have been comparatively "ageless." Thus, time is relative, and a million years, in the earth's early beginnings, may be equivalent in certain significant respects to a mere thousand in the present.

The Atlantean rule of Amilius, like the much, much later decision of the early Israelites to abandon their God-given rights of self-rule and appoint a king to govern them, may have arisen out of a similar tribal weakness and lack of self-discipline as the original thought-form projections found themselves increasingly out of touch with their spiritual origins and more and more given to fleshly entanglements and the ways of selfishness in the earth-plane.

The separation of the sexes had already begun, and this, of itself, was not necessarily counted as a sin as long as the androgynous god-beings in the separation into paired companions (like Amilius and Lilith) retained their essential purity and did not lust after the flesh-forms in the earth. (For as Reading 275–36 put it, though they were thought-forms, *"they had a body!"* But either it was a body-celestial or it was rapidly on its way to becoming an earth-body, trapping the soul-entity in its material encasement through the downward-gravitating desires of the mind-body of the entity.)

Eventually this led to the need to reawaken the drifting souls to the awareness of their spiritual heritage, now half-forgotten. Amilius, as the Elder Brother of all the other souls, and that one initially responsible for their predicament, apparently decided to take personal control of a deteriorating situation. Thus, His long rule began, and under that rule, the Law of One was presumably established. Those who adhered to the Law, based on Amilius's teachings, became known as the children of Light, and in their temples of service they sought to draw the wavering sons and daughters of of God back from the brink of total separation and darkness. However, those who succumbed to the ways of selfishness, and further separation from the Light, became identified eventually as the sons of Belial—an expression signifying lawlessness. Their rebellious ruler was the Prince of Darkness, whose domain was in the earth-plane. The forces of Darkness thereafter waged constant battle with the spiritual rule of the Light, Mind, the Word, embodied in Amilius.

Here, as it were, we encounter the prelude to that turbulent phase in Atlantean history, showing Amilius's growing perception of the problem:

In the period, then—some hundred, some ninety-eight thousand years before the entry of Ram into India—there lived in this land of Atlantis one Amilius, who had first noted . . . the separations of the beings as inhabited that portion of the earth's sphere or individuals. As to their forms in the physical sense, these were much rather of the nature of thought-forms, or able to push out of themselves in that direction in which its development took shape in thought—much in the way and manner as the amoeba would in the waters of a stagnant bay, or lake, in the present. As these took form, by the gratifying of their own desire for that as builded or added to the material conditions, they became hardened or set—much in the form of the existent human body of the [present] day, with that of color as partook of its surroundings much in the manner as the chameleon in the present. Hence coming into that form as the red, or the mixture peoples—or colors; known then later by the associations as the red race. (364–3)

Yet, to comprehend the growing evil in their midst, we need to examine certain other passages that reveal the extent to which some of the more wayward entities were abusing their abilities to call upon the Creative Forces for the fulfillment of their desires in any direction:

These, then, are the manners in which the entities, those beings, those souls, in the beginning partook of, or developed. Some brought about monstrosities, as those of its (that entity's) association by its projection with its association with beasts of various characters. Hence those of the Styx, satyr, and the like; those of the sea, or mermaid; those of the unicorn, and those of the various forms. (364–10)

In Atlantean land during those periods when there were the divisions between those of the Law of One and the sons of Belial, or the offspring of what was the pure race and those who had projected themselves into creatures that become "the sons of men" (as the terminology would be) rather than the creatures of God. (1416–1)

The other group—those who followed the Law of One—had a standard. The sons of Belial had no standard, save of self, self-aggrandizement.

Those entities [termed "things"] that were then the producers (as we would term today), or the laborers, the farmers or the artisans, or those who were in the positions of what we call in the present just machines, were those that were projections of the individual activity of the group [known as sons of Belial].

And it was over these, then, and the relationships that they bore to those that were in authority, that the differences arose. (877–26)

Ah, yes. Differences indeed! Those same differences found their karmic echo, perhaps, in the slave-owning era of our own land, when a privileged class sought to suppress the human rights of others for their own material gain. They lost.

But let us revert to that earlier reference to "the entry of Ram into India." It may provide us with yet another clue to the ancient ticking of time on our anthropological clock.

Ram, or Rama, was one of the first of the great initiates, and he was the founder of the Vedic teachings. (Literally, *ram* means "the leader of the peaceful flock.") Rama's period in history is uncertain; some have estimated 5,000 B.C. or perhaps even earlier. But let us take the given date. Reading 364–3 tells us that Amilius's reign in Atlantis apparently began about one hundred thousand years before the days of Rama in India. Or more precisely, some ninety-eight thousand years ahead of the latter. So, there we are: 103,000 B.C. Take it or leave it, as you wish.

On with our story!

Despite the efforts of the children of the Law of One, the Atlantean race and culture seemed doomed to eventual self-extinction through the increasingly destructive activities of the sons of Belial. Great technological advancements, which had gradually supplanted the declining spiritual power of the race, only led to worse abuses. First, there was the mighty crystal, whose prisms could gather and harness the incredible energies in the rays from far-off Arcturus or the sun of our own little solar system; originally under the direct control of the priests and priestesses of the Law of One, that control was gradually subverted by the sons of Belial, leading to the first of several great eruptions that proved to be the eventual undoing of Atlantis. Lasers and other destructive forces were also unleashed; and as given in Reading 195–29, "That thrown off will be returned"—not necessarily in the same form but with a similar degree of destructiveness, for that is a spiritual law. Yet the wayward Atlanteans paid scant heed to *any* law. The first of the eruptions, breaking up the proud continent into a series of islands, did not deter those who acknowledged no power but their own. Nor did the second cataclysmic upheaval serve to chastise them.

And so the realization came to Amilius that a "second creation" would be necessary, bringing into the earth a flesh-form man, but of pure origins, who would arise from the impending ruins of Atlantis and propagate himself from his own kind, repopulating and replenishing the flood- and earthquake-ravaged planet over which he would be given dominion. His name would be Adam, or *adama,* meaning "the red earth."

As a prelude to Adamic man's appearance, however, there were to be forerunners who would prepare the way. For "preparations were made," it says of that advance era in Reading 3579-1, "for the advent of the souls of men to be brought to their relationship with God." (A similar cycle of preparation, in fact, exists today, if Cayce was right, as we await the advent of a new age and a new race in the earth, and Reading 5749-5 indicates that Edgar Cayce himself entered as a "forerunner" of the approaching new order. We shall shortly see that he was apparently repeating his ancient role in a similar capacity.)

To continue:

The second influx of souls, under the direction of Amilius, began with those chosen to be forerunners. Androgynous beings, even as the soul-entities in the first influx had been, they nevertheless differed from their ancient predecessors (of whom some were themselves, in fact, now returning) by being "flesh-form" entities. From their number, in time, the very purest daughters would presumably be selected as the channels for the initial projection by Amilius of the five racial groupings of Adamic man, the five colors, the five primal nations, that would become known historically as the forebears of modern man—in brief, ourselves.

One among those forerunners of the second creation, however, was to have a special role to play. Now that Amilius, the Maker, would no longer be able to commune directly with those flesh-beings projected by himself (for as the soul-entities took on flesh-form, His higher vibrational rate would automatically separate Him from their three-dimensional view), He recognized the need for a representative in the earth at that time. Such a representative, though also a flesh-form, would adhere to the Law, counseling men everywhere in the ways of peace and brotherhood, as opposed to more disruptive and violent solutions to their problems. It was all a part of the Divine Plan emerging, so that the coming Adamic Age could be safely ushered-in.

And so, Asapha entered. We shall meet him in the next chapter.

Meanwhile, Amilius foresaw yet another necessity in His unfolding plan for the eventual salvation of mankind. It involved an act of enormous Self-sacrifice. Yet He never wavered.

He now realized that He himself would have to enter into one of the five proposed prototypes for the new, flesh-form race, and He chose to come as Adam, the Son of man, entering His own creation a second time but now as a *fleshly* projection of Himself, Amilius, the "Upper Adam." Though androgynous and without earthly father or mother, He would be a mortal, and subject to mortal limitations. In this way, He—Mind, Light, the Word— would become a flesh-form Pattern for all of the souls trapped in the earth, as He led them through a cycle of numerous incarnations, slowly and painstakingly, out of the self-imposed prison of their earthly vibrations and back to their original, unfallen estate as One with Him, in the celestial body and the heavenly realm.

It has been said that we are His brethren, *His individual selves—* men in the earth, but gods in the making. And where does the evolving soul go when fully developed? Back to its Maker, as a cell reborn in the Body of God:

And ye must be one—one with another, one with Him—if ye would be, as indeed ye are—corpuscles in the *life flow* of thy Redeemer! (1391–1)

4. When the Two Were as One

In the beginning, there was presented that that became as the Sons of God, in that male and female were as in one.

—*Edgar Cayce Reading* 364–7

Jesus said: On the day when you were one, you became two.

—*The Gospel According to Thomas* (Logion 11)

THE COUNCIL OF FORTY-FOUR
(Asapha and Affa; Egypt, 50,722 B.C.)

In February 1925, Edgar Cayce obtained a follow-up life reading for himself.

As often turned out to be the case with such follow-up readings, whether for himself or others, there were surprising new disclosures in this one. It was as if the spiritual progress made by an entity in using the information in a former reading to further its soul development determined its degree of readiness to learn more about its past lives. And in knowing more about its past, and the fruits thereof, the earnest seeker after truth would obviously be that much better equipped to shape the course of its future. For all our yesterdays are a collective image of what we are today, and the living present, with its opportunities, is like a sharp sculptor's chisel with which we may change the shape of the image, modifying the shadow it will cast upon our tomorrows. The good in our past should be an incentive to new achievements; whereas the flaws, if seen and acknowledged, can be erased and the marble restructured to a more perfect likeness of our ideal.

In Edgar's case, with that particular reading, the revealing new information was of a mixed nature. He learned more about a downward-gravitating cycle in the earth, during the Trojan wars, that adversely affected his ability in the present to control his wrath or displeasure in certain situations. But he was greatly encouraged to learn of a very early incarnation that had been omitted from his initial life reading. It fitted between his initial entry in the beginning, with Amilius, as one of the sons of God in that first influx of souls and his memorable Egyptian cycle as the priestly Ra Ta, who had journeyed under a psychic compulsion to that sunlit region of the world from his adoptive homeland on the slopes of Mount Ararat to fulfill a unique destiny.

Now he discovered that he had come as a forerunner in the *second* influx of souls, "when the forces in flesh came to dwell in the earth's plane." The reading continued:

The entity was *among the first* to inhabit the earth *in that form,* and was from the beginning in the earth's forces. In this we find the larger development in the entity, for then [the soul was] able to contain in the Oneness of the forces as given in the sons of men, and realizing the Fatherhood of the Creator.

In the present plane we find that ever urge to be drawn nearer to the spiritual elements of every force. Hence, in the summing up and use of these, let the entity keep the spiritual forces ever magnified, in action, deed, and in truth, For, in earth's plane, every element of the physical or mental, or spiritual nature, is judged by the relation to spiritual force. (294–19; italics added)

And there the matter rested. The reading included no elaboration as to Edgar's identity or purpose in that first flesh-form incarnation. However, the reference to "the larger development in the entity" in its ability "to contain in the Oneness of the forces as given in the sons of men, and realizing the Fatherhood of the Creator" provided a clue of sorts: One could infer from such a laudatory reference that it had been a notable incarnation, probably affecting the lives of many. The spiritual lessons gained and applied must have been significant, in fact, since their influence upon Cayce in the present was given as "that ever urge to be drawn nearer to the spiritual elements of every force."

A few months later, a seemingly unrelated series of readings was given while Cayce was still residing in Dayton, Ohio, before the oft-urged move to Virginia Beach. Those readings, known today as the "5748" series, were primarily concerned with an ancient gathering of forty-four world leaders among the sons of men to discuss ways and means of ridding the planet of fearsome beasts then overrunning the earth in certain areas.

Based on a very precise date of 50,722 B.C., as supplied some years later in one of the Search for God readings (namely, 262–39, given in February 1933 at Virginia Beach), that urgent conclave must have occurred after Amilius's departure from the Atlantean scene; for the five nations of early mankind were now in their formative stages and already being inhabited and ruled by the sons of men. Also, by our calculations, it was a period some thirty-nine thousand years before Adam's advent during the next return of the Age of Virgo, which marked the commencement of our present Grand Cycle of the Ages. Finally, it preceded Cayce's Egyptian incarnation as Ra Ta by about forty thousand years. (Actually, a highly questionable and most unlikely dating for the great conclave had been supplied in one of the original Dayton readings, 5748–2, suggesting a time frame of some ten-and-a-half million years ago! But Hugh Lynn had properly sensed that this date was flawed, reflecting a sudden malfunction in Edgar's psychic calculator, and it was he who made the inquiry resulting in the corrected dating, 50,722 B.C., given eight years later. For it was obvious to him, as it must be to any astute researcher, that the period covered by the particular readings in question concerned the *second* influx of souls, not the first.)

If anything emerges with certainty from the Edgar Cayce readings, it is the incontrovertible fact that great events on the stage of human history, as well as in the realm of so-called natural phenomena, tend to occur in a cyclical pattern. Scientists, too, have observed this fact to some extent, without being able to explain it. Thus, when I pored over the details in the 5748 series and began analyzing the teachings and activities of that early Egyptian leader who had drawn together the forty-four world representatives of his day, seeking a peaceful rather than a destructive solution to the dilemma then facing mankind, the parallels with the later Ra Ta cycle—occurring in essentially the same environment —were stunning. For one thing, both were primarily active in the "second rule" of their respective epochs, although the one—Asapha—came as the ruler, whereas the other—Ra Ta—appeared as a spiritual leader, though with a ruler's supreme authority in his final years. Their teachings were based on essentially the same spiritual precepts, supporting the universal laws. Both were peacemakers. And, finally, both appeared on the world scene at identical times of crisis, using their spiritual powers of persuasion to rally all other world leaders under a common banner, re-establishing unity of purpose through the Law of Oneness: "The Lord thy God is One!"

Implicit in these parallels, of course, was the obvious likelihood that the Ra Ta era in Egypt was simply a "repeat" cycle, with appropriate variations, of the great spiritual accomplishments in that earlier Egyptian epoch, when a priestlike ruler, named Asapha, had assembled the Council of Forty-four. Thus, given the workings of mass karma at a planetary level, what more logical deduction could one make than to conclude that the selfsame entity had led both cycles? He who had ruled in the earlier Egyptian cycle had returned to the familiar scene, impelled by the same spiritual forces set in motion by Amilius on both occasions, to take a directing role in the spiritual affairs of the planet in what was to be a permanent closing of the Atlantean epoch and a critical developmental phase in the infant Adamic Age under way in the days of Ra Ta.

Yet another intriguing aspect of the Ra Ta cycle, linking it by spiritual roots to the earlier, under Asapha, was the fact that the priestly Ra Ta had purportedly received psychic guidance from the beginning, compelling him to lead King Ararat and his people out of their mountainous homeland into Egypt. Why Egypt? Many reasons, as we shall later see. But one was undoubtedly an answering chord from within, from that earlier cycle, if our speculation is sound. Additionally, compelled by one knows not what atavistic promptings, Ra Ta had conducted archaeological research in a portion of the Sahara where he had presumably reigned some forty thousand years earlier as Asapha. In the Ra Ta diggings, the site of a large colony of so-called things, bearing tail-like protuberances, was uncovered. Ra's research established that they had been sun worshipers, even as those natives in his own day, and that they had apparently migrated to the Sahara region many thousands of years earlier to escape persecution at the hands of the sons of Belial, who had treated them as automatons. It was presumably in their new land, coming under Asapha's benign rule, that they became sun worshipers, envisioning their new king, or pharaoh, as the incarnate Sun-god. (The historical parallels are stunningly obvious. It is like a tune replayed, with only the octaves altered.)

Finally, in confirming the cyclical pattern of history, there is a much more modern parallel, which I am somewhat reluctant to commit to writing, though its time has surely come. It is a story, I am told, with no documentation to support it. Nevertheless, it was related to me by Gladys Davis Turner, Edgar Cayce's longtime secretary and a virtual member of the Cayce household after her initial employment in 1923. It pertains to an incident in Edgar's psychic career that predated her arrival on the scene, of course, since it concerned Woodrow Wilson's vision of a League of Nations and its dramatic impact upon the Paris peace conference in 1919. The readings say of Wilson's ill-starred efforts that the Christ himself sat at the peace table, in the presence of that very sincere and humble president of the United States. What is not mentioned in any of the readings, however, is the "background" story; I relate it here.

During World War I, Gladys explained, David Kahn—a close friend and lifelong spokesman of Cayce's—became associated with two first cousins of Woodrow Wilson. Through that association, arrangements were made for Edgar Cayce to come to Washington and give a "very private" reading for President Wilson in connection with the proposed peace plans. The whole affair was treated with absolute confidentiality, and Mr. Cayce was not even permitted to be accompanied by a recording secretary. But it is believed that Wilson's famous Fourteen Points may have emerged—perhaps verbatim—from that Cayce reading. Failure of the other Allies to accept Wilson's idealistic proposals, and subsequent senatorial opposition, reportedly broke Wilson's heart, though he was awarded the Nobel Peace Prize in 1920. If ours is an accurate account, the League of Nations concept originated, in part, with Cayce, who, much earlier, as a representative of Amilius in the earth, had twice before attempted to bind the nations of the world together in peaceful cooperation in his two Egyptian cycles; as Uhjltd, the nomadic Persian ruler whose appearance followed Cayce's Egyptian incarnations, his activities had been along much the same lines. (History does indeed seem to repeat itself, but more particularly so if the same soul-entity is allowed to reincarnate with a new opportunity to play out a variation of its former role under fresh circumstances that favor its efforts.)

As a recent postscript to Wilson's tragic failure, I found these words by Haynes Johnson, in the June 26, 1983, edition of the *Washington Post,* strangely moving: "It is said that when Woodrow Wilson went to France at the end of World War I, everywhere expressing his dream of a League of Nations that would banish war from the Earth, the millions who turned out to cheer him did so with an emotional fervor that was frightening in its intensity and spontaneity. Reporters who accompanied him wondered whether even a Caesar or Napoleon had ever stirred such an emotional outpouring from the masses."

(Indeed! Or a *Christ?* . . .)

If our narrative seems to have strayed somewhat off course in its pursuit of parallels, the purpose of such a diversion will now become plain. Actually, it has led us full circle, back to our starting point. For we find that the first reference, by name, to Asapha (or to Affa, as his companionate soul, or female counterpart, in the androgynous flesh-body of that particular incarnation) occurred in a reading that dealt with the Christ appearing down through the ages as a living Presence in the hearts of certain individuals deemed worthy of carrying on His work in the earth-plane. The reading indicated that this had been an observable pattern in human history ever since the Master's initial entry as Amilius, in the beginning. Then, in a passage that quite plainly identifies Asapha as that Egyptian leader who convened the Council of Forty-four, we read: "He [the Christ, Amilius] has walked and talked with men as in those days as [of] Asapha, or Affa, in those periods when those of the same Egyptian land were giving those counsels to the many nations [an obvious allusion to the Council of Forty-four], when there would be those saving of the physical from that of their own making in the physical" (364–8).

The karmic consequences implicit in the above reference to the "saving of the physical from that of their own making in the physical" is worth noting. Later, we shall see how Asapha sought to invoke aid from the Divine Forces in meeting the threat to mankind from the beasts overrunning the planet rather than resorting to violent solutions that would obviously perpetuate the karmic cycle.

Before proceeding with other details of the story, we must pause to consider a second reference to Asapha, in a reading given scarcely a week after the reading just cited, in April 1932. This time, it was disclosed that Cayce's Persian incarnation as Uhjltd, the nomadic ruler, had followed *two* early Egyptian incarnations, one as Asapha and the other as the priest Ra Ta. Somewhat curiously, though, the reading assigns an alternate name to Ra Ta, "Adonis." Yet I found this easily clarified with a bit of research. Gaskell identifies Adonis as a symbol of the Higher Self—the incarnate God born in the soul. "Adonis," he continues, "was conceived of the Divine Father and born of Myrrha—the purified lower nature." (How closely this parallels the account given in the readings of Ra Ta's entry through a daughter of Zu, but without earthly father!) Gaskell continues: "The incarnate God is therefore bound by the Divine law of the reincarnating cycle, and has to pass through short periods of earth life or physical existence, with intermediate periods of astral and mental existence of longer duration" until the soul is made perfect. Gaskell then cites Hippolytus: " 'Now the Assyrians call this [mystery of soul development] Adonis (or Endymion).' "[1] These mythological trappings, of course, should not be misconstrued to suggest that Edgar Cayce, as

Ra Ta, was a soul-entity any more godlike than the rest of us. In fact, a Cayce reading on the Ra Ta epoch is careful to lay to rest any such misconception, based on Ra Ta's unusual birth and appearance, as well as that he was later worshiped as the Sun-god by the native Egyptians: "Ye say, then, that such an entity was a god! No. No— ye only say that because there is the misunderstanding of what were the characters or types of spiritual evolution as related to *physical* evolution in the earth at that period" (281–42).

Here is the specific quotation on Cayce's two Egyptian incarnations, first as Asapha and later as the priestly Ra Ta (or "Adonis"), preceding his Persian experience:

In the first, we find that the entity Uhjld [Cayce] was an incarnation of Asapha and also of the priest [Ra Ta], both experiences being in Egypt— or Adonis and Asapha. In entering, then, we find, in the land then known as Iran [Aryan land?], there were those that had held true to those teachings that had been propounded by the teachers [note plural] in the Egyptian. (294–142)

Meanwhile, picking up again the main thread of our story, it is time to review some of the highlights of that Council of Forty-four in the days of Asapha and his companionate entity, Affa.

We find, to begin with, that "the first ruler of groups" in those days when the five nations were in their formative stages had established himself "in that place in the upper Nile, near what is now known as the Valley of Tombs" (5748–1). He was succeeded by Asapha, whose authority apparently extended beyond his own immediate realm, since it was he who determined the rulership in the other tribal spheres of the planet where emergent mankind was gathered together for its own protection and evolutionary development. In addition to the Sahara and the Nile region, under Asapha's personal rule, this included Tibet, Mongolia, Caucasia, and what is now Norway; also the southern cordilleras and Peru; and those plateau regions now known as Utah, Arizona, and New Mexico. As for the portions of Atlantis still intact, most notably Poseidia, these were not mentioned, presumably because their inhabitants held themselves aloof at that time from the more "primitive" sons of men and their problems. Moreover, the beasts that terrorized other portions of the planet may have been of no direct concern to the Atlanteans, who had long since eliminated them from their broken lands.

Asapha's approach to the problem, resulting in the convening of the Council of Forty-four, was expressed in this manner:

In the second rule [headed by Asapha] there came peace and quietude to the peoples, through the manner of the ruler's power over the then known world forces. At that period, man exchanged with the forces in each sphere that necessary for the propagation of the peoples of the sphere then occupied. In each of the spheres given was the rule set under some individual by this second rule [i.e., Asapha's] in now Egyptian country, and the period when the mind of that ruler brought to self, through the compliance with those Universal Laws ever existent, then that ruler set about to gather those wise men from the various groups to compile those as that ruler felt the necessary understanding to all peoples for the indwelling of the Divine Forces to become understood and to break away from the fear of the animal kingdom then overrunning the earth. (5748–1)

The next reading in the series pointed out that the number of souls then in the earth-plane was 133,000,000. Asapha's rule lasted 199 years. It was in his twenty-eighth year that he "began to gather the peoples together" to study the grave situation confronting them, "surrounding himself with those of that [Egyptian] land and of the various lands wherein the *human* life dwelled at that period. The numbers of the people that came together for the purpose then numbering some forty and four [44]" (5748–2; italics added).

In the next reading on the subject, we have this interesting observation by the sleeping Cayce:

Then, we have the gathering together then of this group, from the farthest places—forty and four [44]. As we see, this number will run through many numbers, for, as we find there is the law pertaining to each and every element significant to man's existence considered and given in one manner or form by the groups as gathered at this meeting. (5748–3)

Whatever its significance here, students of numerology will note that 44 is one of the four so-called master numbers, which retain their given value; the other three are 11, 22, and 33. Let the interested reader pursue that arcane matter further if it appeals to his or her mystical sense. But we will leave it at this juncture to continue the thread of our narrative.

Asapha's advice to the council was to avoid the use of warlike or destructive measures to cope with the murderous beasts that threatened their existence. It was hard advice, and many members of the council apparently demurred. It offended them. They felt a need for swift and violent action. Yet Asapha held firm to spiritual principles:

> And the first as was given by the ruler was, then, that the force that gives man, in his weak state, as it were, the ability to subdue and overcome the great beasts that inhabit the plane of man's existence must come from a higher source. (5748–3)

After many moons of debate, the wisdom of Asapha's counsel was demonstrated in a startling manner, as the hand of God resolved their dilemma for them in an unexpected fashion. We find an account of what happened contained in this excerpt from a reading for Mr. [5249], who was told that he had been one of the forty-four council members at that memorable conclave in the tents of a prehistoric time:

> The entity then was among those [forty-four] who were of that group gathered to rid the earth of the enormous animals which overran the earth, but ice, the entity found, nature, God, changed the poles and the animals were destroyed, though man attempted it in that activity of the meetings. (5249–1)

If Cayce was right, a similar shifting of the poles will occur at the close of the present century and the dawning of the next. It will signal the dayspring of the Aquarian Age and the fifth root race. It will also follow closely on the heels of yet another prophesied event, which Cayce predicted would occur in 1998: the Second Coming of the Lord. What changes may we expect to see take place upon our planet in the wake of such a wondrous synchronicity of major events?

AGE OF VIRGO
(Aczine and Asule; Atlantis, 12,800 B.C.)

In one of her life readings, the entity [288], who had incarnated in the late Atlantean epoch as a ruler in Poseidia named Asule, asked an interesting question and received an interesting answer:

Q–1. *In Atlantis, was I associated with Amilius? If so, how?*
A–1.   One as projected by that entity as to a ruler or *guide* for many, with its associating entity [294, Edgar Cayce]. (288–29)

The date of that androgynous incarnation had been given as 12,800 B.C. in an earlier life reading for [288] that explored her past associations with [294], or Edgar Cayce, who had been her twin soul in the beginning:

We find these [two], as in the present earth's plane, have had many experiences together, and their soul and spirit are well knit, and must of necessity present each that they may be one. For we find *in the beginning* that they, these two (which we shall speak of as "they" until separated), were as one in mind, soul, spirit, body; and in the first earth's plane as the voice over many waters, when the glory of the Father's giving of the earth's indwelling of man was both male and female in one. (288–6; italics added)

But whereas the male aspect had apparently been dominant in the initial projection as a thought-form being, during that first influx of souls, as well as in the days of Asapha and Affa in Egypt, now the female counterpart took the ascendant role in this late-Atlantean flesh-form appearance in Poseidia:

In *flesh-form* in earth's plane we find the first [if we omit the male rule of Asapha] in that of the Poseidian forces, when both were confined in the body of the female; for this being the stronger in the then expressed or applied forces found manifestations for each in that form. . . . The experiences there were as these: These two were [involved in] the giving of the spiritual development in the land [Atlantia], and the giving of the uplift to the peoples of the day and age.

In 12,800 B.C. we find together. . . . The desire remained in the One, for which the Oneness was created. (288–6; italics added)

The first reference to a given name for the androgynous flesh-being in the Poseidian rule was "Aczine":

Q-1. *Will you please give us the names of the personalities?*
A-1. We have given the personalities. The names of individuals as were in the earth's plane, in the first (Poseidia) that of Aczine. (288-10)

Curiously, though, all subsequent references to that Poseidian incarnation in [288]'s life readings give her name as "Asule." On this basis, it seems to be a reasonable speculation that the name Aczine, which Cayce had given originally, applied to his own identity as the companionate soul.

This late Atlantean incarnation took place in the Age of Virgo—a time, by our calculations, when Amilius implemented His plan to project into the earth as the Son of man, or Adam, appearing as an androgynous flesh-being in the fabulous Garden of Eden. (Reading 364-4 describes the lost Atlantis as "this, the Eden of the world," so we may assume that Adam's earthly paradise was somewhere within that realm, or what then remained of it.) But after the separation of Adam's companionate self, or twin soul, Eve, sin eventually entered. They were driven from the garden. Eastward they fled, where, of the five racial forms of the new root race then emerging, they became the progenitors of the red in its final condition as flesh-form man.

Sin entered, too, in the fair city of Alta, where Asule, with her companionate soul, Aczine, reigned over the Poseidians, lending much assistance to the common people of that day. Apparently Asule was one of the few remaining androgynes in Atlantis during that period of its last flickerings of glory preceding its final demise. The date, by our estimation, was perhaps half a millennium before Adam's appearance in the land. Many, the readings indicate, were envious of Asule's androgynous state and her spiritual powers of projection, reminiscent of the activities of the sons and daughters of God in a former era. In an age of flesh-beings, her status was unique, and it bespoke the spiritual purpose of her rule in a land where the sons of Belial had not ceased to work their mischief. Observing their ways, Asule eventually yielded to certain temptations. With the desire no longer remaining "in the One, for which the Oneness was created," the entity [288] sought carnal gratification "with one of lower estate"—an animal-like being, or "thing," presumably, brutish in its passions—"and through this treachery of one not capable of understanding, it brought physical defects in the limbs of these [companion souls] then contained in the one body in physical form." A comatose state resulted, with "karma exercised in coma," and "there was brought the separation," or the entering into the land of the Unknown (288–6).

It is a story with obvious parallels to Adam's "fall," in that same general epoch heralding the birth of humankind. Thus, not inappropriately, Asule's fateful choice can be expressed in the same biblical terms applicable to Adam's, a bit later on: "As given in the injunction from the Maker: 'I have this day set before you good and evil. Choose the light or the darkness' "(288–6).

That fateful incarnation marked the last androgynous appearance of [288] and [294]. Indeed, the androgynous state apparently terminated permanently with Adam's advent, not to be resumed until man could put off the flesh and regain the body-celestial. Yet, in examining their subsequent entries into the earth-plane as separate entities, both [288] and her companionate soul seem to have tried in their varied incarnations (we shall take note, along the way, of [294]'s exceptions) to re-establish, not only for themselves but for the rest of fallen mankind, a condition of oneness with the Maker:

At present we find they are again together, still in different divisions, positions or circumstances, each paying out that which has been gained or merited. . . . In this [present experience] they are again united in soul and in spirit force, and through the joy and the pleasure of selfless service they may again know the meaning of these as given.

They need only remain in the future faithful one to the other, ever giving, ever retaining those joys of the relations that bring and give of self in service to others; and these bring joy, peace, and again uniting of body, soul, and spirit in the next [a reference to Cayce's prophesied return in 1998?]. Remain faithful, therefore, unto the end; gaining those joys through daily acts of selflessness for and with others, remembering that in these manifestations they (and all souls) become knit one with the other. (288–6)

As for Adam, his sin opened his eyes:

Q–3. When did the knowledge come to Jesus that He was to be the Savior of the world?
A–3. When He fell in Eden. (2067–7)

A surprising glimpse of the paradisiacal garden is provided, incidentally, in the following excerpt from one of the readings, which tells us that Adam and Eve were not altogether "alone." They had other visitors and "watchers" than the serpent, and perhaps other temptations than the apple:

. . . *the garden called Eden*. There we find the entity was among those who looked on the activity of the mother of mankind. The entity was among "the things" and yet was touched in person . . . in heart . . . and sought to know the meaning . . . for it saw then the fruit, the leaves, trees, which had their spiritual meanings in people's lives. (5373–1)

What, precisely, was the sin of Adam? Was it carnal knowledge of Eve? or cohabitation with "one of lower estate," as Asule's sin had been? We are reluctant to speculate. Yet a definition of the "original sin" was given in Reading 262–125: *willful disobedience*. That is knowledge enough for our purposes. And its corollary, arising from guilt, is the initial impulse to blame another: "The *woman* Thou gavest me, *she* persuaded me and I did eat!" (262–125).

Finally, here is a philosophical summary of the matter, which the reader may enjoy wrestling with:

Adam . . . first discerned that *from himself,* not of the beasts about him, could be drawn—was drawn—that which made for the propagation of beings in the flesh, that made for that companionship as seen by creation in the material worlds about same. The story, the tale (if chosen to be called such), is one and the same. The apple, as "the apple of the eye," the desire of that companionship innate in that created, as innate in the Creator, that brought companionship into creation itself. *Get that one!* (364–5; italics added)

After giving us that walnut to crack, just for openers, the next paragraph of the reading cuts into the core of the apple:

In this there comes, then, that which is set before that created—or having taken on that form, [capable of] projecting itself in whatever direction it chose to take, . . . for were He not the Son of the living God made manifest, that He might be the companion in a made world, in material manifested things, with the injunction to subdue all, being all in the material things under subjection—by that ability to project itself in its way? knowing itself, as given, to be a portion of the whole, in, through, of, by the whole? In this desire, then, keep—as the injunction was—thine self separate; *of* that seen, but *not* that seen. The apple, then, that desire for that which made for the associations that bring carnal-minded influences of that brought as sex influence, known in a material world, and the partaking of same is that which brought the influence in the lives of that in the symbol of the serpent, that made for that which creates the desire that may be only satisfied in gratification of carnal forces, as partake of the world and its influences about same—rather than of the spiritual emanations from which it has its source. Will control—[or] inability of will control, if we may put it in common parlance. (364–5; italics added)

The Adam in us all, Cayce seems to imply, must be overcome by the Christ within us.

This does *not* rule out the use of the procreative function, however, as two souls come together in oneness and purity of purpose. This function, as a natural consequence of the human condition as it came to exist after Adam, was properly defined in one of [288]'s readings, respecting her love match with Uhjltd in the Persian incarnation, as the giving of self to "the sex desire between the two for the developing" toward the spiritual ideal of oneness, in the act of procreation; for "in that we find it counted as righteousness in both" (288–6). The outcome of that particular union, as we shall find explained more fully in a later chapter, was a son named Zend, who was an incarnation of the Master and a man of peace and virtue—the evolving Christ, who had been the fallen Adam.

It was at once a blessing and an absolution for all concerned.

Each Grand Cycle of the Ages, lasting some 25,920 years, marks the precession of the equinoxes through the twelve signs of the celestial zodiac. Because it is a backward-moving passage, following the earth's polar wobble in its infinitely slow gyrations, the Great Year cycle begins with Pisces and ends with Aries. This, of course, is just the reverse of the Sun's annual orbit through the twelve heavenly signs from Aries to Pisces.

At present, we are about to complete the 2,160-year backward passage through the Age of Pisces, the sign of the Fishes; and we straddle the cusp of the coming Age of Aquarius, the sign of the Man. By traditional calculation, assuming that the Piscean Age had its beginnings about 160 B.C., in the days of Hipparchus, the famous Greek astronomer who "rediscovered" the precession of the equinoxes, this means that the current Great Year will not reach its close until A.D. 23,760, as it passes into 0° of the Age of Aries.

But let us take a more esoteric view of the subject, one, I think, that has not previously been explored in its full dimensions. It will undoubtedly upset a lot of applecarts. No matter! Apples are not all that sacred to us: we consider the trouble they brought to man in the beginning. The beginning—that is just where we wish to start; for it is our premise that the advent of Adam occurred in the Age of Virgo, the sign of the Virgin. (On this point, we are not only able to present supportive evidence from the readings, in correlation with the generations of Adam's progeny as recorded in Genesis, but we shall draw on E. W. Bullinger's bold hypothesis, presented almost a century ago to a world then unprepared to receive it, that the original zodiacal map—probably conceived by Adam or Enoch—was really no more nor less than the heavenly pattern of a Man, the seed of a Virgin, who was destined to become a crucified Savior, and eventually return to claim His own.)

And so, if we are to adopt the last Age of Virgo (ca. 13,119 to 10,960 B.C.) as the commencement point for our present Great Year cycle, where will it end? If we are no longer headed full circle back to Aries, as the traditional map of our Great Year journey would have it, where then are we headed? Anyone familiar with the twelve signs of the zodiac and able to trace them in clockwise rotation will easily see that we are headed toward Libra, the sign of the Balance. And interestingly enough, it is the only sign in the zodiac that is not a creaturely sign; it is, rather, a symbol of Judgment.

Prepare yourself for a stunning surprise.

Edgar Cayce, in one of his own life readings that drew on his ancient wisdom as the High Priest Ra, in Egypt, in association with the Master as Hermes, had this to say of mankind's evolutionary destination:

> This building [the Great Pyramid, of which Hermes was the master architect] . . . was formed according to that which had been worked out by Ra Ta in the [Libyan] mount as related to the position of the various stars, that acted in the place about which this particular solar system circles in its activity [a reference to the zodiac], *going towards what?* That same name as to which the priest was banished—*the constellation of Libra,* or to Libya were these people sent. (294–151; italics added)

The mysterious "Hermes," who enters our story in the next chapter, was actually none other than the prophet Enoch, an incarnation of Adam. (Not only do the readings themselves seem to support this interpretation as to His true identity, but it has long been an accepted fact in Islamic tradition and esoteric lore.)

Finally, then: If Cayce foresaw the Age of Libra (ca. A.D. 10,641 to 12,800) as our ultimate destination, does this mean that Adamic man will reach his final fulfillment and spiritual regeneration in that age of judgment? Will the earth, as we know it, exist no more, as a regenerated mankind leaves it permanently behind to ascend heavenward on the etheric current of the universal vibration? These are cogent questions for us. Add another: In glimpsing Libra as the terminal point of our long journey, can it be doubted that Cayce equally knew that Virgo marked our beginnings in the flesh, as Adamic man? We posit the strong likelihood that Cayce, as the exiled priest Ra Ta in the Libyan mount, may have received instruction in the arcana of the zodiac from that great initiate, Hermes, also identified as Enoch, and an incarnation of Adam himself.

This speculation leads us, now, to a consideration of Bullinger's hypothesis, mentioned earlier. It has a most interesting part to play in our unique view of the Virgoan age.

The thrust of Bullinger's theory, presented in an obscure book titled *The Witness of the Stars*,[2] is that the original zodiac, of which our present-day version is a scarcely recognizable copy, was a mystical depiction, drawn in celestial symbols, of an ancient prophecy attributable perhaps to Enoch or even to Adam. That prophecy, of which recognizable echoes are found in various books of the Old Testament, tells of the coming of a Messiah—that Lamb slain from the foundation of the world, a sacrificial offering for the salvation of a lost mankind; the Son of God, born as a man and dying as a man; crucified, and resurrected; a Redeemer, who would return after two thousand years to claim His own.

In Bullinger's presentation, there is also a symbolic relationship between the twelve zodiacal signs and the twelve sons of Jacob, suggesting that Adam, Seth, or Enoch—the supposed originators of the zodiacal legend—had precognition of the entire genesis of Jewish history and the evoluton of the Messiah as that "Branch" out of the stem of Jesse.

Bullinger, a direct descendant of the great Bullinger of the Swiss Reformation, was an Anglican clergyman and a renowned scholar, as well as a formidable linguist. No fanatic or Christian fundamentalist, he backed up his startling hypothesis with a scholar's logic and the true researcher's indefatigable thirst for detail and documentation. Consequently, his book is an impressive *tour de force*. I can only refer the interested reader to that source, for there is not space here to give a full presentation of his elaborately developed theory. Suffice it to say that the opening of events occurs in the sign of Virgo. Thus, Bullinger's theory implies, without directly saying so, that the true primogeniture of the zodiac—far more ancient than modern interpretation will allow—must apparently lie at a point somewhere in Virgo, rather than 0° Aries (or at a disputed point in Taurus, as the siderealists insist) and that Adamic man must have had his origins within that Virgoan age, namely, somewhere between 13,119 and 10,960 B.C. But this unpublicized aspect of his portrayal of events, which could readily have ruffled the feathers of a great many prominent scientists and theologians of his day, mercifully went unnoticed. Bullinger chose not to draw attention to it, although it could scarcely have escaped his personal awareness. Such a disquieting deduction, actually assigning a celestially oriented time frame for Adam's appearance in the earth, could only be made by looking at Bullinger's armada of evidence through the long-range lens of the 25,920-year precession of the equinoxes. This was not at all his point of focus. Rather, his lineup of celestial and terrestrial data unfolded along the more familiar annual path of the solar ecliptic, thus sidestepping the potential controversy his highly original interpretation of the zodiac could easily have ignited if viewed through the opposite end of the astrological lens. In short, the perspective presented by Bullnger was a "forward" progression through the twelve signs, starting with Virgo and ending with Leo, in keeping with the annual cycle of "birth signs," rather than the reverse order of the Grand Cycle of the Ages.

In the sign of Virgo, Bullinger shows that the name of this sign in the Hebrew is *Bethulah,* which means "a virgin," and in the Arabic, "a branch." This introductory theme is skillfully developed with numerous biblical quotations, moving on to celestial facts. For instance, the first constellation in Virgo is Comah, meaning "the desired," or "the longed for." The more ancient zodiacs, Bullinger tells us, pictured this constellation as a woman with a child in her arms. He specifically cites from the astrological lore of the Persians, the Chaldeans, and the Egyptians to support this interpretation. In fact, in more precise symbolic terms, we learn that the ancient Egyptian name for the constellation of Comah was *Shes-nu,* which translates "desired *son.*"

Next, in the constellation of Boötes (we are still in the sign of Virgo), golden Arcturus is interpreted as meaning "He cometh," alluding to the Christ. (In Edgar Cayce Reading 827–1, we find Arcturus identified as that star which guided the shepherds to Bethlehem, while Reading 900–10 tells us that "the man called Jesus" went on to Arcturus "as of the developing"; so here we have an interesting parallel with Bullinger's scholarly findings.) Within that same constellation, a star in the spearhead of Boötes the Shepherd— "the Coming One"—is *Al Katurops,* meaning "the branch," as well as "treading under foot." *Nekkar,* meaning "the pierced," is another star in this same constellation.

Thus, with scholarly mastery, Bullinger carries us through the various zodiacal signs with their individual stars and asterisms, patiently depicting the Messiah's agonizing journey through the earth and His eventual triumph and Second Coming, with this last phase depicted, of course, in the closing sign of Leo. Here we have the glorious *Orion,* whose foot is coming down on the enemy's head (*Lepus*). And we see *Him* in the Lion of the Tribe of Judah (symbolized by Leo), about to tread down that Old Serpent *Hydra,* the Devil.

Regrettably, as Bullinger's scholarly annotations make abundantly clear, Greek and Latin corruptions inherited as fixtures of modern astronomy and astrology have clouded and nearly obscured the ancient symbolism. But the symbols are there. The story, which is written in the heavens, is as enduring as His Word.

Leaving Bullinger now, we must journey back in time to the generations of the early patriarchs, as given in Genesis. If, as the readings suggest and various extant legends maintain, Enoch and Hermes were one, and if Enoch was indeed a reincarnation of Adam, as given in a number of esoteric sources as well as in the Cayce readings, then how does this serve to pinpoint Adam's appearance in the Age of Virgo?

Quite simple, really.

The Cayce readings introduce Hermes (Enoch) as the master architect of the Great Pyramid, which was supposedly constructed in a one-hundred-year period from 10,490 to 10,390 B.C. (as already mention in Chapter 2). Now, the biblical account of the days of Enoch, as found in Genesis, states that they numbered three hundred sixty and five years. Yet, rather than saying that he died, we find this cryptic allusion to a physical "translation" of some kind: "And Enoch walked with God," says the author of

Genesis, "and he *was not;* for God took him." In the aprocryphal Secrets of Enoch,[3] his transition is explained in these mystical terms: "When Enoch had talked to the people, the Lord sent out darkness onto the earth . . . and it covered those men standing with Enoch, and they took Enoch up . . . and light came again."

It is our speculation that Enoch was transported to Egypt—or, more precisely, to the Libyan mount—where the Edgar Cayce readings indicate he joined forces with the exiled priest, Ra Ta, later returning with Ra Ta and his fellow exiles to Egypt. But now, rather than being known as Enoch in this new land, the stranger and teacher in their midst was called Thoth, or Hermes. But that's getting a bit ahead of our story, for his rightful introduction is in our next chapter.

The point, then, is simply this: Enoch's birth, if we count back some 375 or more years from 10,490 B.C., when construction on the Great Pyramid supposedly commenced, was about 10,865 B.C. The patriarch was six generations removed from Adam, yet the span in years was more than six hundred. Finally, in Genesis 5, wherein the generations of Adam are given, we find a serious gap, which can perhaps be attributed to some early biblical censorship on the part of that sect known as the Sethians. For we find the account of Adam's direct progeny beginning with Seth's birth, and Adam's age is suspiciously given as "an hundred and thirty years" at the time, although He was presumably much older. Why? Because omitted from this censored version is any reference to the earlier days of Adam in the Garden of Eden, or the eventual birth of Cain and Abel. Conceivably, we have "lost" as much as several hundred years—perhaps more. (We are not questioning Adam's total length of days, which was given as nine hundred and thirty years, but we suggest that there may have been some "doctoring" by Sethian zealots in assigning to Adam a relatively youthful one hundred and thirty years at the time of Seth's birth, when he was probably considerably older. By this device, no question arises concerning the unaccounted-for centuries of his earlier transgressions, which simply have no place in this expurgated chapter, presumably a separate scroll or palimpsest.) Anyhow, by our estimation, Adam must have had his Edenic beginnings some thousand years or so ahead of Enoch's time, not a mere six hundred. Otherwise, Adam would still have been alive at Enoch's birth—a circumstance contradicted by the Cayce records, as well as legendary accounts cited by Jung and other scholars, which identify Enoch as the first in a series of reincarnations of Adam, leading up to his final entry in the earth as Jesus.

To summarize: In round figures, we would speculate that Adam probably projected into the earth-plane about 12,000 B.C., near the midpoint of the Virgoan age.

Finally, all of this serves to corroborate our theory about the present Great Year cycle, commencing in Virgo and ending in Libra. Amilius, the Maker of the manifest universe—*including the zodiac*—set the pattern for the zodiacal ages when He chose the "Age of the Virgin" to enter His own creation as Adam, the Son of man, during that second influx of souls, coming among His own in flesh-form to take on the predestined role of a Redeemer.

Only one major question remains unanswered, looming in front of us like some Sphinxian riddle: If there is to be a shifting of the poles at the turn of the century (whether a partial tilt or a magnetic reversal, or perhaps a combination, was not stated), how might this affect our planetary relationship to the constellation of Libra? What surprising realignment with the signs of the zodiac could come about with even a minor shifting of the earth's geopolar or magnetic axis? Perhaps we are destined to meet the sign of Judgment a bit ahead of schedule. If so, only time and planetary tilt can tell . . .

5. An Aryan in Egypt

EXODUS FROM ARARAT

Questionings arose. There was much consternation and dispute among the elders. Clearly, the pale-bodied, blue-eyed boy-child represented both an oddity and a threat to the tribe of Zu. For he was not one of them, yet his unique social status demanded full recognition.

His mother, a daughter of Zu, spoke of visitations from the gods of that area, between the Caucasian Mountains and the Caspian Sea, who had brought about his conception.[1] She declared that his name was to be Ra Ta, signifying the first pure white in the earth.[2] Indeed, she spoke of her newborn son with such an unaccustomed air of authority and purpose that some were strangely moved by her words, while others were made uneasy by them.

All knew of her innocence and purity. And none dared to doubt the integrity of her speech, as a daughter of the leader Zu himself. Yet because of the infant's alien appearance and because he had no father from among the tribesmen to claim him and raise him, it was argued by some among the council of elders that the child should be disposed of. Others, however, warned of retribution from higher forces if such a rash act were to be carried out. For in those days, some 10,600 years before the entry of the Prince of Peace into the earth[3] and only a millennium or so after Adam's advent, the gods were not so far removed from the minds or the activities of the sons and daughters of men that they had forgotten to respect and fear them. So it was decided, instead, with Zu's reluctant approval, that the mother and her newborn son should be sent away—rejected, as permanent outcasts from the tribe. However, they were to be accompanied by a small retinue of "things" (those grotesque remnants of unholy cohabitation by the sons of

Belial with the beasts in the earth, who now labored for the sons of men), and these would protect and serve them in their wanderings.

Thus is was that Ra Ta and his mother eventually found their way to the slopes of that mountain now known as Ararat, and named after the Carpathian leader who had established a home community for a band of his nomadic people in that place. It lay in a northwestern quadrant of that land later known as Persia, or the Aryan empire (today within Turkish borders).

King Ararat, marveling at the child's unusual appearance, immediately welcomed the outcasts to his primitive encampment. He treated them henceforth as his own. Although Ararat condemned Zu's actions, he instinctively sensed that the gods may have had a hand in leading the outcasts into his protective custody for reasons beyond his present comprehension.

The boy Ra Ta grew swiftly, gaining in grace and stature. But that was not all. He began to exhibit an uncanny psychic ability, of which the king took careful note. Often, too, the lad would wander off alone, deep in his trancelike meditations. When asked about these long periods of entering into the silence, Ra Ta reassured the king.

"The gods sometimes speak to me when I am very still," he said matter-of-factly. "It is like a wise voice within me, giving me directions."

The king nodded approvingly.

"That is good, my son," he told him. "Be an attentive listener, then. I believe it is the voice of the Creative Forces that speaks through you, and when you are old enough I shall make you a priest to my people. Then you shall instruct them in the ways of the higher laws, called the Law of One. It is the knowledge all upright men are continually seeking."

Ra Ta was greatly pleased. It was just what the inner voice had told him would be his future destiny.

The king's own son, Arart, was a shepherd in the higher pastures, and somewhat older than Ra Ta. Yet a close bond had developed between them. Arart was skilled in the arts of warfare and

politics, but he also sought knowledge of a moral and religious
nature, which would make him a wise ruler one day. Ra Ta had a
natural understanding of these matters, and whenever he joined
Arart in the higher pastures, the future king would sit, entranced,
as his younger friend instructed him with ease and grace, answering all manner of ethical and metaphysical questions as if from
some inner well of wisdom.

In his twenty-first year, Ra Ta received a prophetic vision.

The vision had come to him as a spiritual directive, and Ra Ta
hastened to tell the king about it. It concerned a whole "new order" of things that was even now in the making, and King Ararat's people were chosen to play a decisive role in the unfolding
pattern of events, along with Ra Ta. Led by the king's son, Arart,
as their new ruler, and with Ra Ta as their spiritual leader and
guide, a pioneering group of some nine hundred souls was to journey many moons southward into the land of Egypt. There, with
divine help, they would conquer the native inhabitants—peaceful-
ly, if at all possible—and set up a new rule in that ancient kingdom, which was materially far advanced though spiritually deca-
dent. Yet Ra Ta's vision nevertheless told him that Egypt marked
the spiritual center of the Universal Forces in the earth. From this
center there were destined to emanate many spiritual changes and
teachings, he explained to the king, that would serve to awaken
the then-developing nations and races among the sons and daughters of men so that they could be made aware of their spiritual
roots and responsibilities. Without such an awakening, Ra Ta
warned King Ararat, mankind could not hope to survive a great
planetary cataclysm that was fast approaching. Nor could the
necessary preparations be made to preserve the sacred records of
the era, as a warning and a revelation to future generations in a
distant age, to be uncovered when the proper time had come.

The king gazed intently upon the tall, alabaster-like figure of his
newly appointed young priest, with his flowing mane of flaxen
hair and eyes the color of azurite. He had listened well to Ra Ta's
inspired words, and it took only one look into the impenetrable

depths of those strange blue eyes to tell Ararat that he must heed the prophecy. The prospect somewhat saddened him; he would be staying behind, with an aging remnant of his tribe, here on the slopes of the great mountain to which he had first brought his people to establish a home community, while his son now followed his earlier example by leading a great horde of hardy pioneers into yet another distant land.

Ararat might have wondered privately at the choice of Egypt, despite Ra Ta's compelling psychic convictions. Yet according to the readings, it was inevitable. A number of factors made it so:

Why Egypt? This [place] had been determined [by those forces guiding Ra Ta] . . . as the center of the universal activities of nature, as well as the spiritual forces, and where there might be the least disturbance by the convulsive movements which came about in the earth [soon thereafter] through the [final] destruction of Lemuria, Atlantis, and—in later periods —the flood.

When the lines about the earth are considered from the mathematical precisions, it will be found that the center is nigh unto where the Great Pyramid [later to be constructed by Ra and Hermes] . . . is still located.

Then, there were the mathematical, the astrological and the numerological indications, as well as the individual urge [determining Ra Ta's choice of Egypt]. (281–42)

The preceding reference to "the lines about the earth" relates, in all probability, to those esoteric measurements called "ley lines," which are apparently determined in some arcane manner by the positions of the stars. It is believed that prehistoric science had mastered the use of these ley patterns in determining the exact positioning of many sacred structures, such as Stonehenge and the Great Pyramid, which still stand today in mute testimony to an ancient wisdom now forgotten.

As for the "individual urge" prompting Ra Ta, alluded to in the foregoing excerpt, this presumably emanated from his own subconscious memory patterns of that much earlier Egyptian cycle as the androgynous ruler Asapha. Now those old memories were drawing him back to the same general locale that had once before served as a world center for spiritually directed activities, during a similar time of planetary crisis. For, as given, "in the earth manifestation and the cycle of time, much repeats itself."[4]

Preparations for the exodus from Mount Ararat, like the long and perilous journey that lay ahead, took many, many moons. Provisions had to be gathered; slings and other crude weaponry had to be fashioned for the coming battle, as well as for the defense en route and the gathering of fresh game along the way; and fearsome beasts of warfare—including bulls, bears, leopards and hawks—had to be specially trained by Arart's warriors and, in some instances, equipped with cleverly wrought spiked collars to enhance their ferocity.[5] In devising this strategy of fear, Arart reasoned that they could thus subdue their potential enemies more quickly, cowing them into surrender without needless bloodshed. Ra Ta's preferred approach to the Egyptians was that of friendly persuasion, which he planned to use in conjunction with Arart's more forceful tactics. Peace, not war, was Ra Ta's goal. He sought eventual unification of Arart's invading forces not only with those peoples in the Egyptian land but with the tribal clusterings of mankind that were now gathering into the separate nations and races of the prophesied new order, thus bringing about a closer relationship of man to the Creator, and of man to man.

Ra Ta and Arart included in their entourage many of those classless beings termed "things" by the Atlanteans, who now served the sons of men as laborers. However, in the new land toward which they were headed, their subhuman status was to be raised by the priest to that of potential equals who, through purification, "might eventually become channels through which blessings, and knowledge of the divine influence and force, might be made manifest."[6]

The caravan of some nine hundred souls at last departed, as Ra Ta and Arart turned their backs forever upon Mount Ararat. The awesome procession, stretching a mile or more in length, traveled mostly afoot, with beasts of burden taking the place of wagons or carriages.[7] It was to be a long and arduous journey, requiring numerous prolonged encampments en route to replenish their energies as well as their provisions. Yet, across the broad plains and rugged hills of Araby lay a shimmering land of promise and plenty.

Egypt! There the River of Life poured its abundant waters upon the green and fertile delta, and the sun shed its bright rays upon a dark-skinned people whose perennial prosperity had gradually led to indolence and materialism. These were mostly the evolving descendants of Asapha's people, from an age only dimly remembered. Now that same Asapha was returning to his own. They would see in the strange, alabaster-pale figure of the charismatic priest an image of the Sun itself, brought down to earth.

Based upon the readings, it was perhaps an understandable confusion:

[For] the entrance into the Ra Ta experience, when there was the journeying from materiality—or the being translated in materiality as Ra Ta—was from the infinity forces, or from the Sun; with those influences that draw upon the planet itself, the earth and all those about same.

Is it any wonder that in the ignorance of the earth the activities of that entity were [later] turned into that influence called the sun-worshippers? (5755–1)

THE VICTORS AND THE VANQUISHED

King Raai was a man of peace. More than that, the elderly ruler of the Egyptians was a man who chose solitude over pomp and ceremony. He had increasingly isolated himself, of late. The king was by nature a philosopher, and affairs of state bored him. Thus, he had paid less and less attention to governing his people in his declining years, preferring to let them govern themselves. This was not too difficult, fortunately, in a land that was sufficiently prosperous and happy to pose no major problems.

Or so it seemed, at any rate.

Then, one fateful day, Arart and his great horde of fierce-looking tribesmen suddenly descended upon the sleeping city of Luz just as the sun awoke.

Terrified farmers, up early to work in their fields, fled in horror at the sight of the approaching warriors, who were flanked on either side by wild, bloodthirsty beasts straining at their leashes. In the vanguard of the strange procession was a tall, white-bodied figure such as they had never seen before, with both of his hands raised aloft. This was the priestly Ra Ta, signaling them to surrender and make peace.

Make peace they did—not only the farmers encountered along their triumphal route, but the startled populace within the city itself. Only a token resistance occurred at the hands of ill-prepared and badly outnumbered guards outside the royal palace. In the midst of the slaughter, however, King Raai came forth. He ordered a halt to the futile resistance by his own forces. Then he graciously surrendered his rulership to Arart, upon receiving assurances from Ra Ta of the invaders' benevolent purposes in accord with the precepts of the Law of One.

So the new rule began, and Arart was designated the first of the "shepherd kings" from the north. (His son, Araaraart, who was to be born some years later in the new land, would become the second to bear that epithet.[8]) We do not know what symbolic significance such an epithet may have carried, if any, but undoubtedly it bespoke in plain terms the invaders' pastoral origins.

The readings say of Raai's act of submission to Arart's forces that, although condemned at the time by some of his own people, it demonstrated a principle that later became the basis for the studies of the Prince of Peace himself.[9] This was undoubtedly the Christ-like principle of laying self-interest aside for the sake of the greater good.

(In his next incarnation, however, Raai lost. This was during Cayce's Persian cycle as the nomadic ruler, Uhjltd, again playing the role of an invader, while Raai—known as Bestreld then—was the keeper of the exchequer for Croesus. Much of Croesus's fabled wealth was apparently due to Bestreld's greedy hoarding. Yet in the actual sacking of the storehouses by the invading forces, the life reading states that the entity Bestreld finally *gained,* in the material loss encountered and the subsequent persecutions. A curious way to "gain," one might say, but from the karmic aspect, apparently a needed lesson was learned. Thus, it is our speculation that in his previous incarnation as King Raai, the entity may have harbored a secondary reason for his hasty surrender, a reason less noble than the first. In short, he perhaps sought to preserve his worldly goods by this action, as further resistance to Arart's forces would probably have cost him the loss of his possessions, and even his life, in addition to his throne. If our speculation is valid, then it serves to demonstrate in dramatic fashion how closely intertwined are the karmic threads of our lives with those whom we daily encounter. Yet, when Raai once again came on the scene as the present-day entity [1734], and found himself drawn to the former priest Ra Ta, who was now Edgar Cayce, it was for a spiritual opportunity in *both* their lives, and a mutual blessing.)

Back to Egypt and our story.

Among the natives of the land, there dwelt a young scribe and teacher of unusual mental abilities, who was the principal sage of a cult known as the Euranians.[10] He was well versed in the esoteric application of numbers, among other mysteries, and he soon came to King Arart's attention. This compelling young intellectual and occultist, although once removed from power by Arart's fearful predecessor, King Raai, was still much respected among many of the more influential of the native inhabitants and had a considerable though discreet following.

Now that the new rule under Arart was bringing about many important changes in the social, moral, and religious order of the land, the king sensed the need for a prominent figure among the native populace to stand at his side, as it were, as a trusted councillor or scribe who could interpret to his own people the intent and purpose of the new laws and the new rule being formulated by the king and the priest. In this way, the rising tide of resentment and criticism could be deflected. The influential young leader of the Euranians struck Arart as a most logical choice.

And so, in his thirty-second year, the young Egyptian was invited to share in the pomp, glory, and power of Arart's rulership, while occupying a position parallel, in a historical sense, to that of Jefferson in the drafting of the Declaration of Independence. For, as explained in one of the readings for Mr. [900], who had been that chosen scribe and interpreter, "the scribe set about to give those interpretations in the combination as Jefferson gave that of liberty to [the people] . . . [presenting] those truths as pertaining to man's relation with the higher creative energy and forces."[11]

This appointment occurred in the third year of Arart's dynasty. At the time of the invasion of Egypt by Arart's forces,[12] the youthful scribe was only twenty-nine. Moreover, in many parts of the world in those days, the age of male maturity was regarded to be thirty-three. Yet the king himself was probably not much older than that, and Ra Ta, the chosen priest, had been only twenty-one when he first received his psychic inspiration to undertake the entry into Egypt—a journey that we assume may have taken the invading forces a decade or more, considering the slow and deliberate preparations and the long and frequent encampments en route with such a vast entourage. All the same—give or take a decade in our calculations—it may be seen that the "shepherd king" Arart, the priest, and the native scribe were all relatively youthful contemporaries of one another. Consequently, with their combined energies working toward the development of that ideal as set by the priest, this ruling "troika" must have represented a veritable dynamo of spiritual reform in a land that was far more accustomed to its own former leisurely pace and materialistic goals. Inevitably, the rumblings of discontent, particularly among the former ruling class, began to grow. As the years continued to roll by and the level of reform intensified under Ra Ta's unrelenting efforts, replacing the last vestiges of a materialistic and class-conscious culture with a more egalitarian and spiritually based rule, the discontent became increasingly vocal, most notably among the deposed aristocracy, whose special vulnerability made them all the more rebellious. They protested a lack of fair representation.

It was at this time that King Arart made a totally unexpected move. His young son and heir apparent, Araaraart, who had been born in the new land, was now sixteen. A mere stripling! Yet Arart saw that this very fact would work in his favor. He decided to turn over his throne to the boy, and then make the Egyptian scribe, whom he had learned to trust, a full-fledged member of the royal household, assuming "Aarat" as his family name. He then planned to pit Aarat's considerable talents against the new young

king's, so to speak, by elevating him to the role of a special councillor to the youthful ruler. It proved to be a clever bit of strategy.
The native populace was considerably mollified by this conciliato-
ry gesture, and the various reforms in progress could still proceed
as usual. The retiring king reserved a background role for himself,
and he was confident, meanwhile, that his son, who was quick of
mind and speech despite his tender years, would soon be wise in
the ways of power and emerge as an excellent ruler. He was very
nearly right. But later on, a flawed judgment intervened.

When he was thirty, Araaraart II, as the second "shepherd king"
was called, surveyed the political situation about him and made
what appeared to be an astute decision. In part, perhaps, to under-
cut some of the entrenched influence of his native adviser, Aarat,
but also to create the semblance of a more democratic rule, the
young king formed a cabinet, or council, of twelve advisers,[13]
drawing their numbers impartially from among the native populace
as well as his own people. These twelve, in consultation with one
another and with the king, would aid in deciding the affairs of state.
However, for the crucial position of chief councillor, Araaraart II
retained a somewhat Machiavellian figure named Asriaio, who was
of his father's people from the north and had been chief councillor
in his father's court.

Although these developments appeared to offer expanded representation of the people's interests in the royal court, they also gave
the young king ample leverage against his Egyptian rival, Aarat,
whose voice would henceforth be only one among twelve. Yet it
was a move that was to work against the king's interests in the
end, as he tended to listen more and more to the advice of others
rather than to his own inner voice.

Ra Ta, the high priest, was to be another loser from Araaraart's
political manipulations.

In the beginning, the choosing of Ra Ta as high priest in the
new land, with supreme authority over the native people as well as
Arart's people in all matters religious or spiritual had met with
jealous resistence and much dissension in certain ruling quarters.
This highly vocal opposition had gradually been silenced, how-

ever, as the inspired nature of the priest's psychic powers became more and more evident even to his most vociferous opponents. At last they no longer dared speak out against him. The priest's programs of moral and spiritual reform had gradually made Ra Ta a figure of awe and veneration among the masses. His success was epitomized in the extraordinary results of the purification rituals in the Temple of Sacrifice, where the "things" were being cleansed of such bestial hindrances as the cloven hoof or tails or feathers, among other monstrosities and protuberances, and the Temple Beautiful, where those souls purified in the physical could then go for mental and spiritual training to fit them for higher service to God and man. By some, in their ignorance, the priest was even viewed as a god himself.

The Egyptians, in their cultural advancement over Arart's more pastoral and simple tribesmen, had long enjoyed lighter-than-air travel in gas-laden balloons introduced to them by the Atlanteans in times past. And now that Atlantean evacuees were beginning to arrive in increasing numbers, as their priests and priestesses warned of the impending destruction of Poseidia, and strife with the sons of Belial was accelerating, Ra Ta saw an opportunity to visit other areas of the world where the sons of men were gathered. So he went to India, to the Gobi land, to Og, and to what is now Peru, as well as to Carpathia, speaking to the spiritual leaders in these places about the evolving new order of things and the preparations for the new root race then emerging. Also, he went to the fair city of Alta, in Poseidia, where he conferred with many of the children of the Law of One. One of the leaders there, a great sage named Hept-supht, chose to come to Egypt and assist the priest in the great reforms he was undertaking with the peoples in that land. For he knew, as did Ra Ta, that Egypt was to become a great spiritual center in the days immediately ahead and a place where the records must be preserved, even as was being done in Atlantis already and would be done later by Iltar in Yucatan.[14]

As these more esoteric activities were proceeding in the spiritual affairs of the land, Egypt was also experiencing dramatic developments in commerce and construction and the arts. Under the supervision of Ararat I, and later his son and successor, Araaraart II, mining activities were aggressively pursued in a search for precious stones and gems, as well as such minerals as zinc, copper, tin, and the like. The construction of temples and other edifices went forward relentlessly. Storehouses became commonplace and served as places of exchange or barter in international commerce with merchants from other lands. Egypt was thriving.

It was thriving, but not everyone was happy. Many of the former pleasures had been outlawed by the priest. And his increasingly frequent absences as he journeyed to other parts of the planet to confer with spiritual leaders, became occasions to revive those sinful self-indulgences forbidden by Ra Ta. The concocting of intoxicating brews was one, and another was the sexual abuse of those poor, victimized "things" who were undergoing the various stages of purification and higher development in the Temple of Sacrifice and the Temple Beautiful.

The priest, upon returning unexpectedly from a regional archaeological expedition, learned firsthand of these violations of his edicts, and, to put the matter in common parlance, "all hell broke loose." Moreover, the violations were not only being committed by certain disgruntled native subjects but also by some of Araaraart's own clansmen. Ra Ta went to the council with his complaints.

But what the priest did not know, in his innocently trusting nature, was that several among the councillors themselves were on the side of the lawbreakers. This included the chief councillor, Asriaio, who had succumbed to the evil machinations of Ra Ta's enemies as they sought some way to discredit and overthrow the priest. It was mankind's first conflict between Church and State.

When the Devil can find no other way to get a man, he sends for a woman. And this is what the plotters did.

One of Ra Ta's edicts was that no man should have more than one wife. At the same time, his obsession with developing as many representatives as possible of the emerging white race he himself embodied was well known, for the changing of the pigmentation to lighter hues—though an act not wholly in accord with spiritual purposes, as will be shown in a later chapter—was one of the more remarkable accomplishments Ra Ta had presumably learned from the Atlanteans and had been applying with varying degrees of success in the developmental phases in the Temple of Sacrifice and, later, the Temple Beautiful. Indeed, so eager was he to hasten the law of evolution that it had become a blind spot, as it were, in his own understanding and application of the spiritual laws governing such matters. For the hand of God is seldom hurried, and racial differences served a definite purpose in the Divine Plan.

Knowing the priest's one weakness, then, the plotters moved to exploit it. In the Temple Beautiful was a dancer named Isris, whose fairness of skin and unusual grace and beauty had made her an object of envy and desire by many. The daughter of the second sacrificial priest, she was a special favorite of the young king, Araaraart II. If she could be persuaded that a liaison with the priest would serve a good cause, in producing a truly perfect offspring from their mating, the next step would be relatively easy: one glance from the eye of Isris, followed by the appropriate words, and the priest would be fair game for the plotters' evil arrow.

It worked, of course, as expected. (As an aside, though, Isris's karmic payoff in the present life was near-blindness in one eye.)

When a daughter was born nine months later from the illicit union of Ra Ta and Isris, all that remained was to spring the trap that would convict the offending priest of violating his own edict. The matter went before the king for judgment. Araaraart, who was perhaps less enraged by Ra Ta's infidelity to his own law than by the fact that his favorite dancer, Isris, had been involved as a partner in the sexual transgression, was readily persuaded that Ra Ta should be punished. The question was whether to put him to death, as certain extremists among his councillors recommended, or to seek some less drastic means of meting out kingly displeasure upon the hapless priest.

The banishment of both offenders was urged upon Araaraart by his chief councillor, Asriaio. It was seconded by Aarat the Egyptian.

Thus it came to pass that Ra Ta was sent into exile, accompanied by some 231 souls who remained loyal to him. This included the Atlantean sage, Hept-supht, and the priest's favorite daughter, Aris-Hobeth, whose name meant "Favored One." Both were to be a great comfort to him, along with the sorrowfully repentant Isris, in the years of trial that lay ahead of the priest in the far Nubian mount of their exile.

As for the fair child, Iso, that luckless offspring of the fatal union between Ra Ta and Isris, the vengeful king held her as a hostage. Though well cared for, she was to die of desolation before the exile period ended. The reading for this soul-entity, known as [288], indicated that she was that twin soul of Edgar Cayce's whom the reader has already encountered in earlier chapters.

Meanwhile, as the priest and his party of fellow exiles journeyed southward under a blazing Egyptian sun, Ra Ta reflected ruefully upon the far-reaching and tragic consequences of his momentary weakness. And as he looked toward the purple hills of Nubia that lay ahead, forbidding and mysterious in their bleak majesty, he thought he could hear echoing ever so faintly at his back the mocking laughter of the gods.

THE PRIEST IN EXILE

The Cayce readings on the Ra Ta period refer interchangeably to the place of exile as the "Nubian" or the "Libyan" mount, while the local inhabitants are similarly spoken of as either Libyans or Nubians. Also there is at least one reference to Abyssinia as the general setting. The latter, of course, is today known as Ethiopia; it lies directly below Egypt and the Sudan. Nubia, which no longer exists as a separate country, is now remembered only for the Nubian Desert, in the eastern sector of northern Sudan, just above the northernmost tip of Ethiopia. Thus, it seems likely, in view of the language of the readings, that all of this general area was once a part of the ancient Libyan kingdom—with the Nubian principality occupying only that small, easternmost sector of

Libya's vast desert empire—to which Ra Ta and his band of fellow exiles were either specifically sent at Araaraart's command or voluntarily chose to go.

More probably the latter. We say this in light of the unique associations awaiting them there, which suggest that Ra Ta was again being guided by his psychic promptings. As far as the king's wishes were concerned, we submit that the terms of exile may only have required that the priest be banished to a place outside the borders of Egypt. But if the kingdom of Libya was indeed the king's mandate—and admittedly, Reading 294–151 does say, "to Libya were these people sent"—one may suspect that the selection of the Nubian mount, at least, was Ra Ta's.

In support of this supposition, there is a vital clue to be found in Reading 294–148, suggesting that Ra Ta may already have been familiar with that same mount of exile in the Nubian hills. Although no geographical indicator is included in this particular reference, which would clearly confirm the suspicion, the reading alludes to Ra Ta's return from "one of those visits to the mount." Moreover, it concerns a period immediately prior to Ra Ta's betrayal, when he first discovered evidence of lustful activities and other acts of self-aggrandizement by those in charge in the Temple of Sacrifice. What would have been more natural, then, when the priest found himself sent into a Libyan exile than to return to that same mount where he had so recently been meditating and researching?

The nature of that research, which had apparently been going on for some while, was "delving into what was termed the archaeological conditions of those that had lived in the lands in the periods before,"[15] and remembering that Ra Ta had reigned in Upper Egypt, as Asapha, during a much earlier incarnation, he undoubtedly experienced psychic recall of the whole general area and its ancient inhabitants, over whom he had presumably ruled. In summary, then, the basic nature of Ra Ta's archaeological research appears to have been at the *psychic* level first, even as was to be the case ages later when he reincarnated as a twentieth-century prophet and seer, Edgar Cayce, and gave psychic readings that were to become the basis for much highly promising archaeological research work that still continues in the Middle East and other areas of the world (and may one day be resumed in Iran).

Returning to the days of Ra Ta, here is a revealing reference to the priest's early psychic pronouncements, or "readings," as we would term them, during the initial period of Arart I's rule in the conquered Egyptian kingdom:

> With Ra Ta then beginning with the natives and *those that listened to the uncovering of the records* (in what would be termed archaeological research in the present), gradually more and more adherence was made to those words of this peculiar leader that had come into this land. (294–147; italics added)

Whatever setback Ra Ta may have experienced as the deposed high priest in Egypt, there were now compensatory blessings in the Nubian land:

> With the entering into the Nubian land, there came such a change that there were the bettered conditions in every term that may be applied to human experience. . . . As the priest in this period entered more and more into the closer relationships with the Creative Forces, greater were the abilities for the entity or body Ra Ta to be able to make or bring about the *material* manifestations of that relationship. Hence the peace that was enjoyed by the peoples, not only with the priest but all those of that land. (294–150)

Also, some very interesting activities were begun. Some of their effects, surprisingly, are still with us in the present:

> There were begun some memorials in the Nubian land which still may be seen, even in this period, in the mountains of the land. Whole mountains were honeycombed, and were dug into sufficient to where the perpetual fires are *still* in activity in these various periods, when the priest then began to show the manifestations of those periods of reckoning the longitude (as termed now), latitude, and the activities of the planets and stars, and the various groups of stars, constellations, and the various influences that are held in place, or that *hold* in place those about this particular solar system. Hence in the Nubian land there were first begun the reckoning of those periods when the Sun has its influence upon human life, and

let's remember that it is [was?] in this period when the *present race* has been called into being—and the *influence* is reckoned from all experiences of Ra Ta, as the effect upon the body physical, the body mental, the body spiritual, or soul body. (294–150)

Here it may be useful to pause, and ask ourselves what Cayce meant in the preceding excerpt, in referring to "this period when the *present race* has been called into being." The answer seems to revolve around a simple question of syntax—one of the recurrent hazards, admittedly, in working with the Cayce readings. If the phrase "this period" alludes to Ra Ta's era, not ours (and I think it must), then the reference was undoubtedly to the fourth root race —our own, in fact, and thus the "present race"—at a time when the Adamic Age was still in its infancy. However, mankind is now on the threshold of yet another transformation, which will introduce a new root race, which Cayce has identified as the fifth. But this new development cannot yet be termed the "present race," for it is not yet fully upon us. We are told that its actual beginnings are to be signaled by an event that may still lie a full generation ahead of us: the opening of a concealed Pyramid of Records, buried under the Gizeh complex, somewhere between the mysterious Sphinx and the Nile. (This matter will be taken up in proper detail later in the chapter.)

To continue, then, we find that Ra Ta's esoteric activities in the Nubian land involved all manner of celestial observations and scientific inquiry that form a part of our present heritage.

Of special significance to the researcher in a correlation of Ra Ta's activities with the much later psychic revelations of Edgar Cayce is the uncanny emphasis always given by Cayce to the role of the Sun, the Moon, the stars and the various constellations, not only in their combined effects upon human life, but upon other life-forms as well, and upon planet Earth itself. In fact, in addition to special readings on the subject, every life reading given by Edgar Cayce can be found to include certain astrological reference points in the past and present soul development of that particular entity. Planetary sojourns elsewhere within our own solar system are also mentioned as a part of each soul's experience in the spiritual plane between earthly incarnations. Finally, it is indicated in the Cayce readings that upon completion of its cycle of development within this solar system, the soul-entity moves on, either through Arcturus or Polaris, for higher development in other spheres of consciousness. (All of this esoteric wisdom, whether or not one is prepared to accept the validity of such arcane revelations, apparently came to Cayce in trance-state as a direct outgrowth of his former psychic development as Ra Ta, in the Nubian land.)

The Nubians were a warlike people. Hostility was their natural reaction, therefore, when the high priest of the Egyptian kingdom to the north, whose previous visits to their hills on relatively brief archaeological missions had involved only a small team of helpers, now very suddenly arrived with a multitude of followers and proceeded to establish a home community in exile, choosing a prominent hilltop where the priest's earlier excavations had taken place. Such bold actions were viewed as a threat, at first.

Yet it did not take long for the charismatic priest to win them over by precept and example, as his enlightened teachings took root and brought manifold blessings to the Nubians, as well as to his own people. Among Ra Ta's first converts was a prince of the Nubian land, who was to be one of many among the native inhabitants to accompany the priest and his people on their triumphal return to Egypt some nine years later.

Another important convert was a seventeen-year-old Libyan princess, named Ai-Si, who was also destined to follow Ra Ta back to Egypt. There she became a musician and priestess in the Temple Beautiful and a drawer of "life seals" depicting the key symbols of a soul-entity's unfolding evolutionary pattern in the earth.

Meanwhile, temples of worship were built in the mount and separate abodes where those who chose to live in pairs, as man and wife, could raise their families. This was a distinct departure from the custom in Egypt, where the life-style was strictly communal, and segregated, women from men, except for periods of union in the conjugal chambers. This creation of a "home life" for his people, as Ra Ta had observed in certain of the lands he had visited, brought a new sense of happiness, prosperity, and peace.

Word of Ra Ta's remarkable accomplishments not only reached King Araaraart's ears in Egypt, where the Ruler's heart was already troubled by private feelings of remorse, but those in distant lands soon heard and came seeking.

One of these was the great initiate, Hermes.

Tradition ascribes to Hermes various sobriquets. Generally known to the Egyptians as Thoth, or Thoth-Hermes, the Greeks later gave him the legendary name of Hermes Trismegistus, meaning "thrice great." To the ancient Egyptians, he was the "scribe of the gods," and "lord of divine words"; he was also regarded as "the heart and the tongue of Ra." But to really pierce his identity, we must revert to a little-known Islamic legend, chronicled by îbn Batuta in A.D. 1352, claiming that Hermes was none other than the patriarch Enoch (known as Idrîs to Muslim scholars), and that *it was he who built the Great Pyramid.* In the apocryphal literature, we find ample evidence to support the view that Enoch, who was apparently translated from the sight of his own people in his three hundred sixty-fifth year, when "God took him,"[16] actually spent many additional decades traveling to the four quarters of the earth, warning the people of cataclysmic changes approaching and the need to draw closer to God. It was he, in fact, who is believed to have warned Noah some few centuries later of an impending flood.

The Edgar Cayce readings, as already noted in an earlier chapter, identify Enoch as an incarnation of the Master, whose immediately prior appearance in the earth had been as Adam. But it may be even more surprising to some to learn that there are in existence certain ancient scholarly sources, cited by both C. G. Jung and Manly P. Hall in some of their writings,[17] wherein Adam and Enoch and Jesus are presented as one and the same entity in different incarnatons. Another incarnation mentioned, further confirming the Cayce readings, is that of the priest-king Melchizedek, who appeared to the patriarch Abraham; but that is another story.

The synonymity between Enoch and Hermes was eventually

uncovered by some of those close to Edgar Cayce. The readings had made repeated allusions to Hermes as an incarnation of the Master, most notably in Reading 281–10, in response to a series of questions by Miss [69]. She was told of her association, as Isaholli, with the Master during the Egyptian period. Since she had attended the priest in his period of exile, when Hermes first appeared among them, the inference seemed logical: Hermes and the Master were one. And although his role at the time seems to be shrouded in mystery, it was undoubtedly significant.

In Reading 69–1, we find what appears to be an elusive reference to Hermes as, simply, "the teacher": "The entity [69] among those who waited on the holy place from which the ministration of that given as moral, penal, and spiritual precept, that both from the priest and *the teacher* of that period" (italics added). But in Reading 281–43, it is more plainly given: there it refers to "what the Teacher of teachers taught" in Egypt.

Hermes was later to accompany the exiles upon their return to Egypt, where the readings tell us that he was the master architect of the Great Pyramid. It should not surprise us that the Master of masters had such a pivotal role in its construction; called the Pyramid of Understanding, it was designed as a temple of initiation, to which Hermes would return in a later age as Jesus, undergoing His youthful initiation with John the Baptist under the supervision of the Essenes, preparing himself for His sacrificial role. So, at least, the readings tell us . . .

To further confirm our identification of the "Teacher of teachers"—that obvious sobriquet for the Master—with Hermes, there is a second reference in Reading 69–1; Isaholli's role, upon the return to Egypt, is given as "the active agent between the king and *the teacher* and the minister [i.e., the priest]" (italics added).

Long were the years of exile; and as messengers from Egypt brought to Ra Ta word of increasing turmoil and strife among the native Egyptians and Araaraart's people, with many added troubles from the rapidly accelerating influx of Atlanteans fleeing from their doomed homeland, the strain upon the priest was great. He who had come into Egypt with an inspired vision and a purpose now feared that all of his earlier accomplishments would come to naught as the result of the discord and divisiveness that had arisen in his prolonged absence. His sorrows were further increased by word of the death of his infant daughter, Iso, who had been held hostage by the vindictive king.

Despite the visible blessings from the continuation, here in the Nubian mount, of the work he had begun decades earlier in Egypt, Ra Ta yearned for a reconciliation with his own people, and also with the young king who had sent him into banishment. He and his present companion, Isris, had paid dearly for their indiscreet union, which the priest had innocently viewed at the time as an acceptable means of serving the development of the new race. He now acknowledged to himself that he had been mistaken, although the punishment had surely been disproportionate to the crime. After all, the law he had been tricked into breaking was not the king's law but his own, as high priest.

In the ninth year of exile, when word finally reached Ra Ta that the king had revoked his order of banishment, and that the priest was to be fully pardoned and restored to his former position of supreme spiritual authority, it was a moment of bittersweet triumph for "this poor, decrepit outcast,"[18] as we find him described at the time.

The priest's followers greeted the news with mixed emotions. Many of them, in fact, had established close ties of a familial nature with the Nubians and would be loath to leave. Moreover, the king's pardon had come only as the result of tediously drawn-out negotiations between the two camps, and now it might have arrived too late. For their leader was now more than one hundred years old. Those closest to Ra Ta, who had observed his increasing frailty, were concerned lest he fail to survive. It would be a great tragedy indeed if he should lack the strength or will, in his hour of final vindication and victory, to draw a divided people together again and lead them back to the Law of One.

But if others doubted the priest's recuperative powers, there was one who did not. That was the ancient sage and teacher Hermes.

He knew what he knew. And he said nothing. For that was his way.

To many, that ageless figure who had suddenly appeared amongst them from out of nowhere was an enigma. His prophetic utterances were given mostly to the priest, who always listened closely. Like the priest, he could dream strange dreams and prophesy, but the mystery lay deeper than that. The old, bearded one had an uncanny way about him. He had only to close his piercing, gray-blue eyes for an instant, and he could then look forward or backward in time as readily as a hunter gazes straight at the quarry in front of him. All knowledge seemed to be subject to his command.

Yet this mysterious Hermes was ever humble and self-effacing. It was a major part of the mystery. One sensed that under the pearl gray robes there lay the hidden splendor of a god.

A KINGDOM IN TURMOIL

The king's lot had been nothing but trouble right from the start.

Jealousy had been Araaraart II's undoing. In his more reflective moments, the young ruler secretly rued the day he had listened to the conspiratorial voices of those among his councillors who had played upon his special fondness for the temple dancer Isris to rouse his ire against the victimized priest. Had Ra Ta's breaking of the law involved any dancer other than the king's own favorite, his wrath would have been hard to rouse, and in all likelihood the banishment decree would never have been issued. But, then, the young king was not only quick of speech but quick of temper as well. It was one of his failings. And having acted in a certain way, at the urging of others, he had as king, to uphold what many around him, and others throughout the realm, increasingly viewed as a seriously flawed decision.

What the impetuous king himself had no way of knowing, in regard to the strange and rather possessive bond of attraction he had always felt toward the enchanting Isris—an attraction that she had never discouraged—was that they had been twin souls in their entry into the earth-plane in the beginning.[19] One might reasonably cite such a unique relationship as an ameliorating circumstance before passing judgment on the king's harsh edict. In a much later life, in the Holy Land, when the former young ruler in Egypt incarnated as a chastened and loyal disciple of the Master, in the name of Andrew, that same twin soul overshadowed his activities from the Other Side, where she then dwelt, becoming, as might be termed, a "guardian angel." Still later, when he met much of his former karma in a highly demanding twentieth-century role as a dedicated and supportive son of that same priest he had once sent into exile, it was now as his beloved mother that Isris entered. (This time she was his "guardian angel" in the flesh.)

But let's return to our ancient setting. We are in Egypt, just following the king's fateful decision to send the hapless priest into exile with his offending mistress.

The immediate repercussions had been a political uprising first, followed by a religious war. The political revolt was sparked by Araaraart's younger brother, Ralij, prince of the Ibex region, in a bid to seize power. Indeed, there were those who suspected that it was he who had masterminded the plot against the priest in the first place, as a way of dividing the secular and spiritual rulership and thereby weakening the king's hold on the throne. The ruse did not work, however, and the Ibex uprising was put down. As for the religious strife, overzealous supporters of the ousted priest Ra Ta, led by one Oelom, tried to storm the palace. The rebel leader was slain in the ensuing battle with the king's troops. (In a more rational defense of the priest's cause, this same Oelom was to reincarnate as Cayce's "official" biographer.)

More and more, the native Egyptians grew rebellious in the wake of what was happening, and various royal edicts were now disobeyed with impunity. The incoming tide of Atlanteans escaping from Poseidia's rumblings observed with incredulity and disdain the slow crumbling of law and order in the once-promising Egyptian kingdom.

Araaraart was hard put to find a solution to his dilemma that did not further compromise his shaky rulership. His chief councillor, Asriaio, now genuinely concerned at the unfavorable turn of events, sought to make amends for his former bad advice. That crafty old politician suggested that the king enforce a selective return from Nubia of certain native followers of the priest who had held positions of influence in the temple service, feeling that their return would have a calming effect upon the unruly populace. But the king demurred. It would mark a further show of weakness on his part, he argued.

Thus, things bumbled and bungled along, but conditions gradually settled somewhat. However, overtures were continually being made to the king by various influential individuals to bring back the outlawed priest as the only means of restoring unity and order among the people.

Those whose collective voice counted most with the king were the increasingly vocal and powerful Atlanteans, who now formed a substantial and highly independent community in the land. Therefore, when their leaders began to insist more and more forcefully upon the return of Hept-supht, the Atlantean sage who had come to Egypt some years earlier as one of the leaders of the Law of One who wished to aid the priest, the king was at last obliged to accede to their insistent demands as a matter of political necessity. Besides, Hept-supht's essential neutrality in the whole affair had never been in dispute, and the king may have sensed that his return could prove useful in restoring peace. That was in the third year of Ra Ta's exile.

The return of Hept-supht indeed marked a turning point, although it was to take another six years of skillful negotiation by Hept-supht and numerous other emissaries to bring about a full reconciliation between the exiled priest and the stubborn king.

In finally rescinding the banishment decree, the king effectively acknowledged Ra Ta as the only leader who could pull the country together again and bind up its long-festering wounds. Yet, deep within Araaraart's troubled heart and conscience, he knew that the spiritual purpose and higher guidance that had originally brought his father's people into Egypt had emanated from the priest alone;

and if that guidance were to continue, and the divine purpose to be rekindled, it would require Ra Ta's unquestioned leadership. The king, henceforth, would have to cooperate fully with the priest, in a greatly reduced role that would make Araaraart little more than a figurehead. The *real* authority in the land would be the Law of One.

THE RETURN OF THE PRIEST

A series of remarkable events that, if viewed singly, would seem to harbor no concealed or secondary significance went hand in hand with the return of Ra Ta and his band of loyal followers to Egypt. Viewed collectively, however, as will be the case here, those same notable happenings suddenly point to an unexpected and startling conclusion about their probable origin. So obvious seems that conclusion, in fact, and so momentous are its implications from both a spiritual and a historical perspective, that one must find it all the more astonishing that apparently no researcher has previously stumbled upon it in studying the Cayce readings on the Egyptian epoch. Yet perhaps that is just the point: it must quite literally be "stumbled upon," like some unpolished diamond lying unmarked in an open field, for there are no clear directions to its discovery.

I refer to the carefully concealed but crucial role that must have been played throughout by the great initiate Hermes, that self-effacing incarnation of the Christ, in the unfolding events surrounding most of Ra Ta's latter-day activities. It is as if he had chosen to stand out of sight (even as one notes the paucity of references to Hermes in those readings, despite his identification as the Master), apparently speaking and acting through the priest in all matters. Thus, his hidden role confirms the legendary view of Hermes as "the heart and the tongue of Ra."[20]

To make my point, here is a summary of the succession of events surrounding the priest's return and the years following, all of which are suggestive of the participation of the evolving Christ, as Hermes.

First, immediately prior to the departure from the mount, each of Ra Ta's faithful followers—those who had "named the name of the priest,"[21] as one of the readings phrased it, in words curiously reminiscent of a much later biblical reference to the Christ—received a unique bodily mark from Ra Ta that was to remain with that soul-entity as a "sign" of their spiritual association and oneness throughout all future incarnations in the earth. It was as much a mark of blessing as it was a permanent identification.

Secondly, upon the return to Egypt, Ra Ta was henceforth known only as Ra—a symbolic new designation synonymous with the Sun, or *Son,* with whom the priest was now actively associated; whereas the literal interpretation of the glyphs for "Ra Ta," the former name, was "Sun [brought to] Earth."

Next, the name of the Egyptian capital, the city of Luz (meaning "almond," in one interpretation, "light," in another) was changed to Bethel. And Bethel, if one consults a Bible dictionary, means "House of God," although the Cayce reading on the subject put it this way: "Bethel means, 'Silence is golden' if thou art in the presence of God."[22] In either case, the new designation would appear almost certainly to have been inspired by the Christ, as Hermes. And why so? Because we encounter this stunning biblical parallel in Genesis 28:19, where that incident in ancient Egyptian history in the time of Ra is strangely repeated in Jacob's inspired experience in the Chosen Land, following his mystical vision of the ladderful of angels and his meeting with the Lord, or the Christ: "And he [Jacob] called the name of that place Beth-el; *but the name of that city was called Luz at the first"* (italics added).

In yet another example, there was the six-and-a-half-year period of the priest's regeneration following his return—a process of inner purification that enabled him to carry on the work for an additional hundred years. One has reason to suspect the hand of an initiate greater than the priest himself in carrying out the rejuvenation process, which was familiar to some of the earlier Atlantean adepts but had not been practiced in Egypt. Hermes, of course, was just such an adept, whose own age was a mystery. We find very little detail on this abstruse subject in the readings, but the activation, through deep meditation, of the pineal center—called the seat of the Christed Consciousness—must have been the key.

For we find it stated in one of Cayce's own life readings, "Keep the pineal gland operating, and you won't grow old—you will always be young!"[23]

Lastly, we have Hermes openly identified by Cayce as "the guide, or the actual construction architect"[24] of the Great Pyramid, then known as the Temple of the Initiates, or the Pyramid of Understanding. This is the only instance in the readings on that period in which we find Hermes plainly credited with an active, unconcealed role. The exception is understandable. After all, this particular pyramid was essentially His own great spiritual testament to the future. And here the Great Initiate was to undergo His supreme test as the youthful Jesus (as mentioned earlier in this chapter), spending three days and three nights in the empty sarcophagus in the king's chamber, preparatory to His ultimate role as the crucified Savior and the resurrected Christ. No one else could stand in His stead. It was to be His personal destiny.

The triumphal procession had left the Nubian mount in gas-driven chariots provided by the Atlanteans under Hept-supht's direction, and now they entered the city of Luz to joyous shouts of welcome. Throngs of well-wishers crowded the streets, strewing their way with pink and white lotus blossoms.

Ra Ta was dressed in the simple blue-gray linen robes of the priesthood, but with the cowl dropped back to reveal his withered features, which were nevertheless still etched with the innate nobility of his spiritual nature. The deep-set blue eyes the color of azurite were searching the crowd rather nervously, not sure that the face he sought could be recognized after nine long years, or that the owner of the face would be welcoming him, as were all the others. For it was his young son, Ra-La-Ral, who had remained with the king when the priest went into exile, for whom Ra Ta now looked uneasily with an uncertain heart.

In his way, despite the inner hurt, Ra Ta had been proud of the boy's decision nine years earlier to place a moral principle above filial obligations. For the plucky lad had taken the king's side in the dispute over his father's transgression of the law. That was an act that had surely required much inner discipline, just the sort of quality Ra Ta had always tried to instill in him as an apprentice priest. Yet he had also stressed the need for compassion and forgiveness as priestly qualities, too. And soon he would know if Ra-La-Ral, now a youth of eighteen suns, had learned to temper his sense of justice with the wisdom of the heart.

There was no need for Ra Ta's concern. Already his son had spotted him and had broken ranks from the king's official welcoming party to dash to his father's side for an emotional reunion. They exchanged a long and tearfull embrace.

Then, looking upon the still lovely Isris, the handsome young Ra-La-Ral showed the extent of his maturity by greeting her with a smile that bespoke his total forgiveness. Next, in exchanging a kiss with his little half-sister, Isibio, who had been born to the priest and his companion in exile, Ra-La-Ral sealed his forgiveness with a commitment to matrimony. His subsequent marriage was to be marked by faithfulness to one wife, in strict keeping with the law his father had broken.

From the day of the priest's return, peace and harmony were also restored throughout the land. The king and the priest, and the Teacher of teachers, all worked as one; and the new order took root in Egypt, as the building process began in earnest.

THE CALL OF THE LOTUS

With the return of the priest, a bright new era had begun. And the call went forth to all of the nations to "come and see" what was being accomplished in the land of Egypt.

Among the many who came—spiritual leaders, for the most part, in the lands of their respective origins—it is fascinating to note that more than a few of them, though now in quite different walks of life, reincarnated during Edgar Cayce's lifetime, finding their way to him by some inner compulsion. They showed up, usually, as if by chance. Some left. Others chose to join once more with that same "regenerated priest" who had once called them to the land of the lotus, but this time a place called Virginia Beach, in

America, gathering in what might again be termed "a preparation for the individual activities in the various services to the fellow man."[25]

Indeed, the parallels between the life and activities of the twentieth-century prophet and healer Edgar Cayce and his ancient former self in the role of the high priest Ra, were more than coincidental. Several of the readings pointed to a cyclical pattern that was apparently being repeated for a purpose, in response to a recurring need in our present age.

In a reading given on September 3, 1931, for Edgar's wife, Gertrude, who had been his companion, Isris (later renamed Isis), in the Egyptian period, the question was asked: "Are we passing through a period at present similar to the period of banishment in Egypt?" That question arose because, some nine months earlier, Edgar had experienced a bitter parting of the ways with a former friend and benefactor, Mr. [900], a young Jewish stockbroker, who, incidentally, had been the young Egyptian councillor, Aarat —that one whose advice to the king, along with Asriaio's, had led to the banishment decree. And now, that same entity's sudden withdrawal of financial support had forced the closure of the Cayce Hospital and an end to Edgar's hard-won goal—namely, a place where he could put his holistic healing methods into practice. But the answer given, in that particular reading, was beautifully reassuring:

Rather the period of the return, for those that are associated in the *present* with the desire as of *that* period, for the carrying *on*—see? *Banishment,* that period when contention, distrust, false activities, wonderments at actions, changed surroundings, environs. Is it not nine moons, or months, since change? (538–30)

The reference to nine moons (as contrasted with a cycle of nine suns, or years, in the Egyptian period) was, of course, a reference to the ruptured relationship with [900] back in January 1931. Though the hospital was not reopened, Cayce did receive the cooperative support of a number of doctors who were willing to implement his triune approach to healing, treating body, mind, and soul as a single unit. It marked the beginnings of the now popular holistic healing movement. Foremost among these pioneers was Dr. Harold J. Reilly, whose Reilly Health Institute in Rockefeller Center, New York, was a health mecca serving many prominent figures for several decades. Dr. Reilly was to learn, through a life reading from Edgar Cayce, that he had been associated wtih him in the healing activities in Egypt.

Again, in demonstrating the parallel with Cayce's Egyptian cycle, it was stated in Reading 254–47 that "much is being attempted at this time, even as during that experience" and that "the cycle has rolled to that period when the individual entities again in the earth's experience gather together for a definite work."

Finally, in one of Edgar Cayce's own life readings, the parallels with the Egyptian period were plainly articulated:

It has been indicated again and again through these channels that this period of activity of the entity called Edgar Cayce is a replica of, or follows closely in, the activities of the experience through that called the Egyptian period.

As indicated, there was a period of banishment, a period of reclamation; then came the period of regeneration. (294–197)

That Egyptian epoch, we are told, may be considered one of the most momentous periods in the world's history.[26] If such was the case, then we have no reason to doubt that we are now in the midst of a similarly greater historic era, as the cycle repeats itself at a higher evolutionary level. Yet its more visible signs still lie ahead of us. These will be discussed in a later chapter.

Most prominent among the spiritual teachers who journeyed to Egypt, following Ra's regeneration, were these: Ajax, the teacher from Atlantis; Saneid, from India; Yak, from Carpathia; and the venerated Tao, from Mongolia, or what was then called the Gobi land. They came to learn firsthand from Ra (as the mouthpiece, as it were, of the Teacher of teachers) what were to be those tenets that should be established as a uniting influence for all of mankind, under the Law of One.

It was a wonderful, sharing experience, with only the Atlantean giving somewhat less than the others. He tended to hold himself aloof. For all of his noble wisdom, the poor fellow appeared to suffer from a typical Atlantean trait—a sense of superiority:

> The entity found little of help; finding fault with the king in power, finding little in common with the priest that led; finding those things that measured not to that standard the entity had had in the [Atlantean] land, withdrew on account of the associations—specifically—of the priest with those women, or those of the opposite sex in the land.
>
> Hence builded in self much that must be met, must be counted, must be countenanced in the present experience—if there will be gained that which will make for the soul development. (487-17)

So Ajax lost, in that experience. But the same entity, who was also referred to alternately as Ax-Tell ("Ax-Tell and Ajax being the same, as a united force," explains Reading 1007-3, suggesting that the proud Atlantean may have been one of the last surviving members of that earlier class of androgynous beings), came into the present life with a unique opportunity to meet himself: he chose a close association with the former priest whose faults he had once magnified over his virtues. Whether he made maximum use of his opportunity, the entity alone can judge.

It was indeed true that Ra had a weakness for women. Whether his companion Isis (the former Isris), now venerated by her people and virtually elevated to the status of a queen, may have chosen to lead a celibate life is not known. But it is known that Ra sought elsewhere for companionship. He found it in a succession of lovely, obliging companions through his waning years. And he, too, of course, was building that in self that must eventually be met . . .

Primarily, he was to meet it in a much later incarnation, in his "double" appearance on the early American continent as the wanderer and wastrel John Bainbridge.

It was in and about ancient Delhi, in the land now known as India, that the teacher Saneid first brought to his people "the unifying of the teachings that came from other lands,"[27] for he had gained much from his rich exchange of views with Ra and the other spiritual leaders when he had answered the call to come to the beautiful city of Bethel.

Not too surprisingly, then, it was again in India that he last reincarnated, toward the close of the last century, becoming a teacher of yoga. And in his travels, he of course found his way to America and ultimately to a meeting with Edgar Cayce—a meeting that seemed to confirm, with unusual eloquence, a view so oft expressed in Cayce's psychic readings, that no meeting is by chance. They met as long-lost brothers—as indeed they may have been, once, in the English land (but that story belongs to another chapter).

Another who came to Bethel, in Egypt, was a princess from the Carpathian land, where Arart's people had originated:

And as there arose those periods when there was the invitation (as it might be called in the present) for those of *every* land to become acquainted with the activities of the king, the priest, and those from the Atlantean land of that day, we find that the entity entered into the activities there at an age when—as would be called in the present—it was just reaching maturity—*then* at thirty and three.

There we find the entity was among those not only giving but gaining. For, as is the eternal law, as ye give ye gain in understanding.

The entity remained . . . until there began the exodus of those who were to become emissaries and teachers and ministers in the varied lands to which they were to go as a part of their experience . . .

Aid came through a helpmate who aided in carrying forward the greater development—which arose from that land to which the entity and its offspring and those periods of activity brought the albo, or the first of the pure white race in the Carpathian land. (1472–10)

In a much later incarnation in the Holy Land, this same entity was to draw on what had been gained spiritually during her travels and studies in Egypt and elsewhere. Her role was a blessed one: as the Essene teacher Judy, she personally instructed the boy Jesus in the Law of God and later arranged for Him to be sent to other teachers in India, Persia, and Egypt for His further preparation.

Closer to home, there were two in Egypt who came to a reckoning of sorts.

That wily old chief councillor to two kings survived, but was no longer a power in the land. Yet Asriaio was to be "immortalized" in a most curious and unexpected fashion: it is his impassive and asexual features, under the ancient headdress of the councillor, that adorn the Sphinx, that mystery of the ages.

In a modern-day incarnation, however, he found himself faced with a less desirable destiny:

Q-46. *Is the time propitious to seek [953]'s advice at this time?*
A-46. It is. The individual often stands in their own light, as here. Much good could, and would, come to all through the advice of the individual known as [953]; yet that individual may not be driven, nor does it stand that the work would fail because he does not apply self. Rather does he falter, and again and again will it be necessary for him to come in the more lowly, the more servile, condition, for having failed in the present condition. (254-47)

Sic transit gloria! From the face of the Sphinx to the dust heap of history . . .

And the other, in Egypt? the councillor Aarat, who had joined with Asriaio in urging the banishment of the priest? Upon the priest's return, no action was taken against him. He was simply ignored. His usefulness had ended. In his modern-day role as a benefactor of Edgar Cayce's, the aid given was mutual: no one received quite as many psychic readings as the entity [900], many on such self-serving topics as stock market investments, the interpretation of personal dreams, and advice on various interpersonal relationships. But as [900] gradually came to assume a "proprietary" role in various personal matters in Edgar's life and daily affairs, including the giving of readings, the indignant psychic decided that his independence was of more value to him than [900]'s aid, with all those strings attached. The relationship was severed.

Perhaps both men were somewhat to blame. Each had a share of karma to meet with the other. Moreover, the roots of their karma involved yet another incarnation, after the Egyptian, in Troy (which will be covered in another chapter). But an impartial evaluation of the facts tells us that it was Mr. [900], not Mr. Cayce, who lost. The latter gained, for the real growth in the "work," as it came to be called, began with [900]'s departure from the scene. It is our charitable hope that he will have another opportunity, in a future lifetime. He was in many respects a remarkable man, possessed of a keen intellect and an inquiring mind. Aside from the many readings he received of a strictly mundane and personal nature, he also left us as his legacy a large body of psychic readings requested of Mr. Cayce on a broad range of metaphysical and philosophical subjects.

For he, too, had heard the call of the lotus, though in a new land and a later age, and had sought out the former priest in search of spiritual answers.

THE PYRAMID OF UNDERSTANDING

Among all the mysteries and the marvels of the ages, I suppose it is safe to say that none surpasses in wonderment the Great Pyramid of Gizeh.

Down through the centuries, the Egyptologists have busily propounded a number of "scientific" theories to explain its origins and purpose, as well as the manner of its construction. But none of these conflicting opinions has successfully challenged the long-held esoteric belief that this particular pyramid, far more ancient than present scientific opinion allows, was never designed as a tomb for a pharaoh—Cheops or otherwise—but was actually constructed by early initiates whose advent preceded the known pharaonic culture, and whose construction techniques were highly sophisticated. The pyramid was intended, say the occultists, as a temple of initiation and an astronomical observatory, also embodying in the precise measurements of its odd chambers and passageways a sacred record of coming events for those who can interpret what is writ in space and stone, in shape and angle and elevation.

The Cayce readings, of course, uphold the esoteric view. And they go much further. They not only remove the veil of mystery from the past, but they add much startling new information for our modern-day enlightenment.

One thing we learn, as most occultists have long suspected, is that the role of the Sphinx in the intricate layout of the Gizeh complex under the direction of Ra and Hermes was far more than ornamental.

Actually begun before the priest's period of banishment, the Sphinx was intended to symbolize the mixture of man and beast that needed to be purged and rectified through the cleansing work in the temple services, for "respecting the peoples of that time, much of the animal—that had been fully cleansed in Atlantis— remained with the peoples in the Egyptian development."[28] (The calm, reflective visage of the chief councillor, adorning the leonine body, was merely emblematic, of course, since Asriaio was one of the original Carpathians, whose tribal roots were pure.)

Following the priest's return, the Sphinx was completed; it then took on special significance of a hidden nature. It now became a sentinel, or guard, with a secret connecting chamber from the right paw of the mysterious statue leading to an underground pyramid being constructed nearby, at a point between the Sphinx and the river. The buried pyramid was to become a respository of the records of the great Atlantean civilization, now in its twilight days, and would also house many artifacts from the Egyptian civilization of that day, including certain tombs and tablets, various musical instruments then in use, and similar objects. Finally, it would contain the records of the Christ, presumably placed there by Hermes, giving a prophetic account of his own prefigured destiny—"those records that are yet to be found of the preparation of the man, of the Christ, in those of the tomb, or those yet to be uncovered in the pyramid [of records],"[29] culminating with His Second Coming, in 1998.

One of those whose sarcophagus was placed in the safekeeping of the buried pyramid, along with thirty-two tablets containing records prepared by the entity herself, was that of the priest's favorite daughter, Aris-Hobeth—a name, not surprisingly, that means "Favored One." And herein lies a story, incredibly strange and wondrous, which will have to await a much later chapter.

When the Pyramid of Records was finally completed, it needed to be sealed in a ritualistic manner that would only be comprehensible to a trained initiate. The Atlantean sage Hept-supht, who had supervised the sealing of the now-sunken records in Atlantis before emigrating to Egypt, was chosen for this occult ceremony by the king and the priest and the Teacher of teachers. Hept-supht's very name, in fact, signified his fitness for this sacred role and had probably been given to him as an honorary designation following that earlier ceremony in Atlantis, for it meant, "Help Keep It Shut."

In a dream, or vision, that came inexplicably in the midst of a life reading he was giving for someone who had apparently been there, Edgar Cayce experienced this hazy recall of that ancient ritual and the festivities surrounding it:

> There was a great host of people going out to dedicate a tomb [sic] that was being builded or prepared for someone, and they had seven days of entertainment with all sorts of dancing, prayer being made, and songs. Just before the last service was to be carried [out], I saw someone climb to the top of this pyramid or cone-like thing, and clang a big sheet of metal of some kind, or brass. (294–131)

He sought and received an interpretation:

> This, as must be apparent to those concerned, *was* a raising— it were— of the curtain to a physical happening to the body-physical giving the information, in which the entity seeking [Mrs. 2741] *was* associated. . . . It represents the period through which so many are again attempting to do in realities, physically so, the same as of that period. From this may come the greater knowledge of the period, a better understanding of relationships of individuals and how they fit together, and may be then correlated with the experiences that happen from day to day. (294–131)

Three questions and answers followed:

Q–6. *Was this the . . . Egyptian experience seen?*
A–6. Egyptian; for it was the dedicating of that tomb or first cone pyramid not yet uncovered, and the tomb of so many that were associated

at that time. [Note: Rather than referring to it as a "tomb," most further readings identified this pyramid either as the "Temple of Records," or "Pyramid of Records," but quite obviously it also functioned as a tomb, inasmuch as the preserved remains of Aris-Hobeth and Arart I, among certain other notables, were apparently placed therein.]

Q–7. Who was the individual that climbed to the top and clanged the big sheet of metal of some kind?

A–7. That entity has not yet approached for information. When he does, it will be given.

Q–8. At what time did this happen in this Egyptian period?

A–8. When the king that had entered [Arart I] was preparing for his own demise. The father of the young king, or the ruler. (294–131)

That reading had been given in January 1932. It was September 1933 before the entity identified as having been Hept-supht approached for information and was plainly told: "So, he that keeps the record, that keeps shut, or Hept-supht, was made or chosen as the one to *seal* that in the tomb."[30]

Yet a certain amount of confusion surrounds some of the answers given in that particular reading (378–14), which is at least partially resolved in a follow-up reading given a month later for the same individual (Reading 378–16). Apparently Hept-supht officiated at the sealing ceremonies in conjunction with both the Great Pyramid of Gizeh (then called the Pyramid of Understanding) and the earlier "tomb" pyramid, or Pyramid of Records. This point needs to be fully grasped before we proceed, so here is a confirming excerpt from Reading 378–16:

Much might be given respecting the activities of the entity [Hept-supht] who sealed with the seal of the Alta and Atlanteans, and the aid given in the completion of the pyramid of initiation [Gizeh, or the Pyramid of Understanding] as well as in the records that are to be uncovered [i.e., the Pyramid of Records]. (378–16)

Before continuing, we must establish another fact. According to one of his own life readings,[31] the entity known as "the young king"—or Araaraart II—ruled for only ninety-eight years, apparently dying at age 114 (he had ascended the throne at sixteen, the reader will remember, and at age thirty or so sent the priest into exile). Well, then, in referring to "the sealing of the record chambers," Reading 378–16 specifically mentions the presence of King Araaraart, among others. This plainly tells us that the sealing of the Pyramid of Records must have occurred several decades ahead of the later sealing ceremony in conjunction with the completion of the Gizeh pyramid, or Pyramid of Understanding, begun in 10,490 B.C. and completed one hundred years later, in 10,390 B.C. (Had the king lived to witness that ceremony also, his age would have been 150 or more!)

Thus, armed with these prefatory facts, the informed reader may now safely proceed with what I trust will be a minimum of confusion. The only remaining obstacle to comprehending aright some of the pertinent excerpts that follow lies in the language of the readings themselves, and so I have included some bracketed phrases that may prove helpful in their interpretation. Specifically, the reader unacquainted with the psychic readings of Edgar Cayce must bear in mind that the answers given by the sleeping psychic invariably represented a very *literal* response to the questions asked. Thus, if the questioning was careless or inexact, this would as likely as not result in confusing or misleading answers. As a case in point, let's consider the following:

Q–3. Was the entity [Hept-supht] the one that, at the completion of the pyramid, clanged the sheet of metal?

A–3. Clanged the sheet of metal at the completion of Gizeh [the Great Pyramid, or Pyramid of Understanding], that [had also] *sealed* the records in the tomb [Pyramid of Records, or "tomb" pyramid] yet to be discovered. (378–14)

Now, one could argue that the questioner was taking a lot for granted. After all, a year and nine months had elapsed since the original reference, in Reading 294–131, to the metal-clanging ritual in connection with the sealing of what had been termed, in that particular reading, "that tomb or first cone pyramid not yet uncovered." But inasmuch as Hept-supht had also officiated at the sealing of the Gizeh pyramid, that seems to be where Cayce "came in," in providing the careless questioner with an answer that was wholly accurate, from his sleep-state perspective but *not* so accurate from the mental perspective of the questioner. Again and again, we find this sort of thing occurring in the readings, resulting in needless confusion in the given responses. (It has misled many a "Sunday researcher," I'm afraid, and has resulted in the publication of a lot of distorted interpretations of what Cayce said, or did not say.)

In Reading 378–16, we find a highly informative statement—if it is *carefully* studied. It appears to distinguish between the two ceremonies, some decades apart—one in conjunction with the "tomb" pyramid, or record chambers, apparently having involved great masses of the people, possibly in a tribute to King Arart I and others buried there along with the records, and the much later ceremony, sealing the Great Pyramid, of a more esoteric and restricted nature:

> In the record chambers [Pyramid of Records] there were more ceremonies than in calling the peoples at the finishing of that called the pyramid [i.e., the Gizeh pyramid, or Pyramid of Understanding]. (378–16)

Here is a highly interesting description of the clanging ceremony and other rites that were carried out upon the official completion of the Great Pyramid of Gizeh (as it is now commonly called):

> At the completion of that called Gizeh, there was the mounting of that which completed the top, composed of a combination or fluxes of brass, copper, gold, that was to be sounded when all the initiates were gathered about the altar or the pyramid. And the sounding of same has become, as given, the call—in the varied lands—to prayer, or to arms, or to battle, or to service in any of the activities that became the guiding of influencing the masses in activity.
>
> In describing, then, the ceremonies of dedication or of the activities that began with the keeping of the lines of the priests and the initiates in the order according to their adherence to the Law of One that was initiated in the activities of Hept-supht in this period, the sounding of the head or the top was given to one that acted in the capacity of the headsman—as would be termed in some of those activities of such nature in other portions of

the country, or as nations rose in their service of such natures. And the Priest [Ra], with those gathered in and about the passage that led from the varied ascents through the pyramid, then offered there incense to the gods that dwelt among those in their activities in the period of development of the peoples. (378–16)

In the same reading, we find a fascinating account of the earlier ceremony in conjunction with the sealing of the record chambers (to be buried under the sands), with an allusion as to the future period when those chambers might be opened, and by whom:

For, here those that were trained in the Temple of Sacrifice as well as in the Temple Beautiful were about the sealing of the record chambers. For, these were to be kept as had been given by the priests in Atlantis or Poseidia (Temple), when these records of the race of the developments of the laws pertaining to One were put in their chambers and to be opened only when there was the returning of those into materiality, or to earth's experience, when the change was imminent in the earth; which change, we see, begins in '58 and ends with the changes wrought in the upheavals and the shifting of the poles, as begins then the reign in '98 (as time is counted in the present) of those influences that have been given by many in the records that have been kept by those sojourners in this land of the Semitic peoples.

Then the *sealings* were the activities of Hept-supht with Ra Ta [Ra] and [Isis] and the king Araaraart, when there were the gatherings of all the peoples for this record sealing; with incense from the altars of the Temple and altars of the cleansings that were opened for their activities in the grounds about this tomb or temple of records; and many were the cleansings of the peoples from those things or conditions that separated them from the associations of the lower kingdoms that had brought those activities in all lands of the worship of Baalilal [Belial] and of the desires as from carnal associations and influences. (378–16)

The reference to "the reign in '98" coincides with the date given by Edgar Cayce for the Second Coming of the Lord.[32] In yet another reading, it was indicated that a messenger, identified as John Peniel (an incarnation of John the Beloved), would precede the Messiah's return to earth.[33] And Cayce's own return was prophesied for that eventful year, 1998, when it was indicated he would reincarnate in the role of a New Age "liberator."[34]

Meanwhile, what of the opening of the record chambers? Will this, too, be a New Age event, set for the next generation? It seems likely:

> This [Pyramid of Records] may not be entered without an understanding, for those that were left as guards may *not* be passed until after a period of their regeneration in the Mount, or the fifth root race begins. (5748–6)

Ignoring the given hurdles that would humble and chasten most of us, hope has continued to spring eternal in the breast of many a self-appointed initiate who is familiar with that Cayce prophecy but has failed to note another that will be cited shortly. Consequently, there have been numerous futile attempts by various "psychically inspired" individuals or groups visiting the Gizeh plain since Cayce's death to locate that hidden entrance to the record tomb, which lies jealously guarded by the right paw of the impassive Sphinx.

Yet the readings plainly identified the former Hept-supht as the one who will receive spiritually given directions when the time has come. It named two others who would join him, one of them in the capacity of a guide, and added: "These will appear."[35]

Mr. [378], who had been Hept-supht, died May 7, 1960. His next appearance in the earth, probably scheduled to occur in conjunction with the various changes that will herald the New Age at the turn of this century, will presumably signal the appointed time. It will be a time when the fifth root race begins.

Such a scenario, at any rate, is what logic should suggest to anyone intent on following the Cayce script all the way.

We come, now, to another matter. To some, it is the ultimate enigma. But this is only because they presuppose in the days when the Great Pyramid was constructed a primitive culture devoid of our scientific advantages. Yet any engineering expert who has ever examined the pyramid, noting the esoteric nature of its alignment and measurements, as well as the stunning precision with which the massive blocks of its basic structure have been cut and fitted, has come away a convert to the view that it all involved the work of a truly remarkable genius. And it is believed to have been the prototype for all of the other, lesser pyramids throughout Egyptian history that followed it in declining splendor. In 1880, it was the stated opinion of William Flinders Petrie, a mechanical engineer who had set about the difficult task of measuring the pyramid complex from every conceivable angle, that the amazing accuracy of every detail pointed to only one conclusion: it *had* to be the brainchild of one man only. The reason for this interesting verdict? Petrie insisted that only a single, phenomenal genius, of a type encountered once in a millennium, could have conceived of such a wondrous structure. We would have to agree with him, even while concluding that the Master of men, as Hermes, was just such a genius.

This leads us to a question that only the Edgar Cayce readings, to my knowledge, have been able to answer in a firm, nonspeculative fashion. Yet the Virginia Beach psychic's response was hardly calculated to meet the acceptable criteria of modern-day scientific research:

Q–14. *How was this particular Great Pyramid of Gizeh built?*
A–14. By the use of those forces in nature as make for iron to swim. Stone floats in the air in the same manner. This will be discovered in '58. (5748–6)

The principle involved in the first instance is simple enough to comprehend: inasmuch as air is lighter than water, the weight of the iron vessel must be overcome by a sufficient volumetric displacement of metal with air to counteract the gravitational forces. But how does stone float in the air in a similar manner? Modern-day aeronautical principles (by which stone could, of course, be transported from one place to another) would not appear to have been what Cayce was getting at, inasmuch as he referred to a weight-suspending principle not then (1932) known, that would be discovered in 1958. In that year, Professor W. Heisenberg announced the discovery of a unified-field theory that relates mass, energy, and gravity, and this carries us into that esoteric field of physics dealing with neutrinos and antimatter, among other arcane subjects that are still in their theoretical stages.[36]

We suspect, however, that the frequent references in the Edgar Cayce readings on Atlantis to what were termed the "night-side forces" employed by the Atlanteans in relation to energy-controlling principles may conceal an ancient knowledge that is only now being rediscovered by our physicists.

Fortunately, however, Cayce did not stop with that single explanation. He gave us another. It was of a more spiritual nature, referring to the "activities of those versed in that pertaining to the course from which all power comes." And he continued:

> For as long as there remain those pure in body, in mind, in activity, to the law of the One God, there is the continued resource for meeting the needs, or for commanding the elements and their activities in the supply of that necessary in such realtions. (5750–1)

In practical terms, this spiritual principle or law found its manifestation, apparently, in some mode of antigrativational force employed by what would today be termed the "air fleet":

> And with the return and the reestablishings of those activities from the Priest and other lands, the entity then was rather in the capacity of the aide to *those that used the Universal Forces in fitting the stones,* as well as the preparation of those that dealt with communications with other lands; and was with what would today be called the air fleet. (820–1, italics added)

There, at last, although it will not satisfy the scientific mind, I fear, we have the application of spiritual law at a material level to explain how Hermes and Ra and the other initiates involved in the construction of "the Pyramid of Understanding, or Gizeh,"[37] went about their heavenly Father's business. Jesus was later to demonstrate the same mastery of spirit over matter when he walked upon the water and stilled the storm. And in time, I suspect, a day will come when the scientist and the mystic will be able to look upon such phenomena with a common eye. For both will recognize the oneness of all force, or the Law of One.

It was to help establish this universal law among men that Ra entered the earth; later, having done what he set out to do, he left:

And there came, then, that period when all the pyramid or memorial was complete, that he, Ra, ascended into the mount and was borne away. (294–152)

6. Escape from Sodom

When Lot escaped from Sodom, just before it was destroyed by the ancient equivalent of an atomic blast, he was accompanied by two strangers who had been sent to warn him.

One of those two biblical figures, according to a dream interpretation given to Edgar Cayce on April 1, 1932, was none other than himself. But because the two messengers are described in Genesis 19:1 as "angels," rather than men, this raised a pertinent question, and the response, one might argue, introduced a note of ambivalence:

Q–2. *Did the body actually live at that period as a physical entity?*
A–2. As given, one of those sent as the warning, or warner to the people, as to what was coming to pass. (294–136)

All that was really confirmed, in that answer, was the nature of Cayce's role at the time, namely, that of messenger. The initial question still remained: flesh-body man, or etheric being?

Yet the ambiguity was perhaps intentional (I shall explain this point later). Meanwhile, as anybody who has read the nineteenth chapter of Genesis knows, the two messengers of the Lord who appeared at Lot's door were not ordinary mortals. They had the spiritual power to inflict temporary blindness on the men of Sodom who sought to force their way into Lot's house and seize the two winsome-looking strangers for their unnatural sexual sport, which was the very sin of Sodom (as well as its neighboring fleshpot, Gomorrah, presumably) that had brought the Lord's wrath upon its inhabitants.

It was Abraham, of course, who had interceded with the Lord on his nephew Lot's behalf. And in the preceding chapter of Genesis, we have that famous dialogue between Abraham and the Lord as to how many righteous men might save a condemned city from destruction. Yet Lot and his kinsmen were not wholly righteous, and their lives could only be spared, it turned out, if they would heed a warning to evacuate—a gift of grace for Abraham's sake.

We now come to the most intriguing part of the story.

Whereas the nineteenth chapter of Genesis refers to the Lord's two messengers as "angels," we find them introduced earlier (in the eitheenth chapter), in company with the Lord himself, where the trio are referred to rather incongruously as "three men" who suddenly stood by Abraham as he sat at the door of his tent on the plains of Mamre. Later, following a telepathic incident involving Abraham's wife, Sarah, who was sequestered inside the tent, the trio rose up and looked toward Sodom whence they were headed. The Lord is debating whether or not to reveal to Abraham what is about to befall that sinful city where his newphew Lot dwells. The narrative continues in this fashion: "And the men"—apparently a reference, at this point, to those two out of the three who carried out the mission to warn Lot—"turned their faces from thence, and went toward Sodom: but Abraham stood yet before the Lord."[1]

This is not the first time we have met the Lord as a fellow mortal. We encountered him in previous chapters as Adam, the Son of man, and later as Enoch, or Hermes. And now, I suggest, we are meeting him as the priest-king Melchizedek, that further incarnation of the Master, according to the Cayce readings. He who was "without father, without mother, without descent, having neither beginning of days nor end of life, but made like unto the Son of God"[2]—the biblical description of that special incarnation—is presented in the readings as *"Melchizedek, in the perfection"*[3]; and, again, as "that one who had manifested to Father Abraham as the prince, as *Melchizedek,* the priest of Salem . . . *a living human being in flesh,* made manifest in the earth from the desire of Father-God to prepare an escape for man."[4] (italics added).

Whereas we are told that "no man has seen God at any time,"[5] the *Lord* is always plainly visible to Abraham, whether leading him out of the city of Ur, or as he entered the land of Canaan and builded an altar unto the Lord, "who appeared unto him,"[6] or bestowing His blessings upon Abraham in a number of instances.

(Following Abraham's victory in the "battle of the kings," we find the Lord openly identified as Melchizedek and being regarded with a familiar reverence by the patriarch as he receives a blessing. Their prior acquaintance is implicit in the nature of their meeting and Abraham's obeisance. It coincides with a view found in the occult literature of the Hebrews that Abraham received directly from Melchizedek the original Teaching, which was then handed down as the Hebrew Kabbala.[7])

The days of Abraham, as given in Genesis, follow Noah's by about six hundred years. The Great Deluge, occurring in Noah's latter years, may, by at least one account, be given an approximate dating of 9600 B.C., thus placing Abraham's advent somewhere in the vicinity of 9000 B.C. (The source of that dating for the flood, incidentally, is a *scientific* one: a team of University of Miami geologists, in 1975, uncovered convincing evidence of a great flood in that precise period of antiquity, based upon radioactive dating of tiny seashells found in layered sedimentation.[8] The synchronicity of this scientific evidence and Cayce's psychically given date of 10,390 B.C. for the completion of the Great Pyramid and the preservation of the records of late Atlantis, in Enoch's time— some seven hundred years earlier—is too remarkable to ignore.)

Meanwhile, it is our speculation that both Ra and Enoch (or Hermes)—along with a third, unnamed being—made their next manifestation in the earth simultaneously, in the days of Abraham and Lot. And while we can identify the former Enoch, now, as Melchizedek, the former Ra must remain a nameless entity. Was he, like Melchizedek himself, projected as a sort of "fourth dimensional" being, physical in appearance but essentially beyond mortal limitations? So it would seem. Yet this is not to imply that he had reached the same level of spiritual development as the Master himself (appearing as Melchizedek), but we suggest the possibility that the former priest, as a fellow initiate, may have been brought into the earth-plane in a thought-form body *at the will of the Master* to fulfill a specific mission in what was probably a brief appearance only.

If so, it explains the otherwise inexplicable events recounted in

Genesis. More than that, it explains the elusive answer, given in the reading cited at the outset of this chapter, as to whether or not Cayce's appearance in Sodom had been as a strictly "physical" entity. Probably not, in our normal sense of the term.

In his appearance as Ra Ta, the readings had revealed that Cayce's entry into the earth-plane—"or the being translated into materiality," as it was termed—"was from the infinity forces, or from the Sun," whereas his next-given cycle, as Uhjltd, in the Persian experience, was "from those centers about which thine own solar system moves—in Arcturus."[9] This reference to Arcturus was unusual. What it indicated, in effect, was that the soul-entity had reached a point of soul development, as Ra, that enabled him to leave this solar system and go on to Arcturus for the further development, thus precluding the need for additional earthly incarnations. Yet he apparently chose, as an outgrowth of his close association with the Master from the beginning, to link his karma to the Lord's. It ultimately led to his further entrapment in the flesh, and a number of downward-gravitating cycles eventually, before the full cleansing and the upward climb again. But his reentry in the days of Melchizedek and Abraham was presumably in a status somewhat akin to Melchizedek's own at the time. (Arcturus, incidentally, has been identified as that star of the Christ-child, over Bethlehem, or *"His* star";[10] not only was it termed "the center of this universe,"[11] but we find it identified as that sphere to which the risen Christ went "as of the developing."[12])

All of this suggests, therefore—if my theory holds—just why an evasive answer was given to Mr. Cayce concerning his appearance in Sodom. If the full truth about his bodily projection had been given, including the probable nature of his Arcturian association with the Master of men at that time, there is some doubt as to whether his as-yet-unpurified nature (as Edgar Cayce) would have been spiritually prepared to handle such information with appropriate humility. If that sounds presumptuous, let it be pointed out here that Mr. Cayce's incarnation as Lucius, head of the early Church at Laodicea and author of the Gospel according to Luke, was not revealed to Edgar until his sixtieth year, in 1938. When it was finally given, there was this humbling explanation for the long delay: "If this had been given in the first," said Reading 294–142, "there would have been a puffing up"!

In fact, a certain unstableness of character, exhibited in his youthful years as Lucius and again much later in his "double" appearance as John Bainbridge, needed to be fully met and overcome in his incarnation as Edgar Cayce. This was done. But at the time when Edgar sought that dream interpretation, back in 1932, relating the vision of himself as one of the two messengers sent to warn Lot, the full interpretation revealed that the vision, though quite real enough, had actually come as a warning, now, to *himself*. He was told that he was being tested "as by fire," even as Lot and his family had been. Lot's wife had looked back, and it was radiation, actually, that caused her death, as she lingered in her departure from the past. Lot, moreover, had ignored the advice of the Lord's messengers to flee to the mountaintop and instead chose the familiar comforts of the nearby town of Zoar. Though he later changed his course, it was too late: he had already abandoned his spiritual opportunities, proving his unworthiness.

The comparison with Lot's case (for it was not quite a "parallel") lay in the fact that the Cayces, in the past several months, had been obliged to move from house to house in Virginia Beach as their rented residences were sold out from under them. There was great discouragement, plus the temptation to "abandon the mountaintop" (represented in this case by Virginia Beach) and return to one of the environs of the past, beset by fewer problems. But the so-called problems actually represented the spiritual testing and the growth.

Cayce was warned, in consequence, to hold to that advice already given to him through the Universal Forces, which had directed him to Virginia Beach in the first place as that environment best suited to his psychic development and his spiritual growth.

Needless to say, he heeded the warning. It was only a short while later that he was led to the brown-shingled residence on Arctic Crescent that was to become the Cayce home for the remainder of Edgar's lifetime. Meanwhile, in a reading given some years afterwards, it was disclosed to the Cayces and their increasingly large coterie of followers in "the work," as it was called, that Virginia Beach was "the center—the only seaport and center—of the White Brotherhood."[13]

That term, "the White Brotherhood," is a familiar one in occult literature for the fraternity of initiates, or adepts, that has existed from the days of early Atlantis and the Law of One.

The fiery nature of Sodom's destruction and the strange suddenness with which the "three men" in Genesis (including Melchizedek, or the Lord) were able to appear or disappear invites a short sequel to this chapter.

In the biblical account of the holocaust at Sodom and Gomorrah, the Lord caused "brimstone and fire" out of heaven to rain upon the two iniquitous cities. The next morning, Abraham arose and went to the place where he had stood in the presence of the Lord on the previous day. It must have been a small hill or rise upon the level plain; for from this spot he was able to survey all the land round about, and where Sodom and Gomorrah had been, the smoke "went up as the smoke of a furnace."[14]

Cayce, too, in his dream, saw it "raining fire and brimstone" as he and his companion, along with Lot and Lot's wife and two daughters, were fleeing from the stricken city of Sodom. "What had been called, 'she turned to a pillar of salt,' " Cayce recounted, "was that they really passed through the heat—as came from the fire from heaven, and all were tried as by that. I got through the fire."[15] (Yet radiation, too, was suggested in the warning, "Look not back!")

Brimstone, of course, is a sulphurous compound such as would be emitted by a volcanic eruption. But there are no volcanic mountains, active or inactive, surrounding the Jordan valley, where Sodom and Gomorrah were apparently located; and there are no other "natural" phenomena that could account for the destructive, fiery rain. One is left with two options: either it was a wholly supernatural manifestation, or it involved an aerial attack of some kind, using firebombs or, more probably, advanced weaponry comparable to lasers or atomic bombs.

From whence?

The airships of the Atlantean era had vanished from the earth soon after that culture was eclipsed by earthquake and flood in the latter days of Ra and Hermes, a full millennium or more before the days of Abraham and Lot.

Well, then, dare we speculate that Melchizedek and his companions—traveling, perhaps, from a planetary body in Arcturus's realm—had come in a spaceship, from which the attack on Sodom and Gomorrah was launched at the Lord's direction?

That's pretty far out, admittedly. And anything bordering on "sci-fi" or "ufology" is strictly frowned upon by all of the official spokesmen for the Edgar Cayce Foundation and its affiliate organization, the Association for Research and Enlightenment, at Virginia Beach. (The critics of parapscyhological research are strident enough as it is, without providing them with additional grist for the mills of malice and mockery.)

At the same time, no serious researcher in the Cayce phenomenon can afford to overlook an aspect of the readings that is all too often swept under the rug in a gesture of acute embarrassment. For the Edgar Cayce readings *do* appear to confirm the existence of extraterrestrial visitations to our planet.

Let me cite a couple of examples.

In a life reading for a woman who had been "among the priestesses of the Mayan experience" in Yucatan during a previous incarnation, mention is made of "those that were visiting from other worlds or planets."[16] And Edgar's secretary, Gladys Davis, had appended this note: "(Psychic experiences of prehistory? Space ships, flying saucers?)" But a more careful study of the reading reveals that the incarnation in question, like the Mayan culture itself, was relatively recent and by no means "prehistoric," as the notation suggests. In fact, the reading alludes to the coming of Cortez's eleven-ship armada that landed on the east coast of Mexico in April 1519, for it states that the entity's Mayan incarnation "was just before that period when those as from the east [i.e., Spain] had come." There is also a reference to the dreadful blood sacrifices that had become a part of the Mayan's religious practices in that latter-day period and which proved so horrifying to Cortez and his men.

In yet another reading, touching on the Atlantean incarnation of a twenty-six-year-old male, we find this interesting statement: "For the manners of transportation, the manners of communications through the airships of that period were *such as Ezekiel described of a much later date*"[17] (italics added).

The Book of Ezekiel is a book of visions. Written in the sixth century B.C., the very first chapter contains a strange account of an unusual sighting by the prophet:

And I looked, and, behold, a whirlwind came out of the north, a great cloud, and a fire infolding itself, and a brightness was about it, and out of the midst thereof as the color of amber, out of the midst of the fire.

Also out of the midst thereof came the likeness of four living creatures. And this was their appearance; they had the likeness of a man.

As for their rings, they were so high that they were dreadful; and their rings were full of eyes round about them four.

And when the living creatures went, the wheels went with them: and when the living creatures were lifted up from the earth, the wheels were lifted up.[18]

What Ezekiel saw, Abraham in his day might also have seen. But if it was the chariot of the Lord, he would very probably have kept his wonderment to himself.

7. "O King! O Uhjltd!"

The sands of time have buried much of history, but in the cycles of recurrence, what once lay buried may again be revealed to us. We have only to await the ever-blowing winds of change, which bespeak the shifting nature of human destiny.

In a cave not far from Shushtar, in modern-day Iran, lie the buried bones of that ancient leader, teacher, and healer Uhjltd, awaiting discovery by future archaeologists.

Radiocarbon dating of his remains may reveal with some degree of certitude the age in which he lived. The Edgar Cayce readings, as already noted in an earlier chapter, are less than exact on this point.

Yet there is at least one substantial clue, which many have passed without notice. Let us dig it up.

"Ask your Uncle Dudley," the grown-ups around me used to say whenever I asked bothersome (meaning unanswerable) questions of them. Then they would laugh. It was, to my offended juvenile ears, a totally nonsensical expression that hardly merited my youthful notice or contempt. Yet I usually gave them my standing reply: "But I haven't got an Uncle Dudley!"

Well, I have subsequently found him. And it is a rare irony, now that the present chapter has introduced a particularly bothersome question, that it is precisely to "Uncle Dudley" that we are able to turn for an answer.

Dudley Wentworthe, according to Reading 962–1, was a well-respected figure in early-day Manhattan, who served as a keeper of the records for the English and Dutch settlers there. Both competent and kindly, he was also possessed of a phenomenal memory for detail, which earned him that still-familiar expression in his honor: "Ask your Uncle Dudley!"

Long before he was Dudley Wentworthe, however, Mr. [962]

had lived in the days of Uhjltd, though first as a keeper of the treasury in the household of Croesus (a royal name synonymous with wealth and greed, in a lineage that must have been ancient and cyclical) before giving up a life of self-indulgent luxury to join Uhjltd's people in "the city in the hills and the plains." Yet one small piece of treasure, handed down to us in the life-reading of that entity, was a "gift" from his unusual memory, for in probing the akashic records of [962] in his Persian period as Ixelte, Mr. Cayce struck gold—a dating:

The entity then was among the keepers of the treasury during the first and second Croesus; for this was among the *early* experiences, being some seven to ten thousand years B.C. (962-1)

That is not very precise, admittedly, but at least it dispels any doubt as to the antiquity of Uhjltd's rule, which clearly lay in the embryonic era of the great Irano-Aryan empire then emerging.

Gladys Davis's largely speculative dating for the Uhjltd era, found in one of her footnotes, was 8058 B.C. The added ' '58" finds its meaning in a reference Cayce had once made to the fact that many significant periods of change throughout human history had commenced in the fifty-eighth year of a given century (even as the prophesied changes in our time were set to occur from '58 to '98).[1] In any case, Gladys's intuitive dating falls within the time frame just cited from Reading 962-1, and it also appears to fit reasonably well into the time frame suggested by the following question and answer from yet another reading:

Q-3. *By what name if any, was the "city of the hills and the plains" [established by Uhjltd] referred to in biblical history?*
A-3. This will be found referred to as a place of sojourn of some of the children of Cain, as combined later with some of the children of Shem. (288-48)

The area was already a deserted one, however, when Uhjltd arrived, which meant that the descendants of both Cain and Shem had long since abandoned those parts. Yet if biblical sources are correct, Shem's prolific descendants were never far away, but existed wherever one might travel in Persia or Arabia. Shem, it will be remembered, was a son of Noah, and one of the early forebears of Abraham, to whom the Lord had promised that his seed would be as numberless as the stars. Better known as the Shemitic, or Semitic, peoples, they settled in time throughout Lydia, Syria, Chaldea, parts of Assyria and of Persia, and the entire Arabian peninsula. Almost certainly, their tribes had even intermingled with the scattered tribes of Ra and Zu, from whence Uhjltd sprang.

Finally, in another question dealing with the correlation of the Uhjltd period with biblical history, it was asked if there was a parallel that could be drawn between the two epochs. "Of Cushi," was the terse, rather enigmatic, reply.[2]

Well, let us see. Cushi, of course, was that bearer of bad tidings to King David, who told the truth of Absalom's death after the other runner, having overtaken him, had shielded the king from sorrow by claiming, "All is well." Joab, leading David's forces, had succeeded in routing the disloyal troops under Absalom at Gilead, after the latter, in a move to usurp power from his father, had "stolen the heart" of Israel. The traitor had fled, with Joab's men in pursuit. Yet the still loving, forgiving king had sternly counseled his commander Joab, "Deal gently with Absalom!" Joab, however, ignored the advice. He dispatched the traitor when Absalom got caught by his hair in a tree as he rode through a thicket. The parallel, then, in the experiences of King Uhjltd and King David lay not in the realm of their historicity (for their lives were several millennia apart); rather, it was a parallel in the sense of their personal tragedy and betrayal. For there was one among King Uhjltd's trusted subjects who, through guile, corrupted the loyalty of a portion of his followers. As a result of the treachery, the king's beloved wife, Ilya, was assassinated; so, too, in the end, was Uhjltd himself.

It was in the days when there was the final breaking up of the tribes of Ra and Zu.

Eujueltd, a nomadic leader whose domain was a constantly

shifting one on the borders between Araby and Persia, lived with his clansmen from one of the scattered remnants of the tribe of Zu. In his desert wanderings, he met and fell in love with one of the fairest descendants of the legendary tribe of Ra, Slumdki.

Out of their union, Uhjltd was born.

In addition to certain Caucasian traits, it was said of Uhjltd's nomadic ancestry that it combined the strength of Egypt and the mysteries thereof with the glories of India and its equal quotient of mysteries. His parents, in coming together, had chosen that their bodies might become the channels through which a "manifestation" might come to the sons of men attesting to the glory of God. And so, like the priest Ra Ta in the same entity's Egyptian incarnation, Uhjltd entered the earth-plane as one who came with a purpose. His name (pronounced "Yew-ult") meant "exaltation"[3] —not the exaltation of self but of the Creator, which Uhjltd was to accomplish by becoming a peacemaker striving to unite the warring factions around him. This he did by living and teaching that eternal precept "the brotherhood of man and the Fatherhood of God." Later, his son Zend, an incarnation of the Master, was to expand upon this principle in presenting to the world one of the first elaborate systems of religious thought, embodied in what became the Zend-Avesta. But it was left to the first Zoroaster, a grandson of Uhjltd and the son of Zend, to disseminate and popularize those teachings, under the name of Zoroastrianism.

As a young man, however, Uhjltd was trained in the ways of the bedouin. What we would regard as lawlessness was viewed by the hard-pressed nomads as a necessary and normal way of life. Passing caravans were plundered. There were raids and counter-raids upon rival tribes. But the common enemy, as well as the most lucrative target for attack, was the Perisan king, Croesus, with his fabled wealth and reputation for cruelty. In addition, he maintained in conjunction with his major stronghold a training school for maidens, which offered a tempting prize to the amorous bedouins, whose camps were often short of women.

As for the Persian ruler and his protectorates, these were constantly attempting to overcome the nomads, of course, and to keep open those vital trade routes between Persia, India, Egypt, the Aegean land, the Caspian, and those peoples from the north (the Ukraine), as well as the Macedonian land (what later became known as Greece).

The ruler of Persia during the initial phase of the Uhjltd period is believed to have been Croesus II, who was presumably succeeded in the latter days by his son, Croesus III. In one of those stunning karmic patterns so common throughout the Edgar Cayce readings, both of these former kings reincarnated in the present century, found their separate ways to Virginia Beach, and obtained life readings. In the portion of his reading covering that particular epoch, the entity who had been Croesus II learned that he had been "a hard-hearted guy" who consistently abused his authority in dealing with others.[4] Though more of a humanitarian in many ways, particularly as related to educational concepts, his successor, Croesus III, was told that he had been "hard on those with too many ideas,"[5] suggesting that he did not approve of the reforms taking place in that city of the hills and plains ruled by Uhjltd, even though peace had by then been established between their two kingdoms.

Uhjltd was not the only son sired by that great nomadic leader Eujueltd, and the lovely Slumdki. Others followed who were of a less idealistic bent than their peace-loving brother. The second son, Oujida, typified that sibling rivalry so common in many families, and his love of battle apparently endeared him to his father, whereas Uhjltd remained his mother's favorite. Oujida commanded the faction of the clan that led the most daring and destructive raids, as if to show up Uhjltd's more gentle nature as a form of weakness, though he was obliged by the rules of the clan to acknowledge Uhjltd's overall leadership—at least on a ceremonial basis—as the elder brother. The father's role in unwittingly fostering the growing dissension is implicit in the following excerpt:

The entity [Eujueltd] forsook the ways, with the bodily forces that came through Oujida and the other sons, yet with the establishing again—

though broken in body, though turbulent in self through the trials that had been taken on through those periods of oppression and depression, came again to the son [Uhjltd] for the help, the aid; and the new awakening came to the entity. (707–1)

It was in one of Oujida's earliest and most successful raids that the differences between the two brothers posed the first test of wills. A combination of bold strategy and lucky timing had enabled Oujida's forces to break into the fortress of the Persian king, seize a portion of the treasury, and escape with a number of female hostages from the royal training school. Only later, upon returning to his father's camp, did Oujida discover that among the maidens was the adopted daughter of King Croesus himself. Elia by name, the rebellious maiden warned her bold captor of the fierce reprisals that would surely beset his people unless she were set free. Her anger served only to rouse the fires of passion in Oujida's breast, for the maiden was lovelier than any he had seen and made lovelier still by the flush of anger in her face and the glint of fury in her sea green eyes. Yet, even in his passion, Oujida did not lose sight of the urgent need to appease his elder brother, Uhjltd, whose gentle, smiling rebuke could be more terrible than all the angry words of a maiden. So, to blunt the anticipated reaction from Uhjltd for his brash behavior, Oujida dragged the captive Elia to his brother's tent, bowed low before Uhjltd, and offered the daughter of Croesus as his share of the booty.

A smiling Uhjltd declined the offer, which only added to Elia's anger the fresh rage of humiliation. Yet, looking upon the compassionate face of this unusual leader whose visible strength and grace stirred something deep within her, Elia felt an inner confusion that she could not explain. It is possible that Uhjltd was feeling somewhat the same emotion, though carefuly suppressed, for these two, in their former incarnation, had been joined in matrimony as Asua and Ra Ta. Asua, in fact, had been the young priest's first wife. They had been permanently separated when he went into exile with his new companion, Isris (Isis).

Now a strange new scenario unfolded, laden with awe-inspiring karmic overtones for those of us who can read the footnotes to the script. For Oujida now took Elia to wife himself, and she bore him a daughter. That daughter was none other than the entity [538], who had been Ra's companion, Isris. Unable to cope with the hardships and imagined insults of her new life in the camp of the bedouin, and unmindful of the needs of her infant daughter, Elia plunged a knife into her bosom and thus took her exit from that experience. The motherless child, Inxa, was now abandoned by Oujida.

And what of Oujida? Had he played a role in the Egyptian period? Indeed he had. As Arsrha, he was that master mathematician who laid the foundations for the Sphinx at the same time that Ra and Hermes were beginning construction of the Great Pyramid. Was there built into his psyche on that occasion a secret resentment and rivalry toward the high priest, whose greater monument was dwarfing the significance of the Sphinx? Perhaps. (At any rate, the bonds of karma seemed ample enough to go around!)

A cycle of years went by.

As he rode up from the south on his dapple gray charger, Uhjltd reflected upon the changes wrought in his life during the past decade. Most of the time had been spent in the land of Egypt, amongst his mother's people and the priests there, learning of the ancient mysteries. As a consequence, he had acquired much wisdom that he was now eager to apply. But upon his return, nine moons ago, he had found his father's people badly divided and caught in a series of devastating raids and counterraids with the Persians, which also affected a number of neighboring tribes. The badly splintered nomadic tribesmen were in need of a strong leader who could unite them. They had looked to the returning Uhjltd as the obvious choice, and he had accepted the challenge.

Now thirty-three, Uhjltd was indeed an imposing figure. Tall, and straight as an arrow, with a well-proportioned body, his thick, raven black hair framed a noble face that few could fail to admire for its combined gentleness, beauty, and, withal, masculine strength. The piercing gray eyes, under thick, dark brows, lent an aura of great mystery and hidden spirituality, while the firm chin and aquiline nose were the hallmark of a born leader of men.

Yet Uhjltd's approach to the problems of his people, which was to bring an end to the constant raids and begin to engage in legitimate commerce as a means of livelihood, had met with resistance from Oujida and some others, who clung to the former ways and secretly resented the solutions Uhjltd proposed. Uhjltd knew of this, in his heart, and it saddened him.

This particular day, he was riding up toward the stronghold of the Persian king, a lone emissary in search of some means of communicating to Croesus and his people the desire of his own tribesmen, under his leadership, to put an end to their past differences in the interests of a common peace.

It was a bold move. Some might term it foolhardy. But Uhjltd saw a treaty of peace with the Persians as the essential first step in establishing a new era of peace and prosperity for his people.

The sun was low in the distant hills when Uhjltd finally reached the well on the outskirts of the Persian citadel. In the shade of three palm trees there, he rested himself and his horse. Suddenly, he saw a young woman approaching, like some beautiful mirage in the falling light across the desert sands.

When she finally spotted him, she was startled. She almost dropped the jug she was carrying.

Uhjltd laughed good-naturedly and hastened to reassure her:

"Woman, I mean you no harm. I am only here to rest my horse for a while and to draw some fresh water from your well to slake our thirst."

The maiden now eyed him cautiously, and with covert approval. He was strikingly handsome, with a surprisingly courteous and gentle mien for a bedouin.

"Sir, you are welcome to rest and drink here," she said, somewhat surprised to find herself addressing this nomadic stranger without the customary contempt she felt toward those villainous marauders who had captured her childhood friend and companion Elia a decade earlier. It was only by luck that she herself, whose royal father was a brother to the king, had escaped a similar fate.

And Ilya had vowed eventual revenge. But she could not be certain that the smiling stranger who was now regarding her with such close interest was a bedouin of that same fearsome tribe. He did seem different from any nomad she had ever encountered or heard of. In his presence, she found herself growing strangely moved, and not in full control of her emotions. Yet she knew she must remain on guard until she could learn his identity.

"My name is Uhjltd," said he, as if reading her thoughts. "I am recently returned from my mother's people, in Egypt, to rejoin my father's tribemen to the south of here. I come in peace."

The name Uhjltd was like a dagger in Ilya's heart. She was sure she had heard it spoken in connection with those nomadic tribesmen who had carried off Elia into captivity years earlier and continued to harass her people with raids upon their caravans. If she was right about him, this bedouin must be made to pay.

"Does a bedouin ever come in peace?" she asked.

"I would welcome an opportunity to prove it," responded Uhjltd. "As a leader of my people, I have come here, alone and unarmed, to negotiate peaceful terms with those within your gates, so that we may live together in the future as brothers, rather than as enemies who must constantly war upon one another."

Strange words from a bedouin, thought Ilya, somewhat bitterly. But she hid her dark thoughts and instead smiled beguilingly.

"Meet me here on the morrow, at dawn," she told him. "Let me see if I can arrange such a meeting as you propose, for my father is a man of some influence in the court."

Uhjltd's piercing gray eyes searched deeply into the sky blue orbs of the smiling maiden. Her pale, exquisite face and shapely figure, the burnished gold tresses beneath her veil, and the lilting voice like the sounds of the nightingale had all combined to captivate him utterly. Were her words to be trusted? He did not know. But if it was a ruse, he would willingly be her captive. In any case, some deep instinct told him he could trust her.

"I shall be here," he said, "awaiting your return at dawn tomorrow."

She turned to go.

Uhjltd called out after her, "May I ask your name?"

"Ilya," came the bell-like response, as she gave him a parting glance over her shoulder.

Thus did these two, who had been as one in the beginning, each come to find their other self, though not yet recognizing this wondrous fact or its fateful implications.

True to her word, Ilya appeared at the well at dawn and led Uhjltd, who had set his horse free to graze on the sparse desert grasses, in through the gates of the city.

Almost at once, however, he was seized by the waiting guards, and Uhjltd realized, too late, that the maiden he now loved as dearly as life itself had tricked him. Yet he could not hate her. His people, he knew, had given her ample grounds to seek revenge upon him.

However, as Uhjltd was being dragged away to the tower, where he would be bound hand and foot by chains until his captors could decide his fate, he suddenly caught sight of Ilya in the background. Never in his life had Uhjltd seen such a look of utter remorse, as she suddenly covered her tearful face with both hands as he was led away. And in his heart, Uhjltd felt a secret rejoicing: if she loved him, that was all that mattered. His fate was secondary.

To Ilya, though, the fate of the prisoner now beame a matter of primary concern. She knew she must right a grievous wrong and find some way to set the bedouin free. And she knew where to turn for aid. Her former instructress, who was well acquainted with the guard Endessoseu, could help the two of them gain access to the tower. Together, it might be possible for Ilya and the older woman to loosen the chains that by now were undoubtedly shackling poor Uhjltd by his wrists and ankles to the tower wall. It was a spiteful and primitive custom introduced by Croesus, which only moments before Uhjltd's capture Ilya was ready to approve, but such are the curious inconsistencies of the heart when one is smitten by the sudden arrows of love that logic finds no nesting place.

It was not until the third day, as the sun arose, that Ilya and her accomplice were able to gain secret entrance to the tower room where the imprisoned bedouin, weakened by a diet of bread and water, slumped in his heavy chains. At sight of Ilya, however, Uhjltd's strength returned with the fullness of his joy. It was not long before his two liberators had succeeded in loosing his chains, and he was free.

He lingered for a moment, not knowing how to express the depths of his gratitude and his love.

Ilya urged him to flee, pointing the way to the parapet.

Once on the ground, Uhjltd let out a low whistle that reached the alert ears of his dapple gray charger in the desert fields nearby. But as he rode off, with a backward glance over his shoulder at the tower wall where his accomplices now stood, he saw a dreadful sight: guards, alerted to Uhjltd's escape, now rushed up behind the two unsuspecting women and pushed them angrily over the parapet.

Not for a moment did Uhjltd hesitate, despite the obvious danger of exposing himself to the fury of the guards. He rode swiftly back to where his wounded liberators lay hurt and bleeding and placed them astride his strong mount. With himself in the middle, holding the reins, they raced away under a hail of rocks and epithets. The epithets fell harmlessly enough upon Uhjltd and his two frightened companions, but the stones wounded Uhjltd in the back and shoulder and in the same leg he had already seriously injured in his drop from the tower wall.

Yet they rode on. There was no alternative, until they could come to a place of relative safety where they might rest together and dress their wounds.

Such a place of refuge, Uhjltd sensed, might be found among the cliffs and boulders of the rolling hill country that bordered the southern plains.

Sure enough, just as night was falling, they came upon a well-concealed cave in a deep ravine, and inside the cave, there was an inviting grotto with a spring of clear, fresh water. Uhjltd knelt in that place and lifted his voice in a prayer of thanksgiving. He felt Ilya's tender touch upon his shoulder, joining him in the quiet meditation that followed.

Day followed day, and as the bonds of their love grew ever stronger, so did the healing of their bodies progress with miraculous swiftness. Drawing on his recent years of training with the Egyptian priests in his mother's land, Uhjltd now raised his own psychic energies, and Ilya, under his guidance, was soon able to do the same. Thus, they practiced the laying on of hands to help one another, and to aid the recovery of the badly wounded instructress, who nevertheless showed ingratitude by frequently rebuking Ilya for her present troubles. It was an attitude that hindered her healing, and she lapsed into a coma.

On the second day, Uhjltd had uncovered a hidden cache of provisions covered by rocks outside their cave entrance. It consisted of dried dates and figs and sacks of grain stored in airtight goatskin pouches, apparently left there by a passing caravan to meet their future needs when again passing that way. There were also oils and spices. Uhjltd called to Ilya, and they gave thanks to God for this further blessing.

It was on the sixth day that Uhjltd spotted a small party of horsemen riding across the plains. Even at a distance, he recognized them as his own kinsmen, and though his wounds were not yet properly healed, he rode out to greet them.

Uhjltd rejoiced to see among their number his much younger brother, Ulado, and there was a tearful reunion. But as Ulado poured out to him the story of all that had happened in the camp since Uhjltd's departure, it became apparent to Uhjltd that he could never go back, but must wipe the dust of that place forever from his feet.

"Many of your own loyal guards have now set their hearts against you, my brother," said Ulado, "and Oujida and some of the others are fighting among themselves to take command. They had all assumed that you were either dead or captured. Worst of all, the prayer ground you sanctified for the morning and evening worship has been desecrated: the camels are tethered there now, and it is covered with dung! The five of us here have left in disgust."

In that moment, between his anger and his sorrow, Uhjltd received a sudden vision. It became clear to him what he must do.

With an arm about Ulado's youthful shoulders, their former leader now spoke to the small, loyal band:

"Here in this place," he announced to them, "I shall build a great city among the hills and the plains. Its name shall be Is-Shlan-doen. Only those who seek the ways of peace and brotherhood may come here. It will become a great center for healing and worship, and commerce shall also thrive, for I intend to offer trade and protection to all the passing caravans. Yet it will not be the wealthy but the downtrodden and the outcasts, such as yourselves, who will make this a mighty city."

Ulado looked about him, somewhat bewildered by his brother's visionary words. All he could see was a broad expanse of empty plains and hills. Yet he knew that Uhjltd always spoke true and that he often saw things that others saw not.

"Tell me, my brother," Ulado asked eagerly, "what shall I do to get started?"

"Go back to our father's camp," said Uhjltd, "and speak only to those you can trust. Tell them to strike their tents and join us!"

The group would have left at once to obey their leader's orders, but he restrained them. He told them of Ilya and the other, who had arranged his escape, and who were now with him in the cave in the hills.

"Soon Ilya and I must go to Egypt for special provisions and to bring others here to help us. So bring extra horses, and one of our women who can watch after the badly wounded one, who is now in a deep sleep."

As the five rode off, Uhjltd returned to the cave, where Ilya was awaiting him.

That night was a night for love.

Out of the union of their bodies, in that first blissful encounter, as soul met soul in the kind of yearning and longing that only two who had been as one from the beginning of time could understand, came forth the seed that would produce another incarnation of the Master, as the entity Zend:

With bodies oiled and dressed from the cave spring, [they] repair to their couch of skins, and there watch the sun's slow sinking over the desert sands. And in this fading hour they first find the answer of body to body in the soul's awakening, as they melt into one; giving then an offering to the world, who, in the form and in the stature of the great leader [Zend], gave the first philosophy of life and love to the world, coming from this union. (288–6)

The city in the hills and the plains grew and prospered. Under Uhjltd's strong leadership and with a common ideal to motivate them, wonders were being accomplished in what had become a vast communal enterprise dedicated to serving man and God.

Applying to the barren plains those same irrigation techniques already common in Egypt, Uhjltd had workers divert the streams from the nearby mountains into special channels that watered the land so that crops might grow and fruit trees flourish. Meanwhile, the hills were found to be rich in precious stones and minerals, which soon became a profitable source of commerce. Caravans came and went from India and Egypt, from Mesopotamia and Syria, and also from Carpathia and Greece, or the Athenian land.

Most of all, Is–Shlan-doen was gaining fame as a center of spiritual learning, where the healing arts were also practiced under the tutelage of that remarkable leader. A place of refuge for the oppressed from every land, the city had quickly swelled into a billowing sea of tents. The many scattered remnants from broken clans who found their way to Is–Shlan-doen kissed the ground at their feet and called it Paradise.

But if it was an earthly paradise to some, to the Persian king, Croesus, it had become an intolerale threat. Much of his former commerce with the outer world had now shifted to Uhjltd's fair domain; worse still, certain of his most loyal subjects were now beginning to grumble about the unaccustomed hardships they were encountering, without benefit of the former revenues and accompanying privileges. Some even dared to speak openly of the better living conditions said to exist in Is-Shlan-doen.

So the angry king sent forth raiding parties to attack this new threat to his security, but his demoralized troops were repeatedly repulsed by Uhjltd's superior forces. Finally, Uhjltd saw that this oppressive Persian ruler, who had rejected overtures of peace, must be taught a lesson in the bedouin manner: with a vast following of loyal warriors, Uhjltd attacked and conquered the stronghold of Croesus. To ensure more peaceful relationships in the future, Croesus II was forced to abdicate, and his youthful son Croesus III ascended the throne in his stead. Trade relations and friendly intercourse were established between the Persian citadel and Is-Shlan-doen, and many of the conquered Persians actually chose to shift their allegiance to the charismatic and kindly ruler who had subdued them.

Meanwhile, in those early stages of Is-Shlan-doen's development, Uhjltd chose to confer many phases of civil rule on his respected and aging mother Slumdki, who had been living in exile in Egypt since her husband, Eujueltd, had chosen to join forces with Oujida's trouble-making faction of the clan. Thus, during her few remaining years, Slumdki was to become, in effect, a ruling queen:

> The entity then among those peoples of the nomads, and the mother to the ruler who *conquered* the Persian peoples; giving much to the ruler, Uhjltd, in that period, through counsel, advice, and coming as an aid *to* those peoples that were subdued, and teaching much *in* the land—in ensample; that, though there were condemnations, and there were the misunderstandings in the purpose of the raids, or the conquering of the peoples, the entity held *little* against the peoples, and became the ruler, the Queen, of that divided land. In the name Slumdki. (2708–1)

As for Inxa, the abandoned daughter of Oujida, her care had initially been in the hands of Slumdki, following Elia's willful and tragic suicide. Now, however, she came increasingly under Ilya's loving tutelage and also began to assist in the raising and training of the infant Zend. When a second son, Ujndt, was born to Uhjltd and Ilya, Inxa became his happy nursemaid.

Of the offspring of Uhjltd and Ilya, we find it stated:

Just the two children did the entity [288, Ilya] have in that period, both sons; who later became as rulers, or leaders in those activities from which teachers arose—as the teachings of Zend, and the expansion of those activities through other lands. (288-48)

Apparently, though, there was an *adopted* daughter, in addition to the two natural sons. Miss [993], who learned in her life reading that she had been with Edgar Cayce in the Egyptian experience as a member of "the household of the king, and an attendant with the priest in the temple that was called beautiful," found that she had entered in the Persian cycle, as well, where she again assumed a favored role as one of those in "the household of the ruler or the leader Uhjltd, who led these peoples, and the daughter of this leader. In the name Uldha."[6] (She may have been a natural daughter born to Uhjltd through an earlier liaison, predating his encounter with Ilya. But if so, no hint of such a relationship can be found in any of the numerous readings relating to the Persian cycle. Thus, it seems more probable, with the many refugees who showed up at Is-Shaln-doen, that Ilya, recalling her own early years of companionship with the adopted daughter of King Croesus, chose to adopt one of these orphaned children and raise her as her own in memory of that childhood relationship.)

As for the entity Inxa, the karmic roots of her Perisian cycle are fascinaing to consider. As Ra's companion, Isris, in her former incarnation, she had been that channel through which Iso, the twin soul of Ra, entered the earth-plane. That child, of course, had to be abandoned when the king ruled that Ra and Isris must be banished to the Nubian land for breaking the priest's own law against multiple marriages. Iso, it will be remembered, died in early childhood, feeling desolate and purposeless. And now it was the former Isris, or Isis, who had found herself born under parallel circumstances, as the daughter of [369, Elia], who had been the legitimate wife of Ra in her past life. Upon [369]'s suicide, as Elia, in the

Persian experience, the motherless child Inxa found herself also abandoned by her father, Oujida. Yet, ultimately, it was Ilya (the former Iso) who apparently came to her rescue, making Inxa a virtual ward of Uhjltd's household, and a nursemaid to her sons, until she reached marriageable age.

(Ah, how inexorable is the fulfilling of the law!)

Another entity who came under Inxa's nursing care, apparently, was the badly wounded instructress, Irenan, who had aided Ilya in arranging Uhjltd's escape from his tower prison. Although not fully clarified in the readings, it is believed that this was the entity [295], whose present-day resentment toward [288] (who had been Ilya) apparently had its roots partly in that Persian cycle, based upon the following question-and-answer sequence concerning [295]'s Persian incarnation, although the contention stemmed from much earlier differences between them in Atlantean times:

Q–4. *[Concerning my karmic relationships with 288]:*

A–4. In Atlantis; much that made for contentions—and the *manners* of expressions are those influences in the present. In Persia; and also in France. They [288 and 295] are necessary one to another, that they may meet those things. Not as amiss, but they *meet* them in Him that said, "I condemn thee not, if thou sinnest no more!" [Note: Miss 295 had been Mary Magdalene during the Master's incarnation as Jesus.] Rather give life than pleasure. Rather give joy than pain.

Q–5. *What happened in Persia?*

A–5. The entity rebelled against those conditions that were brought about by associations in that experience.

Q–6. *And I left?*

A–6. And the body left.

Q–7. *What was the association that I rebelled against?*

A–7. Against the mate [Ilya, 288] of the teacher [Uhjltd, 294]. (295-9)

In an unusual reading given in 1934 concerning the joint soul development involved in the present associations of [294], [295], and [288], an ominous warning note was included in Cayce's response to Miss [295]'s specific inquiry about her relationship to "the work of Edgar Cayce in this life": "Were not His [Jesus's] blessings on thee as He purified thee, as He condemned thee not?"

the answer was given, in part. "Know that thy place, thy purposes, thine development, lie close with those developments of the work . . . leave not those words that are words of life to thee!"[7]

Despite the warning, Miss [295] left, abandoning her role in the work for petty reasons, even as she had done in Persia.

The Greek traders, a wily lot, had long had a covetous eye on Is-Shlan-doen.

Back home, they spoke to their military leaders about the great prize such a prosperous city would represent if it could only be captured. But it was recognized that Uhjltd was a powerful leader, and that the base of his power lay in the peculiar nature of his teachings more than anything else. It was some odd notion about the brotherhood of man and the Fatherhood of God, and the people were strongly united because of their common religious convictions. Thus, if some means could be devised to undermine those spiritual teachings, which were central to Is-Shlan-doen's present impregnabilty, Uhjltd's power base might begin to crumble around him. Then an invasion force of Athenian warriors could easily take over the divided city.

The first contingent of Grecian maidens arrived at the gates of Is-Shlan-doen without rousing any suspicions. They displayed their charms to Uhjltd's appreciative tribesmen, and many were soon diverting the men from their daily tasks to pursue a more amorous occupation. Their techniques were subtle, of course. Songs and music, affecting a certain affinity toward the community spirit of the place, aided them at the outset in winning converts. It all seemed so innocent and harmless. But many around Uhjltd soon grew suspicious, as did the leader himself. Yet Uhjltd insisted that they should simply turn the tables on their comely visitors and convert them to the ways of Is-Shlan-doen. Surprisingly, Uhjltd's technique of "counterinsurgency" began to work quite well. Many of the maidens were truly impressed by the virtuous new life-style observed around them and the obvious good it had wrought in the happy lives of Is-Shlan-doen's inhabitants. They decided to seek mates for themselves and settle down, forgetting the subversive purposes that had brought them thither. Others, however, did not lose sight of their original objective.

The influx of Greeks continued. Among their numbers, now, were men as well as young women.

Xuno, who was to become the trusted companion of Inxa, was one of these. Uhjltd himself came to like and trust the young man, who was as good an instructor for his sons Zend and Ujndt as Inxa, their doting teacher. The boys now learned twice as much, and twice as fast. But whereas Ujndt showed a propensity for combining idealism with practical judgment—qualities that were one day to make him a highly effective leader in the secular realm —Zend displayed a more mystical bent. And though he was destined to become a great religious figure, the readings suggest an excess of zeal, which hindered him somewhat in that particular incarnation.[8] For, like any other man, the Master was an evolving soul-entity, who entered again and again and on some occasions "failed to keep the whole law."[9]

It was at about this time that the reconstruction of Is-Shlan-doen (called Toaz by the Greeks) was begun. Tents were gradually replaced by permanent structures of wood or stone, and in this activity, Uhjltd and those close about him in the managerial roles, as it were, found themselves too busy to note the gathering forces of subversion, particularly between scheming Greeks and Persians, whose numbers were now quite substantial.

Uhjltd's right-hand man, Esdena, who had also undergone spiritual initiation in Egypt, was what could be termed "a pacifist of no mean estate"; and though others had attempted, from time to time, to subvert his loyalty, it was unshakable:

Many were they that attempted to supersede or to bring about crosses between that leader Uhjltd and the entity, then Esdena, of [Uhjltd's] mother's own people; for Esdena, *too,* was among the initiates of Egypt that came to an understanding with those activities that were begun there; came as from among the initiates in the land where there had been those trainings for many of those teachers in and throughout the earth. The entity gained during that experience. (826-2)

Similarly, Uhjltd's personal emissary, or secretary, though he had formerly been in the employ of the Persian monarch, was not privy to any developing plot among his own peoples—in evil connivance with the Greeks—to overthrow Uhjltd, or he would most certainly have warned him. This entity, named Edssi, though he had faltered at times, was loyal to his new king.

And so it was that Uhjltd and Ilya, relaxing long enough from their official duties to pay one of their infrequent visits to Ilya's reconciled relatives in the distant Persian court, one day rode unwittingly into the waiting jaws of death.

The exact nature of the betrayal leading to Uhjltd's assassination, along with Ilya's, is not made clear; nor is the identity of the specific individual or group responsible disclosed. A dark suspicion, however, falls on the figure of Inxa's Greek companion, Xuno. Whether he might have been among those who accompanied Uhjltd and Ilya on their visit to the Persian court or, more likely, furnished "inside" information on their planned itinerary to a special band of assassins who were permitted secret entry into the stronghold of the Persian king, is left to speculation. But what is made clear is that the assassination, taking place in the Persian court, was timed to coincide with a raid by the Athenian forces (the Greeks), upon Is-Shlan-doen, in which a number of Uhjltd's key lieutenants, including Edssi, were murdered. Rather pointedly, the attackers are referred to as "the entity's [Inxa's] companion's people," meaning Xuno's compatriots, and inasmuch as Inxa had become suspicious of Xuno's true allegiances, she took flight immediately after the raid with two of Uhjltd's children, Ujndt and Uldha, to a place of safety. Meanwhile, it is said of Zend's welfare following "the overrunnings by those from the Athenian land" that he was sheltered by the entity Iahn,[10] a Uhjltd loyalist, who aided in establishing Zend in another portion of the land, "a place of refuge," where Zend "rose to be the ruler in that experience."[11]

The Persian court is identified, if only by allusion, as the place where the double assassination occurred. In a reading that refers to

Ilya's girlhood companionship with Elia, the adopted daughter of Croesus II, which was brought about through the influence of Ilya's father (a brother of the king), it adds that it was "in this same place where the entity spent the days with [Elia]" that "the life, as known, was [later] taken by the invading forces from the south and east," and this is followed by a reference to the entity [288]'s present "aversion to those cutting instruments, for in that manner the bodily destruction came."[12]

The involvement of a trusted friend of Uhjltd's and Ilya's is implicit in yet another reading referring to the assassination. And one might clearly suspect that the traitor was a Greek, for it was as a Trojan that Cayce entered the earth-plane in his next incarnation, coming as the warrior "with a vengeance, attempting to wreck," and those with whom he did battle were none other than the Greeks.

Here is the appropriate excerpt, followed by another, that will provide the finale to our story of that tragic event:

And only with the treachery of others afterward was this life in the female taken. Hence the dread of knives in one [288] and the distrust of friendships in the other [294].

Again we find the male [294], with a vengeance, attempting to wreck, comes as the warrior [Trojan period], though the other [288] we find remains long in the land of nirvana and awaits the coming of her other self. (288–6)

Both suffered physically, and they each bear in the body at present a mark designating these conditions. On the female body, just below the left breast, to the side and on the edge of breast itself, the mark, and an answering one on the body of the male, in the opposite proximity of the breast. (288–6, Note: [288] has confirmed the presence of such a mark.)

If Is-Shlan-doen fell to the invaders, presumably it was later retaken by surviving remnants of Uhjltd's decimated leadership. The entity [2709] is identified as that one who became the king of the nomads after the death of Uhjltd and was known as Uhjltd the Second. Yet he lost in meting out punishment upon "those who were innocent" (perhaps suggesting an indiscriminate slaughter of the Greeks), although he later gained "in being the servant of others," and "the *ruler* of a great land and peoples."[13]

"O King, O Uhjltd," we find the message proclaimed in one of Edgar Cayce's life readings dealing with a series of dreams and visions for which he had sought interpretation, "there must be the purifying of the body from those of the elements . . . that would hinder from giving the greater light to those that would follow thee in any direction."[14]

Implicit, it would seem, in that admonitory reference to Cayce's Persian incarnation as Uhjltd the King was a recognition of its unusual role in his overall soul development. In fact, in a subsequent reading, we find Edgar Cayce's Persian cycle cited as a primary source for much of his present ability, enabling him to cast "the carnal mind" aside, in trance-state, "so that there speaks then as the oracles—or to that Throne."[15]

But if Cayce achieved high marks for the level of spiritual development attained in his Persian cycle, following his equally meritorious Egyptian period as Ra, his next several incarnations saw a pattern of reversal setting in, as is apparently common in the testing and purging of each soul. For, though he were once the priest, the king, "yet he faltered in the next return, and the next return, to earth!"[16]

8. The Siege of Troy

The golden apple of Discord started it all: it was just as one might have expected of such a dubious gift from a vengeful goddess.

Not so expectedly, however, the Edgar Cayce readings now bring to the ancient legend of Troy not only a confirmation of its underlying truth (as many historians have long suspected) but a bizarre and ironic twist to its ending.

The karmic sequel to that Trojan tragedy, with its ancient cast of characters, moved into the twentieth century as at least two of the chief protagonists—Hector and Achilles—reincarnated in strangely altered roles. Moreover, their separate entrances on stage, in different scenes and acts from each other, managed to shape a number of major events in the life of Edgar Cayce.

One needn't wonder why, particularly. After all, Cayce himself had been a participant in the original drama. In the name of Xenon, he had been a warrior defending the main gate of the besieged citadel when it fell to the subtle wiles of the attacking Greeks from without and their Trojan accomplices within. In mortal rage and humiliation, the outwitted Xenon then took his own life.

This impetuous act of "self-effacement," as the readings termed the suicide, was to haunt the entity throughout all of its successive lives. It was to appear and reappear at the subconscious level as a stumbling block, in one guise of self-guilt or another, until, as Edgar Cayce, the entity finally learned to meet and overcome it in patience and love, through the forgiveness of self and others. The lesson is best expressed, perhaps, in this wise counsel from one of the Search for God readings: "Stand aside and watch self pass by!"[1]

Paradoxically, this still involves an act of "self-effacement," but in a diametrically opposite sense, according to the Cayce readings.

Rather than letting the lower self dictate the terms in a maudlin gesture of self-destruction, as in the case of the suicide victim, the human will is subordinated in an act of voluntary surrender to the Divine Will, thereby enabling the Higher Self within to regain its original mastery. A look back at Edgar Cayce's selfless devotion, this time around, to a high spiritual calling in service to God and man suggests that he achieved a complete reversal of his destructive Trojan experience. And so it becomes a matter of unique interest, I think, to note that the Cayce readings sometimes employ the term "self-effacement" in its positive, or spiritual, sense, meaning the conquering of the lower self; at other times, as originally encountered in this chapter, the term is used in an opposite, or negative, connotation, implying self-destruction of the physical body.

Clearly, Edgar Cayce was one who intimately knew the two polarized extremes of "self-effacement," for both had become a part of his soul's experience along the way.

Gods and goddesses, and even a golden apple, may be viewed as fanciful trappings in the telling of a historic and all-too-human tale, but they color the events in accord with the times in which they occurred, thus adding a uniquely "Greek" dimension that is hard to ignore in a proper retelling of the ancient drama.

It began when the sea nymph Thetis was married to the noble Peleus, a mortal. From their godlike union was destined to spring an invincible warrior named Achilles. Invited to the nuptials were all of the goddesses but one. That one, whose name was Eris, or Discord, made her slighted presence known with the gift of a golden apple, hurled among the startled guests. Her pretty gift carried an inscription: For the Fairest.

Jupiter was asked to choose among the three final contestants for the prize, who were Juno, Minerva, and Venus. He wisely declined the honor. So the beauteous trio sought a mortal judge instead. On Mount Ida, they found the graceful youth Paris, ill-starred shepherd-son of King Priam of Troy.

Paris passed up promises of glory and wisdom from Juno and

Minerva and instead named Venus the fairest goddess of them all. Her reward to him was the love of the most beautiful among mortal women, whose name was Helen. The only fly in the honey jar was that Helen was already the wife of Menelaus, king of Sparta. Yet, when Paris sailed to Greece to find and claim her, Helen found his charms irresistible: she readily consented to elope with him. The result could have been predicted. The scandal shook all of Greece like an earthquake, and it triggered the protracted Trojan Wars, which were waged for nine bloody and indecisive years as repeated expeditions of fearless Greek warriors—heroes young and old—sought to avenge the dishonored Menelaus and retake from her brazen Trojan abductor the fair Helen, whose fabled beauty has been immortalized in verse with that rhetorical question: "Was this the face that launched a thousand ships?"

It is to the *Iliad* of Homer that one must turn for a full account of the internecine strife in both of the warring camps preceding the eventual fall of Troy. Actually, the *Iliad* begins toward the close of the nine-year battle, when a quarrel between Achilles and Agamemnon causes the former to withdraw temporarily from the epic struggle and threaten a return to Greece. Consequently, it is his close companion, Patroclus, who fills the gap, as it were, and is slain by Hector in an encounter with the Trojan forces outside the gates. In a fit of fury and remorse, Achilles now rejoins the battle, determined to avenge his friend's death in fierce and unmerciful combat. His chief target, of course, is the illustrious Hector, who, with his mother Hecuba, wife of King Priam, appears to be the real ruling force in the Trojan kingdom, have usurped the old man's power. Hector's brother, Paris, the lover of Helen who got them all into this fine kettle of fish, seems to have been a proficient warrior and womanizer but little else! Yet it is a poisoned arrow from his bow that finally fells Achilles, following the latter's cruel slaughter of Hector in a struggle of unbelievable ferocity.

The defeat and disgrace of Hector was envisioned in an unusually vivid dream-recall Edgar Cayce experienced on September 19, 1933. Since it is even more graphic than Homer's account of the grisly incident and involves Cayce himself as a horrified spectator at the gate where he stood guard, it is quoted here in its entirety:

I saw the battle between Hector and Achilles, recognizing these two as the individuals I now know as [5717] and [900]. They were both beautiful of countenance. Both had matted black ringlets on their heads, which reminded me of Medusa. The hair seemed to be their strength. I noticed that Achilles was very hairy, while Hector only had hair on his neck— which was a different color from the hair on his head. I saw Hector dragged through the gate which I was guarding, into a large arena; and was dragged around the arena several times. Although he was losing, and had lost, quite a bit of blood—leaving the ground and stones bloody as he was dragged along, I noticed that he hadn't wholly lost consciousness. Eventually, the horses—in turning very swiftly, with Achilles driving— caused Hector's head to be dashed against the pillar on the gate near me, and his brains ran out. Before he had even lost the life, or the quiver of the muscles and nerves, I saw the carrion birds eat the great portions of his brain. (294–161)

Following that awesome battle of the titans, the actual fall of Troy comes as an anticlimax. Yet it provides a justly famous and dramatic ending to the story.

The Greeks, still faced with a stalemate, struck upon a brilliant bit of strategy to turn the tide of battle in their favor. They fashioned a large wooden horse, which was placed on wheels and rolled to a position outside the main gate leading into the Trojan citadel, where it was made to appear as a propitiatory offering on the eve of the Greeks' apparent abandonment of the siege. To complete the deception, they then sailed their ships out of sight. The rejoicing Trojans, convinced that the Greeks had left at last, raised up the gate and rolled the great horse into the city as a trophy. But inside the belly of the wooden beast was concealed a small contingent of the Greeks' ablest warriors. Under cover of darkness, while the citizenry slept, they stole out through a secret panel and raised up the gate to their waiting comrades-in-arms on the other side. The Trojans, completely taken by surprise, had no opportunity to organize an effective resistance. The city fell, and the nine-year siege was ended. A penitent Helen was returned to the waiting arms of Menelaus in Sparta, and after the victors had avenged themselves with a sufficient shedding of Trojan blood, a state of peace was negotiated between Greece and Troy.

The Edgar Cayce readings, in giving the era when Cayce lived as Xenon, set a time frame from 1158 to 1012 B.C., although we suspect the sleeping Cayce meant to show the closing date of the period as 1112 B.C. This would reflect a life span of forty-six years, rather than the unlikely one hundred forty-six, for the hapless Xenon, who took his own life in the prime of his manhood.

This revised dating throws us only slightly off the mark from the hypothetical dating of the Trojan Wars (ca. 1140–1130 B.C.) as worked out by Eratosthenes, who based his computations on genealogies of early royal families preserved in Greek tradition and folklore.

Archaeological evidence suggests that the stronghold of Troy was a truly ancient city, located in northwest Asia Minor near the Dardanelles, that was destroyed and rebuilt some nine different times. The Troy of "good King Priam," as Homer refers—with a certain favoritism—to Hector's sire, was apparently the seventh settlement.

In the Homeric account of things, we find the figure of Achilles darkly drawn and ever vengeful, whereas Hector is portrayed as one of the noblest characters of antiquity. Yet this bias doesn't coincide with what the Cayce readings tell us of the two. Instead, we find Hector described as a "usurper" and "the one without heart,"[2] while we see in Achilles' character "one showing development in moral conditions,"[3] who was concerned with "the release of the oppressed peoples and giving the common people their equality with those who would oppress them."[4] In fact, Achilles had apparently succeeded in winning the covert support of many ordinary Trojan citizens, who not only resented the troubles Paris had brought upon them but were rebellious in their hearts against an oppressive rule. The readings seem to suggest that they only awaited an opportunity to throw their support to Achilles' forces in an eventual overthrow of the tyrranical clique in power established by Hector.

In a life reading for Mr. [2886], who had apparently been one of those Trojans secretly supporting Achilles' efforts to bring down Hector's oppressive reign, we encounter this evidence of widespread disaffection:

In the [incarnation] before this, we find in that period when there were wars within and without, known as the Trojan period. The entity then among those who defended the city and [yet] was among those that rose with him [Achilles] that destroyed the usurper, or the one without heart— Hector; and the entity gained through this experience, and lost in other portions of self's own aggrandizement of power gained. Gaining when in service and in acting the *ideal* that impelled many during that period. Losing in meting to others that that was disliked in self. (2886–1)

But in a rebuke of both Hector and Achilles, there is a reference elsewhere to "the beauty and yet the savagery of those people in the Trojan activity, when Achilles and Hector in their activities brought to many of the common people only the revenge one upon another through the relations caused one with another."[5] So it appears to have been a time of strained and wavering loyalties as far as the masses were concerned.

In an account differing somewhat from Homer's, one of the readings reads like a "spy thriller": an aide to Helen, within the Trojan citadel, instructs her son at the propitious moment to open the gate for Achilles' entry. If we interpret this aright, it means that Achilles was still alive when Troy was taken and did not encounter the mortal wound to his heel from Paris's arrow until the final battle. It also points clearly to the collusion of a certain segment of the Trojan forces. And although the readings confirm the story about the famous Trojan horse, even identifying the builder, Mr. [470], it would appear that its concealed contingent of soldiers had other, specialized missions to perform and left the opening of the gate to a Trojan collaborator by prearrangement.

Finally, in a reading for that one among Achilles' forces, Cajhalon, already identified in the present as Mr. [470], who "was the builder and the actual worker on the horse," reference is made to "the siege as was made following this burning."[6] A most curious comment! Are we to deduce therefrom that the giant "warhorse" was set ablaze as a part of the Greeks' battle strategy? If so, it would have been a cunning way to divert the attention of the Trojan troops from the far greater peril awaiting them in the surrounding darkness of that fateful night.

No doubt it is to the Trojans, although it was a Roman poet who said it for them, that we can credit that historic aphorism, "Beware of Greeks bearing gifts"! And from the perspective of this narrative, it is the suicide of Xenon (alias Cayce) that most tragically memoralizes the bitterness of their surprise.

In October 1923, a successful businessman from Dayton, Ohio, described as a short, powerful man with broad shoulders, brown hair, and blue, searching eyes, walked into Edgar Cayce's photo studio in Selma, Alabama. (In those days, the little-known psychic was trying to eke out a living as a professional photographer, for he had some talent in this direction, and he had recently moved his young family to Selma from Hopkinsville.)

The stranger's arrival was to mark the beginning of a unique and rather extraordinary relationship, whose far-reaching consequences (despite its relatively short duration) could not have been imagined at the time. The stranger had come to Edgar for other reasons than a picture-taking session, for he had heard of Mr. Cayce's unique psychic abilities. In short, he wanted a number of psychic readings and was willing to pay a suitable fee for Edgar's services in this regard. Edgar agreed.

That man, like so many others who appear in this narrative, must be identified by his case number only. In some instances, this is dictated by the fact that the individual is still alive; in the present case, it is in deference to living relatives of the entity. Therefore, I must beg the reader's indulgence as I introduce this new character on stage as simply Mr. [5717].

Because of his esoteric interests, [5717]'s entry on the scene was to mark a dramatic turning point in Mr. Cayce's career as a psychic. In fact, the very first unequivocal reference in the readings to reincarnation—a subject that was strictly taboo at that time in most respectable circles—occurred in [5717]'s initial reading for himself. He was told that he had been a monk in his previous life.

What was not revealed at the time, but came out later, was that he had also been the entity Hector in a much earlier incarnation.

As Hector, he was told that he had been associated with Edgar Cayce and two other men of his acquaintance, [5453] and [4121], for "destructive purposes." Now they were all meant to work together for constructive ends.[7]

Yet it wasn't to be. Despite the obvious debt owed to [5717] for focusing Edgar Cayce's psychic talents on a whole new field of inquiry, with its tremendously rewarding results for future generations, the relationship didn't last. Evidently [5717]'s financial situation had deteriorated rather suddenly, along with his interest, and after about a year in Dayton, lured by unfulfilled promises, Cayce found himself high and dry. Similarly shattered hopes and promises pursued the other two men, [5453] and [4121], in their relationship with the man they had once known as their Trojan leader, Hector. It was as if the ill wind of an unspent karma had come blowing up out of the past to haunt them . . .

Each of them, perhaps, was meeting himself in what could best be described as a "testing" situation for the growth of the soul. It would be unwise, therefore, to try to lay the blame for what happened on a single individual or set of circumstances. "Find fault in no one," was an oft-repeated injunction found in the Cayce philosophy.[8] And the obverse of that coin is exprsssed in this: "Lose self in Him."[9] It is quite conceivable, in fact, that without the numerous crosses he was obliged to bear in certain of his interpersonal relationships over the years, Edgar Cayce would not have risen to the spiritual heights he did, nor would he be remembered today.

Before introducing the next central character in this chapter, it is worth remarking upon a highly curious point. Cayce's Trojan incarnation was marked by the conspicuous absence of any of the primary characters involved in his Persian and Egyptian cycles of development—with but two exceptions. One of these we shall meet shortly; the other was Mrs. [369], who had been his first wife, Asua, in his Egyptian cycle and the adopted daughter of Croesus in the Persian experience. In Troy, she came as one who tended to the needs of the gatekeepers (of whom Cayce was one, of course, as Xenon, in charge of the main gate). Otherwise, it was only minor figures from the Egyptian and Persian cycles who reappeared in the Trojan period, based upon a careful analysis of the various life readings, and the nature of the prior connections would suggest that most of them had negative karmic ties to be worked out with Edgar Cayce in that tragic Trojan cycle. Those of a more "positive" developmental makeup seem to have preferred to "steer clear" of the Trojan mess. Its destructive impulses were simply not destined to become a part of their personal karma. (Such, at least, is a likely explanation of the matter for those who, like myself, seek to explain the inexplicable.)

After Mr. [5717]'s hasty exit from center stage came Mr. [900] —the man who had been Achilles. (The reader will perhaps remember him for his earlier role as the Egyptian Aarat, who was pitted against the young king and also counseled Ra's banishment to Libya.)

It is not surprising that Cayce and his former foe, Achilles, were destined to meet again in the present. In one of his own early life readings, Edgar Cayce had been told that "there is, and has been, and will be many more in the present sphere that were in contact with that plane's forces [in the Trojan experience], that the contact will be, has been, brought in the present sphere."[10] (We have already alluded to the essentially minor and negative nature of most of those prior associations, numbering perhaps a couple of dozen or more.) Yet the meeting again was to seize upon present opportunities for constructive purposes, not to rekindle old enmities; and so, with [900] and Edgar Cayce, it was to become a "trial by fire," so to speak, as each sought to meet in self that which had been sown and to find a unity of purpose that would bind them as one.

A slightly built, amiable young man of Jewish ancestry, who was later to convert to Catholicism, [900] had been introduced to Edgar Cayce in 1924 by a mutual friend, David Kahn. Mr. [900] and his younger brother, [137], New York stockbrokers, hailed originally from Altoona, Pennsylvania, and although still in their twenties at the time, they were well on their way to becoming rich. It was a double bonanza for Edgar Cayce, who had not only found a pair of benefactors, but more important, two men who appeared to be deeply committed to the spirit of the readings and who were endowed with the necessary intellectual curiosity and practicality to assist him in using his psychic talents in the most productive and constructive way. Their first step was to see that he followed the advice given in the readings, which was to relocate in Virginia Beach. And there was also talk of building a hospital, which had been Mr. Cayce's long-cherished dream.

But as the years went by, differences arose. Despite their virtual monopoly on Mr. Cayce's time to conduct readings on subjects of their own choosing, often covering matters of a strictly personal nature, the amount of financial aid forthcoming for the furtherance of the "work," as it was called, was disappointingly small. And as [900] more and more insisted upon exercising dictatorial control in the day-to-day psychic activities of Mr. Cayce and in the running of the organization associated with the work, resentments inevitably developed. Relations reached a breaking point at last, and there was a parting of the ways that was irrevocable.

Yet, out of the rubble of his ruined dreams, Mr. Cayce began to build anew, and the greater part of the work still lay ahead. Another crisis had passed. And Cayce, it seemed, if not [900], had "met the test" in his twentieth-century encounter with one who had been a former foe, as Achilles—yet a noble foe, at that, and one from whom he had been able to learn a great deal even while enduring humiliating pressures.

Some psychological insights into the karmic relationship between Mr. [900] and Mr. Cayce, in part predating the Trojan era, are provided in these excerpts from a paper entitled "Historical Data and Connections of [900]," dated July 23, 1929, that was compiled from the life readings by the Historical Committee of the Association of National Investigators, whose three members were Hugh Lynn Cayce, Thomas J. Sugrue, and Gladys Davis:

[900]'s Relationships with [294]

EGYPT—In this period Ra Ta [294] was raised to the position of high priest of the land and until the division arose he gave much to the peoples through spiritual teachings. You sided with the king [341] against the priest [294] and there naturally arises from this a certain sense of disagreement from the point of principle rather than personal feelings. You and [294] probably worked together before and after the division.

From this then comes the natural respect of each for the other's ability to give an understanding of spiritual truths to the people intermingled at times with conflicting views as to the principle of some condition.

TROY—In the Trojan period [294] was one of the guards of the gates of Troy. He was a student of chemistry by nature and one with considerable temper. There would naturally arise from this appearance a certain amount of antagonism since you were one of the leaders of the attacking forces.

In the present this would take the form of signs of unreasonable temper in you both at times. Be careful of this and understand from whence it comes. Don't try to play Achilles [900] with him for you will find him in moods just as stubborn as the Trojans who held out for seven *[sic]* long years [nine years]. (900–275 Suppl.)

A dream interpretation given for Mr. [900] on September 5, 1927, provides a clue, perhaps, as to the direction the relationship between Cayce and his former adversary was already taking. Here is the pertinent passage:

It [the dream] does not mean the close of day, but rather that the individual [900, in this instance] has become so hardened, so engrossed, so hedged about by the various circumstances and conditions, that the individual is incapable of gaining the proper concept and to do the work as should be done for the development of self toward the mark of the higher calling. (900–340)

Meanwhile, in a "check" life reading that had been given to Mr. [900] on his Grecian incarnation as Achilles, we learn of his aristocratic lineage in the Athenian society of his day, as well as his early training in the martial arts, where he quickly excelled over all others. Yet he was also "one showing development in moral conditions, as was shown in the relation to captives," and "exceptional abilities in mental forces" is also mentioned. The legendary death of Achilles due to a poisonous wound in his heel is confirmed in this manner: "The entity then departed the life in personal combat, wounded in the heel, from which gangrene set-in in body and became blood poison to the system."[11]

A similar check-reading was sought on Cayce's Trojan incarnation as Xenon, which proved highly revealing in a number of respects. It was in this particular reading, in fact, with its reference to 1158 B.C. as the apparent date of Xenon's birth, that the significance of " '58" in connection with earthly cycles of turmoil and change came to light: "For there has ever been during a period of fifty-eight ('58) a cycle, unit, age, year, period or era when there has been the breeding, as it were, of strife." And the reading then expanded upon this theme, showing how it ultimately led to Xenon's undoing, and how the entity's shortcomings were to be met and conquered in the present. Here are the most pertinent passages:

So in that experience strife was bred among the Grecians and Trojans.

Into such an environ came [he who had been] Ra Ta, Uhjltd, for those experiences that should have brought—or were to bring—the strength, the power of resistance in the face of adversity. . . .

In that period the entity was first the student; the student of chemistry, the student of mechanics, the student of those things in the arts. . . . Yet the entity was forced, against its *own* will, into active participation in an open conflict.

There had been little or no opportunity of the [attacking] forces breaking through, for the gates which were prepared against the invaders had withheld any or all the assaults. . . . But then there arose conditions to weaken this power, through the subtlety—which had not been the experience of the entity [an allusion, of course, to the Greeks' "gift horse"].

So the entity found self without the strength in the abilities of self to maintain that at-oneness; for he had come to depend rather upon the abilities of self—which is too oft the undoing of a soul!

In *this* manner, then, did the entity fail. And with the failure came the experience of being an outcast, as one dishonored, as one thought little of; at last losing self through self-destruction. . . .

We have indicated that many of those the entity contacted as individuals then would be met in the present, and that many would become again stumbling-blocks in this or that manner; that many would make for experiences when again there would come the urge for self-effacement from the experiences in the material. . . .

And this is the *great* barrier, the great experience which the entity must meet in the present . . . a regeneration from that experience.

As to the manner or way, then, in which the entity may meet same: it is ever set before each and every soul. In Him put thy trust. . . .

As there was the failure then, so may the grace be through Him to whom, of whom, the entity failed then in that experience; that there may be given the spiritual awakening to many.

For to many the power, the help, the aid which has come in their experience in the present has not only equalled but has surpassed any that was experienced in the period of either Ra Ta or Uhjltd.

For once this effacement urge is overcome, then may there begin the rejuvenation. (294-183)

For the entity [900]—the former Achilles—a roll of the karmic dice brought him the same coveted prize that Venus had awarded to Paris. A life reading for his beautiful young wife, [136], revealed that she was a reincarnation of Helen of Troy. One might speculate endlessly on the specific karmic factors that had conspired to bring them together in this lifetime. It was, unhappily, a marriage that did not last. And perhaps that was to be expected.

As for Edgar Cayce, there was a happier ending to it all for him, and the entity gained. Here is the unusual story:

No more beautiful example may be given to another, no wiser counsel, than that drawn from the depths of one's own experience. Thus, when the distraught family of Mr. [378]—the former Heptsupht, the Atlantean initiate—approached Mr. Cayce in April of 1934, fearful that his sudden disappearance was linked to a suicide attempt, Mr. Cayce was able to draw on the lesson learned from his own tragic experience, in Troy, communicating "soul to soul" with his friend [378] and urging him to avoid the path of self-effacement. Often and urgent were his out-of-body counselings with that wavering soul, whose day-to-day thoughts and footsteps

Cayce could follow in trance-state, until finally the urgent spiritual appeals prevailed over the self-destructive impulse, and the man, without fully knowing what had changed his mind around, came home.

For Edgar Cayce, that life-saving incident was a way of turning a former stumbling block into a stepping-stone.

9. The Sage of Samos

In a strange dream that came to him late in his sixtieth year, on the morning of March 14, 1938, Edgar Cayce was given a partial flashback of a previous-life experience not mentioned anywhere in the readings. The dream concerned a dramatic episode that took place in Egypt, presumably some twenty-five hundred years ago, in which Mr. Cayce identified himself with the ancient Greek scientist and sage Pythagoras (ca. 580–ca. 500 B.C.).

No interpretation of the dream was sought, which is a pity. However, here in its entirety is Cayce's account of the vision he received, which we must consider quite extraordinary:

I was a doctor-surgeon-chemist in Egypt—not Ra Ta but at another period, later. I operated on my friend's wife after she died and saved her unborn baby; I knew she had been my daughter when I was Ra Ta, and I was able for that reason to secure her dead body and cut out the child—a baby girl. I put it under glass and fed it nourishment (which I brewed from hay, leaves, etc.) through the umbilical cord and the viscera which I had cut from the mother and which were still around the baby—with the lungs, heart, liver, kidneys, etc., of the mother. People were clamoring outside, wanting to mob me but afraid they would hurt the baby. I knew who the people were then and who they are now, but couldn't remember when I woke up. This much of the dream was recalled to me when looking at a magazine during the day, when I saw the name Pythagoras—which seemed similar to my name then. (294–189)

What are we to make of such an unusual dream? First, we must consider the dreamer. We know, from examining the abundant evidence in the body of psychic readings and dream interpretations left to us by Edgar Cayce, that his "real" world, like that of the great psychologist C. G. Jung, lay at least as much, and perhaps more, in the psychic realm of his dreams, visions, and trance-state or out-of-body experiences as in the day-to-day, fleshly experiences that count as the only "reality" to most of us.

We should note, too, in this particular case, the dream's meaningful reference to Cayce's Egyptian cycle as the priest Ra Ta and to a former daughter in that incarnation (probably the entity [2329], known as Aris-Hobeth, or "Favored One"), for it was not the first occasion on which Cayce had found himself strangely reunited in his dreams with what we may assume was the same daughter, but in different incarnations than either the Egyptian cycle or the present one. Some few months earlier he had recorded a precognitive dream of extraordinary dimensions, involving the former Aris-Hobeth and himself in a "New Age" encounter that literally boggles the mind; it will form the subject of a later chapter. (I think it may be argued, with some semblance of logic, that these two dreams involving Cayce and a former daughter from his Egyptian experience as Ra Ta—the one precognitive in nature, the other recalling a prior-life episode in the period of Pythagoras—tend to reinforce each other, lending a certain degree of validity to both.)

Finally, this dream fragment is much too vividly "alive" and compelling to be easily dismissed in terms of mere fantasy or symbolism: we are tempted to accept it at face value as a genuine re-enactment in the dream-state of an actual event from a prior life, despite the extraordinary nature of its content.

But even if we accept the validity of the dream, how reliable was Mr. Cayce's postdream identification of his dream-self with Pythagoras? In this regard, could his unconscious mind have played a "trick" upon him when he happened to spot that unusual-sounding name in a magazine after his dream? Here again, we must consider the sensitive attunement of Mr. Cayce's mental and spiritual self to the psychic realm, which at times affected even the least significant details of his waking life. So it appears unlikely, on this basis, that he had picked up that particular magazine altogether by chance or by chance had turned to the particular page containing the name Pythagoras; rather, we would suggest the strong possibility that his Higher Self was guiding him throughout.

Nevertheless, any real test of the matter must lie in the sphere of pragmatic observation and appraisal. To undertake this task, it becomes necessary to journey into the past and examine such historical fragments as we can find concerning the life and travels of Pythagoras, all the time looking for any similarities that will connect the ancient Greek sage of Samos with the renowned "sleeping prophet" of Virginia Beach. At first glance, this may seem to be a nearly impossible assignment! But ahead of us lie a number of surprising revelations drawn from the pages of antiquity concerning that legendary figure Pythagoras, who was a close contemporary, in the middle of the sixth century B.C., of Gautama Buddha, in India; Confucius and Lao-tzu, in China; and the "last" Zoroaster, in Persia. (Concerning the last-named, who is not to be confused with his much earlier namesake in the days of Uhjltd and Zend, we are told that Greek writers distinguish at least six Zoroasters, of whom the last, according to Lucius Apuleius, was a contemporary of Pythagoras. The Greek sage reportedly visited and studied with the Persian magus after being taken captive to Babylon by the armies of Cambyses and released.[1])

Before our search commences in earnest, however, we must remove a few obstacles that lie athwart our path.

To the skeptical eye, Cayce's definition of his dream-self as a "doctor-surgeon-chemist" might appear at the very outset to disqualify his subsequent "Pythagorean" identification. Why? Because the historical view of Pythagoras places him in a much more exalted category: Pythagoras was a scientist, a sage, and a teacher, in about that sequence of importance. However, it can be argued that Edgar Cayce, who was certainly no scholar, was not at all concerned with traditional or historical concepts; he was simply choosing the most appropriate terms to describe how he actually saw himself in his particular dream-incident, which was as a "doctor-surgeon-chemist." Moreover, since Pythagoras was a master practitioner of the healing arts and undoubtedly had a working knowledge of chemistry (as did Cayce also, let us remember, having studied that subject as the youthful Xenon, in Troy), this could readily justify calling him a "doctor-chemist." As for the third sobriquet, "surgeon," it is known that the practice of surgery of any kind was essentially contrary to the Pythagorean principles, which taught compassion toward all living forms; yet there is a subtle distinction to be drawn in this instance. The "doctor-surgeon-chemist" in Cayce's dream was *not* operating on a *living* form, but upon a freshly deceased corpse; certainly his motivation was a compassionate one—namely, to save the life of a still-evolving fetus—that could have justified a departure by Pythagoras from his own avowed principles. (Yet it would appear on the basis of the hostile reaction of the crowd without, who wanted to mob him, that such radical surgery in those days—even to save the life of an unborn infant—was highly unpopular.)

Here another nagging question arises. Did the restless mob envisioned by Cayce include any of his own disapproving followers? Or could they have been Egyptians (since he was in Egypt at the time), or simply ordinary Grecians from the local Greek community? The latter is the most likely assumption, although a number of his own uninitiated students and hangers-on may have been present also. At any rate, in relating his dream, Cayce had said: "I knew who the people were then and *who they are now,* but couldn't remember when I woke up." (A stunning comment!) Finally, the unnamed friend of Pythagoras whose wife had died before she could deliver her child normally may have been Pythanax, a Cretan, as we shall see later, and this leads us to speculate that the hostile mob was probably composed chiefly of fellow Greeks acquainted with both Pythanax and Pythagoras, whether or not it included certain members of the Pythagorean school.

There is now a final point to resolve before we proceed.

Since Pythagoras was an Ionian Greek, from the Isle of Samos, is there any historical evidence that he once lived in Egypt? And even if he did, how does the presence of other Greek colonists in the land of the pharaohs at that time square with the facts of history? Very nicely, in fact. For, in 572 B.C., Amasis II became sole king of Egypt after the death of Apries, and continued the policy of his predecessor, who had welcomed foreigners. It is said that multitudes of Jews flocked to Egypt under the reign of Apries, and there was a similar influx of Greeks when Amasis II offered them valuable trading privileges and, more important, a degree of freedom that was not to be found in the Greek homeland in those days.

Yet it was not as a trader, of course, that Pythagoras had emigrated to Egypt, nor was it in the pursuit of personal freedom, although that meant much to him. Rather, he came as a seeker after wisdom. The seventeenth-century English historian and philosopher Thomas Stanley, drawing on the writings of Iamblichus and other early chroniclers, relates that the youthful Pythagoras was first taught by Thales, at Miletus.[2] But with the rise to power of Polycrates the Tyrant, Thales counseled Pythagoras to go to Egypt and increase his wisdom by studying with the priestly initiates at Heliopolis, Memphis, and Thebes. This he did, remaining in Egypt for twenty-two years, during which time he studied astronomy (which would actually have been "astrology" in those days), geometry, and other subjects, while also gaining initiation into all the religious mysteries of the Egyptian priests. As his wisdom increased, Pythagoras undoubtedly began to gather about himself a band of followers, although the height of his fame as a teacher still lay ahead, when the Pythagorean school at Crotona, in Italy, was to become a world center of learning. (Incidentally, does this not carry echoes of Ra's activities, upon his return from exile, or the center established by Uhjltd, at Is-Shlan-doen?)

Pythagoras was noted for his psychic abilities, and this raises an interesting possibility. When he was about sixty years old, some twenty years after his departure from Egypt at the age of forty, it is said that Pythagoras married a beautiful and intelligent young disciple, named Theano. (His twin soul, [288], perhaps?) She was an ideal companion to the great sage, and the relationship was an unusually close one. When Pythagoras was struck down by a band of brutal assassins at Crotona, at a very advanced age, it was this same Theano who rose up to carry on his work and promulgate his teachings. According to Porphyry, *she was the daughter of Py-*

thanax, a Cretan follower of Pythagoras. Was this same Pythanax the unidentified friend in Cayce's dream, whose wife had died in pregnancy? And did the psychically endowed sage, who had alreay identified his friend's wife as his own daughter during a former incarnation in Egypt [Aris-Hobeth, as speculated earlier, the favorite daughter of Ra], also have psychic foreknowledge concerning the premature infant's identity and purpose—so closely intertwined with his own? It is a plausible hypothesis, and if correct, it would readily explain his willingness to risk his own life and reputation in a bold move to save the living fetus through innovative surgery—*surgery that may even have been psychically performed;* it is just possible, inasmuch as Pythagoras had received initiation into all of the mysteries of Isis and was an acknowledged master, or adept.

Although his essential teachings have come down to us intact, how much is known today about Pythagoras himself? Very little, unfortunately. But the little we know is tantalizing. This is because it reveals to us, however sketchily, a man whose inner being and psychic development bear an uncommon similarity to Edgar Cayce's, as glimpsed through the readings.

To begin, then.

"The little that is known for certain about Pythagoras," reports one source, "includes the fact that he was able to remember twenty or more previous lives."[3] (Already, it seems, we have struck upon an extraordinary parallel between Pythagoras and Cayce.) We can go one step further. In Bulfinch's *Age of Fable,* Ovid is cited representing Pythagoras addressing his disciples on the subject in these words: "Souls never die, but always on quitting one abode, pass to another. I myself can remember that in the time of the Trojan War, I was Euphorbus *[sic],* the son of Panthus, and fell by the spear of Menelaus. Lately being in the temple of Juno, at Argos, I recognize my shield hung up there among the trophies. All things change, nothing perishes."[4]

Though Ovid's account does not coincide with Cayce's, if indeed Xenon was a previous incarnation of Pythagoras, it may be argued with some justification that the Roman poet could have adorned a bare legendary fact about Pythagoras with fanciful details of his own invention. It is known that many of the popular tales in Ovid's *Metamorphoses,* from which the preceding quotation came, were in this category. The chief point I wish to make here is that both Pythagoras and Cayce have been credited with Trojan incarnations, for it may bear some significance.

Apparently drawing from Ovid's tale, Iamblichus and other early historians also mention Pythagoras's Trojan incarnation, although there are differences concerning the details and sequence of this and other incarnations ascribed to him. Of special note, however, was the repeated claim of some of the close followers of Pythagoras that he had been an incarnation of Apollo.[5] Apollo, the son of Zeus, has a legendary synonymity with the sun and also with the Higher Self. This puts us in mind of Cayce's Egyptian incarnation as Ra, or Adonis, conveying an identical symbolism, as discussed in a previous chapter.

A further link between Pythagoras and Cayce is provided by C. G. Jung, who draws on the *Vita Pythagorica* of Iamblichus to relate the fascinating fact that Mount Carmel—known to students of the Cayce material for its historical connection with the Essenes—was also regarded as a "sacred mountain" by the pagan Greeks and Romans, and that "Pythagoras often stayed in the sacred solitude of Carmel."[6] This coincides with information given elsewhere to the effect that Pythagoras sought initiation in the sacred wisdom of the Jews, the Chaldeans, and the Persians, as well as traveling to both Egypt and India to gain initiation into their secret teachings. He was undoubtedly an adept in the art of meditation, and we may logically conclude that his frequent retreats to "the sacred solitude of Carmel" were for the purpose of entering into periods of deep contemplation, from which he gained the necessary spiritual insights to guide him in his subsequent activities. In fact, one writer states that "Pythagoras advised his disciples that it is best to commence one's day in silent meditation, and thus compose one's own soul."[7] (Cayce, of course, always counseled the same.)

Tradition records that the first visit of Pythagoras to Mount Carmel, in what was then Phoenicia, occurred in his early youth on the way to Egypt, after leaving the lyceum of Thales; and it is said that afterwards, on the voyage from Phoenicia to the coast of Egypt, lasting two nights and three days, he remained seated on deck in a trancelike state, taking no nourishment or slumber, so that the sailors marveled at him. (Today we would recognize this sort of trance-state as a condition of *samadhi,* or cosmic consciousness.)

According to Porphyry, one of the notable accomplishments of Pythagoras was his ability to interpret dreams. Here, again, we have a unique parallel with Edgar Cayce, whose dream interpretations take up two full volumes of the published readings.[8] Also, the sage of Samos was a master of the art of divination and prophecy; and the mystical "Wheel of Pythagoras" has survived as one of the most extraordinary examples of esoteric numerology ever devised, containing correspondences to the letters of the alphabet, the seven planets, the days of the week, and the signs of the zodiac. Concerning the ability to prophesy, Pythagoras taught his followers that it was a "divine gift," bestowed as "the reward of consecration to principle and truth."[9] (Obviously he did not have any use for self-serving practitioners of the art, who were probably as common in his day as in ours.)

In another parallel with the Virginia Beach psychic and seer, Pythagoras practiced the healing art with great success, and he instructed his disciples in the use of various herbs for this purpose. He also emphasized special diets, as well as recommending the exercise of moderation in all things. (To anyone who has studied the Edgar Cayce readings on health-related topics, all of this will have a strongly familiar ring.)

One of his more revolutionary methods of treating human ailments concerned the therapeutic power of music, and it is said of Pythagoras that he prepared special harmonies for various diseases. This harks back, of course, to what the readings tell us about the use of music therapy in ancient Egypt, when the high priest Ra employed the "attuning of the music" in the Temple of Sacrifice to purge and purify many of those who were trapped in grotesque bodily forms at that early evolutionary stage. "For those vibrations that in the music as of the spheres," said Cayce in one of the readings—and his use here of the term "music of the spheres" bears careful note, for we shall return to it—"brought that purifying through attuning the vibrations with the destructive forces as manifested themselves in nature, as *tore away* in matter that which hindered the individual, the soul, from knowing and being at-one with that Creative Force."[10]

Undoubtedly the greatest and most enduring contribution of Pythagoras to Western thought and culture lay in the areas of philosophy and science. In fact, it was Pythagoras who coined the word *philosopher*, which he defined as "one who is attempting to find out," as contrasted with the sage, who is "one who knows." Thus, Pythagoras revealed the genius of his wisdom: humility. But today, in recognition of his high attainments, he is more aptly and universally referred to as "the Sage of Samos." We use that honorific here.

His philosophy was epitomized in the famous "Golden Verses of Pythagoras," which taught the doctrine of self-knowledge, temperance, and "sacred virtue." "Of thyself stand most in fear," the verses state, and throughout, there is a foreshadowing of the type of simple wisdom and soul-searching we find echoed again and again in the Edgar Cayce readings:

> Hurt not thy self: Before thou act, advise;
> Nor suffer sleep at night to close thine eyes,
> Till thrice thy acts that day thou hast o'er-run,
> How slipt? what deeds? what duty left undone?

"Men come of heavenly race," the verses summarize the message, "Taught by diviner Nature what to embrace." In conclusion, the Pythagorean disciple was admonished to "keep thy Soul clear from thy bodie's stain," and to abstain from meat "in time of Pray'r and cleansing." Then, "strip'd of flesh up to free Aether soar/ A deathless God, Divine, mortal no more."[11]

The Edgar Cayce readings, twenty-five hundred years later, repeat the refrain in a variety of ways. Here is one, purportedly incorporating one of the lost sayings of the Christ: " 'So are ye gods *in the making,'* saith He that walked among men as the greatest Teacher of all experiences and ages."[12]

Another aspect of the Pythagorean teachings was the symbolic use of the letter Y to represent "the dividing of the way." Every traveler on the path of life comes to that point at which he or she must choose either the right-hand road to virtue and wisdom or the left-hand path to worldliness and vice. Cayce spoke of these two paths as representing soul development versus soul retrogression. And thus, in the life readings, one encounters with repeated regularity those two alternate terms by which a soul-entity's progress or retardation in its various prior lives was assessed: "the entity gained," or "the entity lost."

"Pythagoras was probably the first to maintain that the earth is round," writes Louis MacNeice, in his book *Astrology*.[13] He was also the first scientist in recorded history to comprehend man's essential oneness with the universe and to grasp the heliocentric nature of our solar system. It is to Pythagoras that we owe the well-known phrase "the music of the spheres"—a phrase that, curiously, occurs in a number of the Edgar Cayce readings, where it is introduced with all of the naturalness and force of a totally original utterance. Pythagoras also originated the use of the word *kosmos* (suggesting the notion of orderly arrangement and structural perfection) to signify the universe as macrocosm and man as the miniature replica, or microcosm. Also, it was he who introduced to the Grecian world the mystical pentagram, or five-pointed star —5 being the sacred Hermetic number—and adopted it as the emblem of the Pythagorean School.

The Pythagoreans studied geometry, music, and astronomy (astrology) as interrelated aspects of a divine cosmos, and a basic knowledge of these three subjects was considered mandatory to anyone applying for acceptance as a pupil of Pythagoras. A small inner circle of his students—those who had passed the third and final degree of initiation into his teachings—addressed him by name; all others referred to him more respectfully as "That Man," or "Master."

The contributions of this towering genius to the roots of modern science run broad and deep, and there is not any need here to touch upon them all. But a knowledge of numbers must certainly be mentioned.

Pythagoras had a phenomenal comprehension of the science of numbers, in both its esoteric and exoteric aspects. He was apparently the first of the great philosophers to reach an intuitive awareness of the numerical principles underlying all creation. An accomplished musician (he is said to have invented the lyre, although the Cayce readings suggest an early Egyptian version of that instrument), the idea seems suddenly to have burst upon Pythagoras that music and mathematics, in their essence, are one; this led him to the discovery of the numerical ratios underlying the intervals that the Greeks called consonant and used as the basis of their scale.

Also, it was Pythagoras who originated the symbol of the "tetractys," or Pythagorean Decad, which has its correspondence with the symbolism embodied in the kabbalistic "Tree of Life." Consisting of ten dots arranged in four tiers (four in the bottom row, then three, two, and finally, one at the top), forming an equilateral triangle, the tetractys is defined in the *Dictionary of Symbolism*[14] as follows: "The 'perfect number' of the Pythagoreans and of the numerologists, composed of the Divine monad (One), the dyad (Two), the primeval triad (Three), and the fundamental sacred tetrad (Four)."

It cannot be said with certainty, of course, that Pythagoras and Edgar Cayce were one and the same soul-entity in different incarnations. All of the evidence presented here, though some of it would appear to be impressive and convincing, is, in the final analysis, only circumstantial.

This point conceded, it is nevertheless appropriate to add one further note of coincidence (if that be its name), on which to conclude.

In the life readings given by Edgar Cayce, there often emerged a familiar pattern, in which a soul-entity's accumulated karma would bring the entity into a downward-gravitating cycle for the purpose of meeting much of the negative seed it had sown; then there might follow a cycle of positive development, drawing once more on the higher attainments of prior lives to keep the soul "in balance," as it were, before exposing it again to any negative karma still to be erased. In keeping with this cyclical pattern, as we already observed in Cayce's Trojan incarnation as Xenon, the soul-entity is joined by many fellow beings working out karma of a like nature; for it is a universal law, of course, that like attracts like.

Another observable phenomenon in the readings is for souls to reincarnate in clusters, whether for weal or woe, depending upon the nature of their prior entanglements. And it is in this regard that we have uncovered the "note of coincidence" alluded to previously. (For after Troy came Samos—an upward-moving cycle.)

Of all the people who came to Edgar Cayce for life readings over the years, there was only one who was revealed to have been closely associated with Pythagoras. (If there were others, forming a typical "cluster" familiar throughout the readings, they were simply never identified with that historic period.) Yet the one, Mrs. [1472], was a woman of unusually high spiritual development, who had been a strong force for good in several of her prior lives, contributing to mankind's advance, as had Cayce himself. Her first role in our narrative was in the Ra Ta cycle, in fact, where she entered as a princess from the Carpathian land, and took back to her peoples the teachings of Ra, Saneid, and the other luminaries in that epochal gathering. In the days immediately preceding the advent of Jesus, she was a leader among the Essenes, who had predicted the arrival of a Messiah and made the necessary preparations; and with His appearance, she became an instructor to the youthful Jesus, finally sending Him into Egypt, Persia, and India to learn from the three trusted magi of her prior acquaintance.

Now she learned that she had been a student under Pythagoras and had apparently gained much from that association. Yet, little more was given to her concerning that incarnation, adding that "there are many things we would give unto thee, but thou art not wholly able to bear them now."[15]

Surely, on that humbling note, it is time for us to close this chapter.

10. A Grecian Tableau

A tableau, by definition, is a "living picture" in which a silent and motionless cast of characters is arranged on stage, usually to represent a scene of dramatic or historic consequence.

Such, then, is the nature of this chapter. There is no action involved—no script, no story line—just the still, framed tableau itself, from which viewers must reconstruct in their mind's eye, as best they can, the real or imagined sequence of events leading up to, or away from, the group of characters set before them.

The scene is ancient Greece, and Socrates is dead. Xenophon and Plato, two of his most brilliant followers, have immortalized their noble teacher—the one with a series of "dialogues" due to make their author equally immortal, and the other with his *Apologia Socratis* and other well-known Socratic works. Meanwhile, Philip of Macedonia has brought into his court the illustrious Aristotle, a former pupil of Plato's, to tutor his son, who is destined to make a meteoric mark for himself on the pages of history as Alexander the Great. These events fall generally between the fifth and fourth centuries B.C.

And now we come to our tableau, drawing its motley cast of characters from the Edgar Cayce readings and spanning several generations, from the days of Socrates to those of Alexander. We have no way of knowing what karmic threads brought them all into fleshly expression within the same general time frame, in paths that sometimes cross or connect only indirectly, or not at all, yet that seem to point to some sort of common destiny in which each has a particular part to play, however minor.

Edgar Cayce, of course, was one of these. We meet him as a chemist, named Armitidides, under Aristotle.[1] Very likely he assisted Aristotle with his tutoring activities in the Macedonian court, though playing no major role. Yet he probably came to know the youthful Alexander rather well. (Gladys Davis's notes suggest the possibility that the sleeping Cayce may have meant to say "Archimedes," rather than "Armitidides," but this conclusion appears to be ruled out by the fact that the famous mathematician by that name lived a full century *after* Aristotle; nor was he ever noted as a "chemist.") No, I think we must accept the less noteworthy Armitidides, indicating a relatively "passive" cycle of development for Edgar Cayce in that particular incarnation, which probably followed directly on the heels of his entry as Pythagoras. A great life followed by a humble one would seem to form a fitting sequence in the well-balanced evolution of a soul. Besides, there may have been some "catching up" to do, in a manner of speaking, for it will be remembered that Cayce, in his Trojan incarnation as Xenon, had first studied chemistry before being forced into the role of warrior defending the city's gates. Anyhow, we take leave of him now, at stage left in our tableau, holding a chemist's flask in one hand and a bagful of powders in the other . . .

Whereas the two or three terse lines that made mention of Edgar Cayce's Greek incarnation as Armitidides seemed to suggest its relative unimportance in his overall soul development and in fact were actually incorporated in a reading given for another (Mr. [5717]), this was surely not the case with that soul-entity who had been the noble Xenophon. In our tableau, we find him sharing stage front and center with another great leader of men—and his late contemporary—Alexander the Great. But though the latter was to surpass Xenophon in fame, his soul-record in that incarnation, according to the readings, was that of one who "lost." Xenophon *gained*.

In all probability, Xenophon would have been content to live a quiet, intellectual life as the chronicler of Socrates' teachings and a historian of his times. Fate, however, decreed otherwise. Following the end of the Peloponnesian Wars, and apparently disheartened by the deterioration of Athenian democracy, Xenophon became a general in the mercenary forces of Cyrus the Younger in his attempt to overthrow his brother, Artaxerxes II, king of Persia. But when Cyrus was killed at Cunaxa, his cause collapsed, and Xenophon then led the brilliant tactical retreat of some twelve thousand Greeks in a thirteen-hundred-mile march to Chrysopolis through hostile territory. Later recorded in detail in his famous seven-volume masterpiece *Anabasis,* the account of that long retreat still serves as a valid example of tactical excellence for military commanders. Yet, because of his friendship for Sparta and the Persians, Xenophon was stripped of his Athenian citizenship. He retired at a country estate at Scillus, near Olympia, devoting his days to farming and writing; in 369 B.C., his Athenian citizenship was restored, and he moved to Corinth.

All this background data on Xenophon is included for the dual purpose of both outlining his life and accomplishments and providing the reader with the necessary geographic and historical connections linking Xenophon with certain other characters appearing in our tableau.

Of Xenophon, now known as Mr. [2903], his life reading stated: "The entity then in that of him who led the [Grecian] forces," adding, "Also leading the peoples to the higher understanding of self, and seeking to educate them in that which would give the better influence in their homes. Then in the name Xenophon, and in this we find in the present the urge and ability to so direct the lives of others that the best may come to them."[2]

In a former life, it was disclosed, Mr. [2903] had been one of the twelve councillors to King Araaraart II, and a constructive influence. Named Conraden, he had occupied himself primarily as a historian and researcher—activities that were obviously to pay off well in his later incarnation as Xenophon. Although a life insurance representative in his twentieth-century appearance, his life reading suggested that he should have become a minister, adding that he would have made an excellent one.

After the death of Socrates, who took the hemlock cup rather than renounce the truth to his Athenian judges, his impoverished widow, Xantippe, turned to Xenophon for help. His wife, Airdarel, rose to the occasion by employing Xantippe as a seamstress. And thus it was that Noramline, the second daughter of Socrates and Xantippe, became acquainted with her famous father's chief biographer. For although Xenophon, as well as Plato, had been close followers of Socrates in his latter years, sitting often at the great teacher's feet, the child Normaline came into little contact with the participants at these intellectual banquets.

In the present, both the former Normaline, now [538], and Xenophon's companion, Airdarel, known as [760], obtained life readings that described their respective roles in that Grecian epoch. Their positions in our tableau are relatively minor ones, but not to be ignored; we find them seated at stage right, slightly to the rear. (As the childhood governess of Alexander, [538] holds up a toy.)

The entity [538], the reader will recall, had first appeared on the Egyptian scene, as Isis, companion to Ra, and later in the Persian cycle, where she was known as Inxa, and became an instructress to the children of Uhjltd and Ilya. In a comparison of these two former roles with the Greek experience, her reading stated that "the greater influences and activities have been and are in relationships to those sojourns of the entity through the Egyptian experience and in the 'city in the hills and the plains,' " adding that there was "the more joyous understanding of the purposes and ideals," as well as "the greater advancement," in the two former incarnations and apparently a greater capacity for "the meeting of many hardships from the material angle," as contrasted with the Greek incarnation as Socrates' oft-confused and wondering daughter. Of that less hopeful, more unhappy period, the reading stated that "we find the reasoning influences and forces from the material angle becoming at times barriers rather than the greater expression of the spirituality."[3] Yet, it added that these "were not necessarily retarding periods," although from that Grecian experience "there comes that necessary force for the quieting within" so that the "greater powers" may arise.

It would seem, in summary, that [538]'s Grecian incarnation was essentially "passive" in nature, rather like Edgar Cayce's role at that time, perhaps, as the chemist Armitidides—neither contributing much nor detracting much from the building of the individuality of the soul-entity in that sojourn.

Of the entity [760], who had been Xenophon's wife, Airdarel, a gainful cycle was indicated in these words: "In that experience we find the entity developed, and the influence as we see in the present of the ability to advise and to gain the hearing, as it were, when others fail."[4] It was revealed, incidentally, that she had been in the Egyptian cycle as a daughter of King Arart I, and thus a sister to the young king, Araaraart II.

Finally, this interesting footnote: the former Xenophon and Airdarel reincarnated this time around as brother and sister, and were [538]'s uncle and aunt, respectively. (Thus do our past encounters serve to draw us together again!)

A close associate of Xenophon's, sharing in his early military conquests as well as the famed retreat, was one Xeron. It was an experience in which the entity, now identified as Mr. [5249], "gained spiritually, lost materially, and lost its hope on spirituality, condemning others." Thus, the warning: "In that activity, then, beware. Because of place or position, don't let it change the ideal."[5] In his prior incarnations, this same entity had been one of those among the Council of Forty-four in the days of Asapha and Affa, coming from India for those gatherings; later, in the Ra Ta period, drawn to Egypt by word of the reforms taking place, he came as the entity Kudn, but left, with failing results.

So, again, we find an entity coming into that Grecian experience, like so many others, in a more or less "negative" or unfulfilling role, as might seem to be necessary in the learning of life's lessons. Thus are humility and patience acquired, for later application in a more positive role.

Let us place Xeron somewhat in the shadows, behind his leader, Xenophon, and a bit to the right, holding a spear. That is his muted position in our tableau.

Alexander the Great looms on stage like a young lion. We see his bold visage, unders its shining helmet, fierce and promising. He stands a bit left of center, one foot thrust forward.

The entity [1208], an adored nephew of Gladys Davis, was only three days old when he had a life reading. Thus, he was to grow up with a full familiarity with his past and its implications for the shaping of the present. It must, in some respects, have been rather difficult to learn at an early age, as did [1208], that one's prior incarnations included two great historical personages of totally different character and accomplishment. As Alexander the Great, he had an opportunity—under the tutelage of Aristotle—to bring great enlightenment to the world of his day through the combined forces of a well-trained intellect, idealism, and all the physical gifts of a born leader of men. It was said in his reading that he could have made of the world one nation, but instead, in the use of power for self-indulgence and self-exaltation, he lost sight of his original goal and purpose and "ran wild," as it were. *"Here* the entity lost."[6]

Yet he came once again as the idealistic leader, in the name of Thomas Jefferson, and it may be said that the entity gained throughout, as did the newborn nation that the entity served so well.

In the present, the use of prior talents was optional. In fact, it is always so, with every entity; but with a highly gifted soul, the assumption of power poses potential conflicts. One might be tempted, under the circumstances, to be but a spectator—as already observed with certain other figures in our tableau—and simply watch life pass by. In short, a relatively passive cycle, to date, is what one might conclude about [1208]'s present incarnation. Yet, out of a period of self-observation and relative inactivity may come great lessons for the future.

Arlebon, an associate of Alexander's, reincarnated as Mr. [3657]. In his life reading, he learned that he had been a kind of one-man "corps of engineers," with great mechanical aptitude. And his reading said of him: "If the entity were to take the time to apply self, the entity—being interested in what makes the wheels go round—may come nearer than anyone else to make what would be termed perpetual motion, though don't try it—you've commenced too late."[7] (Alas, poor Arlebon!) Yet, for anyone willing to take up the task, the reading added these tantalizing instructions: "The use of elements as of mercury with electrical forces, and of weights, is the correct principle, as the entity has visioned many a time. But you need sufficient earth to make it a negative force."

Surely Arlebon merits a placement in our tableau adjacent to his distinguished leader—a pace or two to the left, and one to the rear, with plenty of room to hold a measuring rod and other engineering implements in front of him.

Last of all, we come to the entity Eoso, who had been in the Persian rule "when the king was being dethroned by the officers of the Grecian forces under Alexander."[8] An officer of the king's exchequer, imprisonment was the entity's lot, resulting in hard feelings against his captors. (In truth, one could hardly blame him.) We have little information on him in his twentieth-century incarnation as Mr. [2698] and can only assign to him some obscure background position in our Grecian tableau, where he must sit, poor fellow, in the discomfort of chains. If he had a lesson to learn in that experience (as he no doubt did), we hope he was quick to learn it, so that he might more readily become free of his shackles.

A closing note:

There is no evidence that Edgar Cayce's twin soul, [288], chose to enter in that group incarnation. If she has any place in the tableau, it is probably as a faint aura somewhere in the vicinity of the lowly chemist Armitidides, serving as an unseen aide or guardian angel operating from the Other Side. It was in just such a role, in fact, that she was to serve her other self in his next incarnation, as Lucius of Cyrene, in the days when the Master walked in the earth as the proclaimed Messiah.

That experience is the subject of the next chapter.

11. Lucius of Cyrene

"Yes," the reading began, "we have the records of that entity now called Edgar Cayce; and those experiences in the earth's plane known as Lucius of Cyrene—or known in the early portion of the experience as Lucius Ceptulus, of Grecian and Roman parentage, and of the city of Cyrene."[1]

Thus it came about, late in his sixtieth year, that a humbled and astonished Edgar Cayce was finally to learn of his prior-life identification with that "Lucius of Cyrene" mentioned in Acts 13:1 and again in Romans 16:21, who was, as it turned out, one of those "other seventy" disciples appointed by the Lord and sent as forerunners "two and two before his face into every city and place, whither he himself would come."[2] Much later, he was chosen by John the Beloved to be bishop of the flock at Laodicea.

To Edgar, who was now at the height of his career as a psychic, this belated revelation was like the famous balm of Gilead. He had passed through many fires and undergone all sorts of trials and tribulations in laboring to bring his life's work (identified, actually, in one of the readings as "the work of the *Master* of masters"[3]) to the attention of a waiting world. Now that he was on the verge of achieving that long-sought goal, his joy was made complete by the present reading, which identified him as a co-worker of the Christ in the Lord's final incarnation as Jesus of Nazareth. Nothing could have been more gratifying than that. The reason was simple. Ever since early childhood, Edgar had been a devoted student of the Bible, being particularly drawn to the New Testament, where the story of the life and teachings of the Master and the later activities of his disciples in the formation of the early church had always been as *living* words to him. Indeed, no matter how often he had read those precious pages, Edgar had never failed to be strangely moved. Now, at last, he understood why: he himself had been an active participant and witness in tha holy drama.

Yet, lest Cayce might have wondered why this particular incarnation, so important and meaningful to him personally, had not been revealed to him much earlier, the reading provided a pungent explanation: "If this had been given in the first, there would have been a puffing up"! It was self-evident that each entity, each individual, must first gain that necessary growth, through application of the tenets it espouses, and through the lessons learned, before it is ready to receive in a true spirit of humility certain revelations that might otherwise prove a hindrance to soul development.

And it was in this context, perhaps, that the reading on his life as Lucius of Cyrene did not overlook a number of Edgar Cayce's shortcomings in that particular incarnation. He learned, for example, that, as a developing youth and young man, "Lucius was known rather as a ne'er-do-well; or one that wandered from pillar to post; or became—as would be termed in the present-day parlance—a soldier of fortune." (It was a description, moreover, disquietingly parallel to the character sketch of him as John Bainbridge, as found in readings dealing with his dual appearance on the American scene much later—where the entity lost.) "Instability" seemed to be the summary verdict.

Like many in the Greco-Roman society of his day, Lucius had a common-law wife, or mistress. Named Vesta, she was of the Roman nobility, and she bore him two children—a son and a daughter. The latter, however, was apparently born to them *after* Lucius had already taken a legal wife, named Mariaerh—a Samaritan—who was younger than himself. Out of this fact much conflict arose, even dividing the members of Lucius's flock, as well as the members of his immediate family. (It was as if the specters of Ra Ta and Isris had arisen to haunt him.) Moreover, because Mariaerh remained childless during the early years of her marriage to Lucius, this was to lead to much questioning and bitterness all around, which was greatly exacerbated by Paul's preachments against marriage. It was during those parlous days, when Lucius had already risen to the rank of bishop over the Laodicean congregation, that John addressed his famous words to that bickering, divided flock: "I know thy works, that thou art neither cold nor hot: I would thou wert cold or hot. So then because thou art lukewarm, and neither cold nor hot, I will spew thee out of my mouth."[4]

Yet the differences, in time, were peaceably resolved; after a son, Sylvius, was born to Mariaerh and Lucius, their marriage at last became the sacred covenant intended on the day of their first vows.

The readings confirm what biblical scholars have long suspected: that it was Lucius of Cyrene who authored the Gospel of Luke.[5] He probably wrote the Acts of the Apostles, as well, although no mention is made of this. However, most authorities ascribe both Luke and Acts to the same author because of obvious textual similarities between the two books, in addition to the opening verse of the latter, which alludes to the "former treatise." But whereas it is the common view that "Lucius of Cyrene" and "Luke" were probably one and the same entity, inasmuch as the name "Luke" is a derivative of Lucius, the Edgar Cayce readings reveal that Luke was actually an uncle of Lucius's, being the brother of Merceden, his mother. Luke, too, had hailed originally from Cyrene. Though commonly referred to as "the beloved physician," we are told that Luke "was the young physician that never finished and never practiced, yet was known as the physician."[6] We are also told, in the same reading, that he was "close to the brother-in-law of Pilate, and came to know much of those things that went on."

The historical confusion between uncle and nephew is explained thus:

And there is often the confusing of Lucius and Luke, for these were kinsmen; and Lucius and Luke were drawn or thrown together, and with the conversion of Saul (or Paul, as he became) they followed closer and closer with the activities of Paul. (294–192)

Cyrene, the capital of Cyrenaica, had long been a prosperous city of Greeks and Greek-speaking Jews, who lived among the

Libyans on the north coast of Africa in that area now known as Tripoli. Bequeathed to Rome in 96 B.C., Cyrenaica became a Roman province and was united with Crete; it was a very natural union, inasmuch as most of the original Greek inhabitants of Cyrene had come from that Mediterranean isle.

It should not suprise us to find Edgar Cayce, as Lucius, having his roots among the Libyans. It was into Libyan territory that he had been sent as the exiled priest Ra Ta, where the Nubians and Libyans had befriended him. Now, in a much later cycle, he found himself again drawn to that same land—though in a somewhat different locale—probably attracted by karmic associations.

Yet it would seem that his father, Philippi, probably for business reasons, decided to move his young family to Laodicea, in the Roman-ruled province of Phrygia in Asia Minor. An even more prosperous city than Cyrene, Laodicea was famed for its black wool and its banking community. Located on the ancient highway leading up from Ephesus toward Syria, Laodicea occupied an almost square plateau some hundred feet above the green, fertile valley where the Lycus and Meander rivers converged. It was a jewel of the empire, whose polyglot population included Greek-speaking Syrians, Romans, and Romanized natives, as well as a prominent and wealthy Jewish contingent.

One could readily understand why Philippi had relocated to such a promising new environment. Nor was he alone in making the move from Cyrene. His brother-in-law, Luke, also joined them in the exodus, although apparently settling in Jerusalem. Other former Cyreneans included the Christian convert Stephen, who was later stoned to death, and that Simon who reportedly bore the Savior's cross when He grew weary.

It was probably on a youthful visit to Jerusalem to visit his uncle and namesake, Luke, that Lucius first encountered the Master and heard Him speak to the gathering throngs. He was enthralled. The simple Nazarene, speaking in colloquial Aramaic, could somehow reach the hearts and minds of the masses as no trained orator or learned priest could do. But it was not only His gift with words and His spellbinding way of presenting great truths in simple parables: rather, it was an indefinable aura of spiritual authority about the man that excited Lucius. Here was a godlike figure of smiling, compassionate countenance, who needed only to look upon the sick and the lame, and they were healed; or, just as suddenly, with a stern and penetrating gaze of those blue-gray eyes, he could command the demons to depart from one possessed, and they departed. Lucius longed to know this man better. And so, in effect, he became "as one that was a hanger-on, and of the very intent and purpose that this was to be the time when there was to be a rebellion against the Roman legions, the Romans in the authority,"[7] to be led by this one who was now being more openly proclaimed as the promised Messiah. And thus, alas, did Lucius, like so many others among the early followers of Jesus, misinterpret the true mission of the Master. Chosen as one of the seventy, who went forth in pairs to those places where the Master would soon follow, announcing His coming, Lucius still believed in his heart that all of this work was but the prelude to a great social uprising that would soon be announced. "Not peace, but a sword," the Master had once said, and Lucius, like so many others listening at the time, had misconstrued the spiritual import of the words. This even included some among the twelve; for such is the way of young zealots and hotheads.

It was not until word reached him later in Laodicea, where he had returned, that Lucius was to awaken fully to the gravity of his misjudgment concerning the Master's mission of salvation. For, tales of His crucifixion and subsequent resurrection spread like wildfire into the provinces, far and wide, and the faithful were soon flocking toward Jerusalem as iron filings to a magnet. Lucius and his younger sister, Nimmuo, were among these eager travelers to where the waiting apostles were now assembled in expectation of further holy visitations.

When the day of Pentecost arrived, they were there. The event is best described, perhaps, in these words from a life reading for the entity [2390], who had been Nimmuo in that experience:

And then there came the day of Pentecost, when the entity heard that speech of Peter; saw John, James, and the other apostles as they sat—as it were—in awe; when the Spirit had descended as in tongues of fire and sat upon that body of the Twelve. (2390–3)

In seeking an explanation for the Pentecostal phenomenon, Cayce received the following answer to a question in his own life reading on that incarnation as Lucius:

Q–2. *Please explain how all heard in their various tongues the message that was given by Peter in the one tongue.*

A–2. This was the activity of the Spirit, and what the Spirit indeed meant and means in the experiences of the individuals during that period.

For one that was of Cyrene heard a mixture of the Greek and Aryan tongue; while—though Peter spoke in the Aramaic—those that were of the Hebrews heard in the Hebrew language; those in Greek heard in Greek, see? (294–192)

Clearly, Peter's miraculous "gift of tongues" bears no comparison with the current Pentecostal concept called glossolalia, which is usually an unintelligible gibberish that appears to be more emotional than spiritual in its origin. In this context, the entity [2205], who was to learn in her life reading that as an elder daughter of the centurion Cornelius she had been a close friend of both Luke and Lucius, was told:

Ye learned later that it was not necessary that ye speak with tongues, but with that tongue of love—which is the language of all who seek His face. (2205–3)

It was on the day of Pentecost, in all probability, that Lucius first met his future bride, Mariaerh, a Samaritan Jew, whose parents were closely associated with Elizabeth, the mother of John the Baptist, and others among the "holy women" who were now in Jerusalem. Mariaerh, in fact, was among the first ten to be baptized on that memorable day.

As the friendship between Lucius and Mariaerh ripened, so did his commitment to the spreading of the gospel. Now a devout follower rather than a mere "hanger-on," as in the past, Lucius sought acceptance from the apostles, most of whom questioned him because he was of the "foreign group." It was Thomas alone, among the Twelve, who showed a willingness to accept him. Later, as the persecutions began and there came the choosing of those who would go out into the provinces as deacons, Lucius was again rejected, this time because of his close associations with that unproven convert called Paul, or Saul, known as a Roman citizen, despite his claim of Jewish ancestry. Yet, as Paul's ministry began, and the fruits thereof greeted the ears of those in the mother church at Jerusalem, as well as the largely Jewish congregation in Antioch, the attitude toward Lucius softened; for Lucius had not only been accepted by Paul but also by a majority of those in the Caesarean church, where he and Paul were preaching. It was then that Lucius decided to return to his own city, Laodicea, accompanied by his bride, Mariaerh, and establish a ministry there.

Also residing in Laodicea, however, was the Roman mistress of Lucius's earlier years, Vesta, and old ties were renewed. A son by that association, named Pebilus, was now growing up, and it could be argued that Lucius was merely playing the role of dutiful father. However, with Paul's increasingly troublesome preachments against marriage on the part of those who rose to the rank of bishop in the church, the marital relationship between Lucius and Mariaerh became badly strained, as mentioned earlier. Finally, the birth of a daughter, Susana, to Lucius and Vesta apparently led to an estrangement. Mariaerh, childless and desolate, fled to Bethany, where she was comforted by Mary, the mother of the Lord, and by Elizabeth and the aging Judy, that Essene teacher of the youthful Jesus.

Meanwhile, in Lucius's own family, as well as in his congregation, sides were drawn. It took his mother, Merceden, to finally bring him to his senses, just as she had so well put Paul (that "old bachelor," as he was derisively called [8]) in his place:

One need never attempt to justify, but needs only to glorify Him; as ye so well proclaimed through Laodicea, as ye so well put Paul in his place, as ye so well comforted Timothy as well as Peter, Andrew, and brought Lucius to his senses. (2574–1)

Thus, peace returned to Laodicea, as did also a tearful Mariaerh return to the arms of her remorseful husband. In due time, as reported earlier in the chapter, they had a son. Differences now arose between Lucius and Paul, but they also arose between Paul and the leaders of the church at Jerusalem and Antioch as a result of his contentious teachings. (All of which probably serves to prove the essential frailty of us all, including the very saints themselves.)

Yet, if Paul's view on marriage was too extreme, it was not altogether without its merits insofar as celibacy may aid the seasoned spiritual seeker, particularly one who would be a paradigm for others who are seeking. To Dr. [866], a Hindu and a teacher of yoga, who was contemplating marriage, Cayce offered this sage assessment of the matter: "He that marries doeth well; he that marries not doeth better."[9]

That leaves it up to the individual, which seems right. In Lucius's case, however, it was a question not of continence but of fidelity. His marital vows, in any case, had preceded his bishopric, and could not be ignored with impunity. That would appear to be where Paul's judgment was spiritually myopic.

One happy outcome of Lucius's reunion with his wife, which had karmic significance he could not have grasped at the time, was a welcomed rapport with the apostle Andrew, who had formerly opposed him and now became his defender.[10] As his former nemesis, Araaraart II in Egypt, who had sent him into exile, the same entity was now ready, once again, to lend a hand of cooperation to the "returning" priest, or bishop. Their next encounter would be as father and son. Once again, cooperation would be the keynote in that familial relationship, as Edgar and Hugh Lynn.

But there is an interesting side note to all this. In the eventual rapprochement between Andrew and Lucius, in those strife-ridden days of the early church, what role may have been played by the entities [538] and [288], then dwelling on the Other Side? "For they became then what might be termed as guardian angels," we are told; and, more specifically, it is added that "the individual entity [538] overshadowed the activities of Andrew through the Palestine experience."[11]

Let us take a look, now, at some of the karmic relationships involving Lucius and those who were perhaps closest to him in that incarnation.

First, there was his younger sister, Nimmuo, known in the present as the entity [2390]. In the Egyptian experience, as the priestess Tar-Ello, she was one of the latter-day companions of the aging Ra. Again she appeared in the Uhjltd period, as one of those "of the leader's household" who aided in "turning the tide of those influences to that of good" when the Grecian maidens attempted to undermine the various activities at Is-Shlan-doen.[12] Similarly, when the conflicts arose around Lucius and Vesta in Laodicea, when "many—*many*—questioned the purposes of Vesta with Lucius,"[13] Nimmuo, who at first had "felt for and sided with that royal personage [Vesta], even against Paul who had espoused the part of Maria-erh" before Lucius's bishopric,[14] ultimately became a neutral party. Paul was later to side with Vesta against those of Lucius's own household, however, when Lucius became bishop; whereas it is said of Nimmuo that "the entity stood as a mighty power—alone with the *truth* in the lack of condemnation to any!"[15] In short, her influence became that of a genuine peacemaker in that time of strife and turmoil. (Her name, appropriately, meant "One sent".[16])

Vesta, the Roman companion of Lucius, had been one of those in Egypt who came into frequent contact with the high priest Ra in his latter days. (She would later come to know him on a much more intimate basis—again as his mistress, as in the Lucius period —during his second appearance on the American scene as John Bainbridge.) Meanwhile, as Vesta, she must have been a woman of considerable charm, able to rouse both envy and admiration, but in her latter days, the spiritual side of her nature dominated over the sensual, for she became a deaconess in the Laodicean church, living to what was termed "a ripe old age."[17] In the present experience, she has remained a faithful and active force in perpetuating the work of Edgar Cayce. However, ancient rivalries have a way of making themselves felt, sometimes, at the unconscious level, and she once told me, with a touch of wry laughter, that her first and only encounter with the individual who had been Mariaerh, her rival for Lucius's affections, had brought instant antipathy on the part of the latter, who soon thereafter left Virginia Beach and never returned.

The children of Lucius and Vesta were Pebilus, a son, and Susana, a daughter. It is awesome to learn that they both turned up, in due time, to obtain life readings from the psychic who had once been their father.

The entity who had been Pebilus (now Mr. [1990]) incarnated as a newphew of Mrs. [1523], his former mother (Vesta), in the Laodicean appearance. His life reading revealed that he had apparently been among the Atlantean immigrants in Egypt after the priest Ra Ta returned from exile; in that experience, he rose to a position of political power. Later, in Persia, he incarnated under Croesus's rule, becoming one who guarded the king's exchequer, although later abandoning that role to follow the teachings of Uhjltd. Of his experience in the Holy Land as the offspring of Lucius and Vesta, we find that Pebilus "was among those who were blessed as a child by the Master,"[18] which may well explain why he chose to appear in a later cycle on the early American scene as a priest, Father Shaughnessy. There he was to come in contact with his former parents, who were again enmeshed in an illicit relationship, as John Bainbridge and Mae Umbor. Not one to sit in judgment, however, the good Father Shaughnessy acted as a teacher and friend, dispensing—along with the usual blessings—kindness, gentleness, and patience.

As for the daughter, Susana, now [3685], she too had been present with Cayce in his Egyptian and Persian cycles. In the former, she served in the Temple Beautiful, whereas in the latter she was one of the lovely Grecian maidens, numbering among those who became converts to Uhjltd's teachings. Not surprisingly, we find that she was also to reappear in the so-called Dearborn experience of Bainbridge and others, where it is said that the entity, as one Claire Inchworth, gained—although finding the experience "repellant."[19]

Of Merceden, the mother of Lucius (to be distinguished from Sophia, who was the mother of Lucius's younger half-sister, Nimmuo, and apparently a second wife of Philippi's), little is given.[20] In her life reading, however, it is revealed that she had been one who served in the Temple Beautiful, as Hes-It-Pet, during Cayce's Egyptian cycle. There must have developed a special bond between them in that incarnation, however, to cause the soul now known as Cayce to choose her as its channel for entry into the earth-plane as Lucius.

This brings us to Mariaerh, the legitimate wife of Lucius.

We find that she, too, had shared in the Egyptian experience, where she was Shu-Tun, one of those natives of Egypt who chose to go into exile with the priest. In the Persian period, she also appeared, coming as one of the Grecian maidens who later became a faithful follower of Uhjltd's teachings.[21]

Beyond the familial relationships in the Laodicean period, let us look at the entity Silas, who travels through the pages of the New Testament in company with Barnabas and Paul, with Lucius and Timothy and Luke, and was known in his present incarnation as Mr. [707]. Married to the daughter of Nicodemus in those days of the early church, he had previously entered the earth-plane in the Persian period, where we met him as Eujueltd, the father of Uhjltd the King. Thus, a renewal of their relationship, this time in holy fellowship as followers of the Christ, and ever helpful to one another, carries a lovely lesson.

As Lucius, we are told that Cayce entered the earth from Jupiter's realm. It was a planetary influence that bestowed upon him a certain "universality of activity." Though he wavered at the first, those universal influences gained through the Jupiterian sojourn ultimately prevailed. "For the entity gave for the gospel's sake," we are told, "a love, an activity and a hope through things that had become as of a universal nature."[22]

12. Among the Arawaks

"I saw myself not as a physical being, but knew that I was a part of the whole order of things."[1]

It was a most unusual statement, like so many of Edgar Cayce's utterances. That impersonalized identification of himself with the totality of being, as a portion or pattern of the whole, was the keynote to interpreting his account of a strange, allegorical dream that followed.

The dream was a curious mixture of fantasy and reality. Using various species of the animal kingdom as emblematic devices to symbolize the shifting patterns of outlook, behavior, and experience that are a portion of each soul's development through the earth-plane as it gradually moves toward a comprehension of the oneness of all force, the dream intermingled a number of symbolic transmigrations of a creaturely nature with what were apparently actual fleshly incarnations of the soul-entity known as Edgar Cayce, entering the earth in a succession of changing human forms. (In one of these incarnations, for example, we encounter him as the Trojan warrior Xenon; in fact, it is that same dream-sequence already cited in Chapter 8, wherein Cayce, as Xenon, finds himself a helpless spectator at the duel to the death between Hector and Achilles.)

In each of these changing incarnations in physical form, there is a symbolic seeking-out by the soul-self of kindred soul-beings who have shared in the lessons drawn from the preceding allegorical phase at the creaturely level, symbolizing that universal law: like attracts like. In the final analysis, however, the soul must come to understand the oneness of all force. Until then, self must be continually met in the varied phases of experience, as symbolized in the entering together as snails or birds or cows or whatever. Such creaturely projections, of course, as the subsequent interpretation of the dream made clear, were to be understood as mere emblems, corresponding to the variations in human traits or character types. As aptly phrased in a reading that relates to the same theme but in a different aspect, it is like those common expressions drawn from the personification of animal traits, such as, "docile as the horse, as catty as the cat, as stubborn as a mule, or the like."[2] In short, "This is not intended to indicate that there is transmigration or transmutation of the soul from animal to human."[3]

To recap the dream very briefly:

At first, Cayce finds himself in the form of a snail, among other snails; and he is suddenly eaten, falling prey to one of those larger beings he has been taught to fear. Then he incarnates as a man, and dies of a fever caused by a parasite found in snails. (The lesson is clear: it is a vivid illustration of the karmic cycle in action.) As for Cayce's identity in that hapless incarnation, however, we have no clues. So let us move on.

Next, he recognizes himself as a fish swimming in the ocean. Along with many of his own kind, he is caught in an enormous net; as he finds himself being prepared for food, he loses consciousness. Now, suddenly, he is back in physical form, associated with many other humans whom he has known before in other stages of expression. But in a swift transition, he finds himself changed to a cow, with a little calf. The calf is frightened by a sheep dog but is rescued by the shepherd, who turns out to be David. The cow has been enraged by the dog's actions, but in a sudden transmigration, Cayce now finds himself a dog and able to understand the dog's natural hostility toward cows. As a dog, he breaks a leg and is killed by his master in an act of mercy. Now the scene shifts to the arena outside the main gate of the Trojan citadel, where Cayce finds himself as the transfixed guard, watching the deadly duel between Hector and Achilles, as described earlier. Again he passes into the unseen world: "There were many souls near me who had been in physical bodies, yet very few that I recognized. Finally I did meet someone I had known before, so we decided to come to a mother bird—and we were hatched out by a little jenny wren, as tiny little birds."[4] Later, however, a cat gets their own brood of six nestlings, and they swear vengeance on the whole cat family.

Now we come to that portion of the dream relating to an incarnation in the days of Columbus, with which this chapter is specifically concerned. Here we find Cayce among one of the Arawak-speaking tribes of the West Indies, probably on one of the offshore islands of Hispaniola, and able to recognize someone aboard Columbus's vessel as a former companion:

It seemed the time of Columbus' discovering of America, because I was among the people in the land when Columbus came; then I met the individual among the people with Columbus who had been with me as a bird. We were anxious to make a trip on the boat with the people who had come ashore, because we seemed to be the only ones who could talk with them. But we were not allowed to. Then we attempted to get back to the mainland [probably a reference to the main island of Hispaniola] from the [outer?] island. A storm came up, and we were drowned. (294–161)

(As an interesting aside, in one of the readings recounting Cayce's death from drowning in his second Bainbridge cycle we find it stated that "the destruction of that physical has oft been through that of the sudden forces—the water destructive."[5])

In an attempt to interpret certain confusing aspects of the above-cited dream fragment relating to the Columbus period, I think we must first separate the allegorical from the real. Undoubtedly there was someone aboard Columbus's ship (who had probably come ashore with a small landing party) whose soul-being could communicate at the psychic level with Cayce's soul-being as the result of a prior-life association—*not* as birds in any literal sense, but in a type of experience (which may have been a planetary sojourn together, as spirit-entities, rather than an earthly incarnation) that had created a common bond enabling them to seek out and find one another again. It is quite probable, moreover, that this individual was a fellow Arawak, not a European. Columbus's first landfall had been in the Bahamas, before he came upon the larger landmass of Hispaniola, which he mistook as either Cipangu or

Cathay (Japan or China), and it is noted in his journal that he took some Arawaks captive. Captive or not, it is a reasonable supposition that the individual spotted by Cayce was an Arawak from one of the other islands, who had probably been serving as a guide or interpreter to the white men. Cayce may have been a leader among the local Arawak tribespeople and, in forming a ready friendship with the other, was able to learn something about the pale strangers who had come in the big ships with the white wings. Using a form of sign language, he then may have been able to reach a basic level of communication with them. It is easy to imagine the strong fascination the three great sailing vessels in Columbus's expeditionary fleet would have held for the astonished observers, who would have seen them as giant birds moving out gracefully over the mighty waters. Thus, there was a strong desire "to make a trip on the boat with the people who had come ashore"; but that neither Cayce nor his newfound companion from among Columbus's landing party were allowed to join them on their subsequent trip to the main island suggests that they were *both* natives. (If the "companion" had been a European, he—or she—would not likely have been snubbed in such a manner.) So the two adventurers apparently decided to follow the European vessel in one of their own little canoes; but "a storm came up," and they "were drowned."

If the proposition is accepted that Cayce had indeed incarnated in the New World in the days of Columbus, we must ask the inevitable question: What was he doing among the Arawaks?

The answer involves a little bit of history.

The Arawak Indians, it is believed, had their origins in the Andes; but in a migratory pattern, some settled eventually in the Antilles chain, which includes most of the West Indies. They were simple, inoffensive people, who lived by rudimentary agriculture, fishing, and gathering mollusks. Yet they were by no means uncivilized. Before returning to Spain from his first voyage to Hispaniola, Columbus established a small settlement of Spanish pioneers at Santo Domingo. The natives of that region were the

Tainos, an Arawak-speaking tribe, and Columbus commissioned a friar named Ramón Pané to make a study of the Taino religion. Father Pané's account reveals an unusually high development of belief and ritual, the source of which is not known, although some authorities have attributed it to the Mayan civilization. The Tainos also had a relatively elaborate system of rank and government, and their society was divided into four classes: slaves, commoners, nobles, and chiefs. A peaceful people, they had no means of defending themselves against the aggressive Spaniards, who soon obliterated all traces of their unique culture.

Into such a society, then, Cayce may well have incarnated to bring to the Arawak-speaking tribes a sense of unity and higher purpose, probably assuming the role of a chieftain. This is suggested by the apparent ease with which he assumed for himself the role of an interpreter to the white men, along with his newfound Arawak-speaking companion, who, in all probability, was a female of noble lineage from one of the neighboring tribes. (She had been his "mate," remember, in the allegorical experience as "birds.")

Before we take leave of him in that relatively unknown cycle, it is worth observing that this same soul-entity, in a somewhat later incarnation that was to bring him once more into the New World, this time as an English soldier of fortune named Bainbridge, brought with him a gift from the Arawaks. A guide to many of his own bewildered and helpless people in that strange new land called America, Bainbridge was quick to make friends with the Indians of the various tribes, and he moved among them as one of their own.

13. The Two Lives of John Bainbridge

Wandering, yearning, curious, with restless explorations,
With questionings, baffled, formless, feverish, with never-happy heart,
Wherefore unsatisfied soul? and whither O mocking life?

Yet soul be sure the first intent remains, and shall be carried out,
Pehaps even now the time has arrived.
The true son of God shall come singing his songs.

—WALT WHITMAN

FIRST ARRIVAL: A.D. 1625

John Bainbridge, wanderer and wastrel.

Those are the tragic epithets applied in the Edgar Cayce readings to that entity who came—not once, but *twice,* it seems—into the earth-plane, emigrating from England to the early American continent on both occasions in search of himself.

Who had he been, this troubled, restless soul, this soldier of fortune and adventurer with a gambler's instinct and a lustfully roving eye? His identity holds no surprise for us, of course: we have been anticipating his arrival, through references in earlier chapters. Yet it still must come as a shock of sorts to realize that an entity of such great and noble accomplishments in his prior lives as Ra Ta, Uhjltd, probably Pythagoras, and Lucius of Cyrene, and with an equally notable incarnation awaiting him just around the bend of the river of life, as the famous psychic and seer Edgar Cayce, could so suddenly have made the "wrong turn," as it were, in that dual cycle on the American scene as John Bainbridge.

Why? We shall come to that, in time. Meanwhile, between his two seemingly wasted lives as John Bainbridge, Cayce was to enter the flesh very briefly as a love child born to Miss [288]—that one who has been described in the readings as his other self, or twin soul. (In that life [288] had incarnated as a legitimate, but not officially recognized, daughter of Louis XIV, the Sun King. Her tragic story in that scandal-ridden incarnation in the Bourbon court of seventeenth-century France, involving the cold-blooded murder of her infant son on the King's orders, is the focal point of our next chapter, which will include some little-known documentation.) Cayce's aborted French incarnation, if our calculations are correct, was from 1680 to 1685, whereas his first appearance in the earth-plane as Bainbridge was during the first half of the seventeenth century, with his birth probably occurring about A.D. 1600; though the date of his death in that initial appearance is uncertain. His second arrival on the scene, carrying the same name and following many of his footsteps as the first Bainbridge, can be estimated to have taken place about A.D. 1720, with his death occurring thirty-four years later, in 1754.

To get at the karmic origins of the downward-gravitating Bainbridge incarnations, when the wandering soul-entity appeared to be losing its way, we need to go back some twelve thousand years in time to Cayce's Egyptian cycle, then trace the slow ripening of the karmic fruit down through the ages; for one's karmic harvest, it seems, is often the result of a cumulative process.

Despite his great and memorable accomplishments as the high priest Ra, there was an evident weakness of the flesh exhibited by the entity throughout that experience. It was first manifested in the relatively easy manner in which the temple dancer Isris, acting upon the malevolent urging of the priest's enemies, was able to persuade him to break his own law establishing monogamy as the rule of the land and to take her as his mistress to produce the "perfect offspring." Upon his return from banishment, moreover, the priest appears not to have learned his lesson from that bitter experience. For the expiation of a sin, it is not enough to acknowledge the wrongdoing to oneself, as Ra may have done: it is necessary not to repeat it. But Ra used his newfound authority as a virtual monarch to indulge his sexual appetites anew with a succession of companions. Thus the first destructive seed of bad karma was planted and nurtured; and it was Bainbridge who was destined to reap its final fruits.

Meanwhile, in further tracing the karma inherited by Bainbridge, we must also examine what negative seeds, if any, may have been sown by Uhjltd. Although an enormous residue of *good* karma is traceable to that noble incarnation, as could also be said of Cayce's priestly days as Ra, there was bad, as well. For at the end, unhappily, the embittered Uhjltd gave way to wrathful urges, vowing vengeance. Such impulses, we are told, built a very negative karmic image on the screen of his dying thoughts. And the subsequent Trojan cycle, ending in uncontrolled wrath and self-destruction, only added to the karmic burden. In such actions, the entity lost hold of much that it had formerly gained in the realm of spiritual ideals and purposes. This departure from the soul's true path, combined with the carnal urges that had once been the entity's undoing, accounts for most of the negative traits of character exhibited by John Bainbridge. He came as an entity propelled by destructive forces and given to serving self's own interests as opposed to the higher development and the common good. (Such a trend, in fact, was initially in evidence during the early part of the entity's incarnation as Lucius of Cyrene; but there the ennobling Jupiterian influences took hold at last, allowing the soul-entity to regain its mastery over the lower self and thereby fulfill its spiritual mission in that crucial cycle of service to God and man.)

And what of his twin soul, [288]? Just as she had chosen not to enter with Cayce in that fatal Trojan experience, so she remained apart during the dual Bainbridge cycle. Possibly it was due to a recognition on her part that the "other self" could better meet its negative karma alone? Or perhaps her decision to again remain in "the land of nirvana" enabled her to play a more important role as her twin soul's spiritual guide or intercessor, operating on the Other Side. But lest we be inclined to pass judgment on the one who faltered, it is well to note this highly instructive excerpt from the readings about soul development and retrogression; for, if the following words are true, the variations experienced by Cayce are apparently common to most of us and represent a pattern of soul-experience and evolution as set by the Master himself:

Q-5. *From a study of [the life readings] it seems that there is a trend downward, from early incarnations, toward greater earthliness and less mentality. Then there is a swing upward, accompanied by suffering, patience, and understanding. Is this the normal pattern, which results in virtue and oneness with God obtained by free will and mind?*
A-5. This is correct. It is the pattern as it is set in Him [Jesus]. (5749-14)

There is much to be learned, we are told, in the soul's evolutionary ascent to its Maker, but, conversely, there is also much to be *unlearned.*[1] In one of his own life readings, Edgar Cayce was told that "destructive forces have entered in through the entity's physical sojourns, so must the rebuilding, resuscitating, re-establishing, reincarnated forces of the entity be manifest in the present."[2]

A man must be judged by his works, even as the Master gave. On that basis, it is fair to conclude that the soul-entity we know as Edgar Cayce succeeded in "unlearning," or reversing, those destructive forces that had been slowly building in the mental and physical self ever since the initial transgressions committed during his great and memorable incarnation as Ra Ta. Yet it was the dual Bainbridge cycle—particularly the manner in which it closed, as we shall see—that apparently marked the critical turning point.

Through a satiety of sin and self, the soul-entity was able, as it were, to "see Satan plain," moving onward and upward in a cycle of renewal as Edgar Cayce. The modern-day psychic and healer now drew on that well of wisdom within himself, whose clear waters first slaked the thirst of many in his inspired Egyptian period as the high priest Ra, and again as Uhjltd, in Persia, and even in his latter days as Lucius (for the Laodicean bishop, too, became a healer[3]).

Out of his cycles of suffering in many an incarnation and the wandering far afield as Bainbridge had come to the entity Edgar Cayce an even deeper wisdom and an ability to comprehend the shortcomings and needs of others. This was made obvious in the following statement from one of his later life readings:

For to many the power, the help, the aid which has come in their experience in the present [from Edgar Cayce] has not only equalled but has surpassed any that was experienced in the period of either Ra Ta or Uhjltd. (294-183)

Even among those who readily accept the doctrine of reincarnation, many might be tempted to view with justifiable skepticism the notion that a soul-entity could reincarnate *twice* under the same name, in a fairly close succession of lives (roughly a hundred years apart), and in an almost identical behavior pattern, even carrying the entity into many of the former environs.

Eerie, isn't it? Yet the diligent researcher can find other, rather similar cases in the Edgar Cayce readings, though of a less dramatic nature, which lend support to the double Bainbridge incarnations. Moreover, what might at first glance appear totally improbable becomes, upon careful reflection, not only plausible but logical as well. The restless soul, with its unsatisfied longings, may understandably seek a renewed opportunity—a chance to re-live, as closely as possible, its former cycle of experience in the earth-plane, particularly where it had wandered and lost its way. The changes, if any, the second time around under similar vibrations, would of course depend upon the free will application of the entity. But while it is true, surely, that "God's purpose is ever growth,"[4] we have already noted that the soul-entity's chosen path of evolution—or *de*volution, as the case may be—is often a circuitous one, leading downward before leading upward. (In fact, we are told that "there is progress whether ye are going forward or backward! The thing is to move! For there may be circles at times, but *no* standing still for the development of a soul."[5]) Meanwhile, since names as well as places carry their own unique vibrations (according to various occult sources and as confirmed by the Edgar Cayce readings), one can readily grasp the significance of an incoming entity's decision to replicate the former vibrations as nearly as possible if a prior cycle is truly to be re-experienced in its major aspects.

Apparently the urge to reassume the familiar vibrations associated with a given name in a prior life, without necessarily repeating that cycle, is not uncommon. The card index files on the Cayce readings at the Virginia Beach headquarters of the association founded by Edgar Cayce before his death contain under the heading "Names: Similar" dozens of cases in which the present Christian name of an individual is the same as, or similar to, its given name in a prior life. Less frequently, this is also true of the surname. In the case of the former, certain "asides" spoken by the sleeping Cayce during some of the readings suggest that the incoming soul-entity is somehow able to wield an influence at the psychic level upon those deciding what its Christian name should be; whereas in the case of the latter, we can reasonably conclude that the arriving soul chooses a channel with the familiar surname and vibration for its own purposes. Indeed, since the readings point out a common tendency for souls to reincarnate together in clusters, apparently working out "group karma" in this manner, it should not seem surprising, really, that incoming soul-entities migrating toward those fleshly channels with which they bear some former relationship will inevitably wind up, on occasion, with the same surname as before, whether specifically sought or not. As a case in point, Edgar Cayce's grandfather reincarnated as his own great-great-grandson, not only taking the Cayce name again, but retaining (this time as a *middle* name, rather than the first) his former name of "Thomas." The name was psychically recommended by Edgar Cayce in a reading given on the day of birth, but probably at the prompting of the newly entered soul-entity. Meanwhile, the entity [857], who had been an early settler in the Williamsburg area, was told in her life reading that she had retained the same first name this time around: "The entity then was in the name Carol again—Carol Fawncet." In another, and quite astonishing case, a childhood sweetheart of Edgar Cayce's, who had died at "twelve and two," as the reading rather quaintly stated it,[6] reappeared as a young lady who was sent to Mr. Cayce by her fiancé for a life reading. Not only was her prior identity discovered, but it was found that her fiancé—who bore the same surname as her family's in the prior life, in Kentucky—was a reincarnation of her former father. He had died shortly after she did and had now come back in a family with the same surname, although in a quite different locale. The fact that they were both guided to Mr. Cayce, resulting in a close and beneficial association, is quite as intriguing, perhaps, as the fact that both father and daughter were destined to resume their interrupted life together under the same surname as formerly, although as husband and wife.

And so, with this little digression into the seeming "coincidence" of repeated names, it is hoped that a plausible basis has been established for the presentation of this account of the two lives of John Bainbridge, which follows.

Bainbridge is a noteworthy English name. Etymologically considered, *bain* means "straight," or "willing," while a bridge, of course, is normally a passage over a body of water, and may be viewed as the link between two lands—or, if you will, two states of consciousness. John, in its Hebrew interpretation, means one whom "Jehovah has favored."

There was a John Bainbridge born in 1582 at Ashby de la Zouch in central England who was a noted English physician and astronomer. He died at Oxford in 1643. It is fair to speculate that he may well have been the male parent of our central character in his first appearance, the father bestowing his own christian name upon the son. We would estimate that the son was born shortly after the turn of the century—probably between 1600 and 1605, inasmuch as his subsequent arrival in the New World as a young soldier of fortune was to occur in 1625—although the readings neglect to indicate the precise location of his birth in that initial appearance. (In his second appearance as John Bainbridge, which was around 1720 by our calculations, Cornwall is pinpointed as the birthplace.) However, Great Yarmouth, in Norfolk, may have been the location of birth that first time around, or somewhere in nearby Lincolnshire. For we find that John Bainbridge was not alone among the English-born sons of that clan to emigrate to the American continent in the days of its early settlings. Another (who may have been a brother or cousin of John's) was one Jim Bain-bridge, who hailed from Lincolnshire and, in the loose style of life that also typified John's New World experience, "became something of the gambler, and the one to take much of the goods from the peoples that then occupied this shore."[7] The entity lost, both materially and spiritually, for he was severely tortured. We find that he had been associated with Edgar Cayce in the Ra Ta cycle, when he was one of the twelve councillors to the young king; howwever, he had taken sides with the priest and was among those sent into exile. (We might deduce, from this earlier connection, that their relationship in that early Bainbridge appearance involved a close familial link of some sort.) Yet another Bainbridge of that early era, journeying from Yarmouth to "this land of promise," as his reading stated,[8] was the entity who had been that great spiritual leader Saneid, who came from India in the days of Ra and Hermes to aid in the dissemination of the greater truths being taught. In America, however, he "found little opportunity for the full expression of self" among "the varied characters or individualities that were expressing themselves in the personalities of those loosed upon this land." So if he was a relative of the less idealistic John and Jim Bainbridge in that incarnation, they must soon have parted company. Yet it is logical to speculate, in light of what has already been said about soul clusters and the workings of group karma, that these three Bain-bridges had originally entered the earth-plane together for a joint purpose, migrating to the New World in pursuit of a spiritual opportunity that was never realized. One held to his higher principles, apparently, though unable to accomplish by himself what required the aid of the other two; they, lured by the ready temptations of the flesh and the Devil, went their self-serving ways.

And now, to start rolling back the akashic records.

In the early morning hours of October 6, 1925, Edgar Cayce had a dream for which he sought an interpretation in a psychic reading the following day.

The dream, of itself, bears no relevance to our story. But the interpretation was preceded by this startling statement:

Now, in this first, we find there are just three hundred years to the day, hour, in which time, space, as known in the earth's plane, passed since the entity landed in this place [Virginia Beach], see? (294-39)

This 1625 dating for the initial arrival of John Bainbridge in the Tidewater area dovetails rather nicely with a whole series of readings pertaining to individuals with whom he had apparently been associated, directly or indirectly, among the early settlers as well as the natives in the Jamestown-Williamsburg area and environs.

One of these, named Ralph Rousch, was "among those who were hired soldiers who came into the land,"[9] and it is our speculation that John Bainbridge probably came in a similar capacity, functioning as a guide and protector to the arriving settlers in his party. This conclusion gains reinforcement from the following excerpt from a life reading for Mrs. [69], who was present in that experience:

In the experience, then, . . . we find in that period of the first settlers of this particular land [Tidewater area of Virginia] where the entity now resides. The entity then among those who were carried by Bainbridge, in the entering of the land, to the southern clime, as the new settlers in what is now known as the pleasure resort of the south [Virginia Beach]. (69-1)

Both of these entities, Mr. [5281] and Mrs. [69], not too surprisingly, had been associated formerly with John Bainbridge—alias Edgar Cayce—in one or more of his prior lives. We find that [5281] had been among those in the Egyptian land who joined actively in the work of the priest Ra upon his return from exile; whereas [69], as already noted in our chapter on Egypt, attended to the needs of the priest during his period of exile and upon his return became an agent, or intermediary, between Ra, Hermes, and the king. In the Persian cycle, she was one of those luckless maidens in the stronghold of Croesus who was taken captive during the first raid and perished in the long trek that followed.[10] Now, in the Bainbridge era, these old associates crossed paths again, but for what specific purpose we shall never quite know.

It was in May of 1607, of course—almost two decades before Bainbridge's reported arrival in the area—that the first English colonists arrived at what was to be named Jamestown, under the leadership of Captain John Smith. With the marriage some seven years later of John Rolfe, the first Virginia tobacco grower, to Pocahontas, the daughter of the Algonkian chief Powhatan, a period of peaceful relationships was then established between the Indians and the settlers.

All of these names, and others less familiar, crop up in the readings touching upon those with whom Bainbridge was to become directly or indirectly associated in that incarnation that first brought him to the shores of mainland America, and even under the vibrations of that place, later known as Virginia Beach, that was to feature so largely in his later life as Edgar Cayce (as it featured also in his second fateful cycle of activity in the earth as the redoubtable Bainbridge).

In 1929, a resident of Norfolk, Virginia, named Mr. [415] approached the Virginia Beach psychic for a life reading and learned that he had been the entity known historically as Captain John Smith, although he was told that it was not his actual name. (Like so many others in that era, he may have sought out the New World as a place to escape from persecution and the law and so found a new identity to be useful.) He was told that he had given much of self during that experience and had been "in favor with those in power," conceivably a reference to the Indian chief Powhatan and other tribal elders, rather than a reference to the Crown.[11] There is no clear indication that he and Bainbridge crossed paths in that incarnation, but they probably did. Later, Bainbridge was to become sexually involved with one Rising Star, a half sister of Pocahontas, apparently born of a union between the chief Powhatan and one of the women among the first English settlers. It was a tragic relationship for the luckless Rising Star, with her reading stating that "only through the inactivities and the littlenesses in this Bainbridge did the entity then lose, in losing faith, hope, and confidence in the peoples of that color."[12]

In tracing the prior lives of both the entity who had been John Smith and that one known as Rising Star, we discover some fascinating karmic ties with Cayce, though of a diverse nature. Mr.

[415] had come to Uhjltd's "city of the hills and the plains" as one of those Grecians who sought "not to destroy but rather to learn," and he apparently lost his life fighting against his fellow Greeks, in the end, in defense of Uhjltd and Is-Shlan-doen. In Egypt, before that, he had been "among those of the king's command," and one who "brought to the attention of the king the necessities for the return of the priest."[13]

On the other hand, Mrs. [543] appears to have been associated with Cayce during the androgynous rule of Aczine, or Asule, in late Atlantis, when that ruler could divide into male and female. Dissatisfied over her own inability "to change its body to that as would entice or bring those influences into the lives of those the entity contacted, . . . the first stumble began, and in this the entity lost."[14] (Thus, while one certainly cannot absolve Bainbridge of guilt in his gross mistreatment of that same entity in her incarnation as the half-breed Rising Star, we can clearly see that she was in part meeting that which she herself had sown.) During Cayce's Egyptian period, however, she had been one of those in the Nubian land who faithfully followed him to Egypt upon his return from exile. So, to put it in the vernacular, one could argue that she was "one up" on Bainbridge, who nevertheless failed to repay her in kind.

Now we come to a conundrum and a mystery.

In a reading that was actually given for Mr. [5717] (the former Hector), but which touched upon Mr. Cayce's "destructive" cycles as Bainbridge, those two appearances on the American scene were presented in this manner:

> In that of Cayce [294] was first [going back from present] in that of warrior forces in the north country [American Midwest] in and near where the body is at present located [Dayton, Ohio, at time of reading]— camped upon this spot. The destruction of that physical has oft been through that of the sudden forces—the water destructive.
>
> Then in one just previous [bypassing aborted French incarnation, 1680–1685] was in that of the settler of Jamestown, Virginia. Hence the call always of the coast country. (5717-5)

Now, there is nothing mystifying about that first paragraph, which will be found to coincide with all the known facts about Cayce's second Bainbridge cycle, as will be presented a bit further on in this chapter. Rather, it is in the following paragraph that we encounter our conundrum. For, here we find Bainbridge referred to as "the settler of Jamestown, Virginia." Plainly, then, his arrival on the shores of Virginia Beach in 1625 with a party of early settlers, was *not* in a direct transit from England but must have marked a secondary journey down the coast from Jamestown. So we are left with this unanswered question: Had he come to Jamestown in 1607 with Captain John Smith, or was he a much more recent arrival in those parts? (If the former, his name was not among those historically recorded.)

Further complicating the mystery of his actual date of arrival in America is a reading given for one of his many "companions"—an Indian maiden named Dove—who, it turns out, had been acquainted with those earlier settlers on Roanoke Island, in what is now North Carolina. Known as the "lost colony," this settlement included more than a hundred men, women, and children, who arrived in 1587. In August of that same year, the wife of one of those English settlers, Ananias Dare, gave birth to a daughter, named Virginia. Virginia Dare thus became the first English child born in the New World. Three years later, however, when the leader of the expedition, John White, returned from a voyage to England for further supplies, the whole colony had vanished. There was not a trace of them to be found.

That was in 1590.

But after Bainbridge met Dove, they traveled together with certain members of her tribe to various locations in what became Georgia, Alabama, and Tennessee, where most of the members of the so-called lost colony had settled with various friendly Indian groups after being forced to abandon their island settlement for lack of food and security. One among their number, in fact, named Henry Desmond, was later to take Dove to wife after her wanderings with Bainbridge came to a feckless end.

All of this tends to suggest that Bainbridge's initial arrival, coming as a settler to Jamestown, may have been close to John Smith's, in 1607, and that he was possibly approaching middle age when he made that first landing with a group of relocating settlers at Virginia Beach in 1625. Yet, of course, it remains strictly a matter of conjecture.

One among those "lost" Roanoke Island settlers was to end up as an adopted daughter of the great chief Powhatan. Known today as the entity [500], she was none other than that first English child to be born in the New World—Virginia Dare. Powhatan, however, renamed her Alahoi, and in time she became very active in healing and counseling among those peoples who had adopted her as their own.[15] (It was not so unusual, perhaps, for one who had been active in similar work in prior lifetimes with both Uhjltd and Ra.)

Still other personages cross our stage in "walk-on" parts. There is Amos Scott, for one, who was among those early settlers in Jamestown and Williamsburg. He had been associated with Cayce in both the Persian and the Egyptian periods—in the latter as one of the twelve councillors to the young king. In the Bainbridge cycle, "the entity gained, the entity lost."[16] And then there was Myra Rouhel (now Mrs. [405]), who "was acquainted with those characters that have gone down in history: Smith, Pocahontas, Powhatan, and Rolfe."[17] Finally, turning once more to those native Americans, we find the entity Dwoidel, who was an Indian maiden described as "well-balanced in body, in mind, and a helpmeet or aide" to her people "until one that came through the land, in the name Bainbridge, led the body far astray in its moral and spiritual intent in the experience."[18]

It is almost intermission time. Before the curtain falls on Act One of our two-part Bainbridge drama, here is a jolting excerpt from a life reading for Mrs. [884], who had been Narwaua, "a princess of the tribes of Powhatan, Chief of many nations":

Before this the entity was in the land of the present nativity [America], among the peoples of this particular land when there were the incomings of others that made the greater changes that were coming about in the experiences not only of those peoples but a returning and a making for the activities through the children of Belial that had escaped [from Atlantis] to the [safety] lands, and the children of the Law of One that were coming again into the closer relationships and contacts with these. (884–1)

Evidently the ancient forefathers of the American Indians were those sons of Belial of old, who escaped from a doomed Atlantis to what is now the American continent. And the arriving settlers, if we interpret Cayce's words aright, were none other than the former children of the Law of One, "coming again into the closer relationships and contact." If true, it tells us much about the tragic and bloody conflicts between European settlers and Indians that later arose out of that karmic reunion of opposing forces.

Curiously, though, we have found some of the ancient adversarial roles reversed, with such noble figures as the Algonkian chief Powhatan and his daughters acting the part of true peacemakers while the selfish likes of the entity Bainbridge (and there were apparently many among the incoming settlers with self-serving goals) stirred the fires of resentment and turmoil whereever they went.

SECOND ARRIVAL: A.D. 1742

In his second appearance in the earth-plane as John Bainbridge, during the first half of the eighteenth century, the entity "entered upon that of the Saturn forces," we are told.[19]

Saturn, according to the interpretation given in the Edgar Cayce readings, is that planetary sphere of consciousness to which a soul-entity may banish itself between earthly incarnations for the purpose of "rubbing out" certain soul memories and beginning "all over again!"[20] The implications with respect to the first Bainbridge cycle are quite clear. Following "such aggrandizement of the laws of the flesh," the entity sought to "find [its] reclamation, [its] re-molding, [its] beginning again, in the spheres of Saturn's relative forces."[21]

In short, the entity sought the proverbial "second chance," and got it. What it did with it constitutes the balance of our story, in this two-part drama on the lives of John Bainbridge.

Born in Cornwall, England, this second time around, Bainbridge's natal Sun was in the sign of Scorpio, with "Venus as the second influence."[22] (It was beginning to look very much as if he were to be tested anew in those areas of his former weaknesses, for that particular combination of astrological influences was intensely powerful, and it could either "make him" or "break him.")

In Cayce's own life readings, as they pertain to the Bainbridge cycle, one searches in vain for clear demarcation between those comments that may be alluding to the first, as opposed to the second, appearance. From this particular approach (which was the one I took initially), the end result is little short of total confusion and perplexity. Yet it seemed at first the only way to go—until it suddenly occurred to me that Cayce, in giving his own life readings, was obviously being "blocked" by the effects of that former planetary sojourn "in Saturn's forces" between the two incarnations as Bainbridge. He seemed to face no trouble in digging up akashic references to the earlier period when giving life readings for other entities who were in that particular experience (and no trouble in that brief dream interpretation that gave 1625 for his first arrival in Virginia Beach), yet the "blackout," I now began to suspect, had been complete and total for any references to the earlier Bainbridge appearance in his *own* life readings. In short, those particular readings apparently referred to the *second* cycle only.

On this premise, the following excerpt from Cayce's life reading 294–19, which had originally been interpreted to refer to his "early return to the earth's plane" from the first Bainbridge cycle to the second, is now seen in a quite different light, revealing a karmic carryover from Bainbridge to Cayce. For we see it pertaining to his return *in the present*. As Cayce, he indeed found himself "wandering to and fro" through the environs traversed by Bainbridge—but specifically in that entity's *second* appearance (which included Kentucky and Ohio, as contrasted with the more limited wanderings of the first Bainbridge):

Hence the early return to the earth's plane and the wanderings to and fro through many of the scenes that the entity experienced at that [former] time. The entity then we see was in the earth's plane *[sic]* in 1742. (294-19)

It becomes fairly obvious, in a cross-check with various historical facts relating to the period of Bainbridge's activities during that second appearance, that the date of 1742, just given, must actually pertain to Bainbridge's arrival on the American scene, or plane, during that incarnation, and *not* to his year of birth. This conclusion will, I think, become evident to the reader as the story unfolds.

Meanwhile, to assist us in erasing any doubts, we are fortunate in having a reference point provided in the readings for Mrs. [1523], which serves to corroborate our interpretation of that 1742 dating. Mrs. [1523] became the mistress of Bainbridge in a pioneer fortress area that the readings identify, somewhat confusingly, as Dearborn, in the vicinity of present-day Chicago. (Actually, the historical Fort Dearborn was not constructed until 1804, and it was razed in a raid by the Potawatomi Indians—incited by the British—in 1812. So Cayce may simply have given the Dearborn name to identify the approximate site of an earlier fort, in the time frame of the French and Indian War, which broke out in 1754. On the other hand, had Cayce's numerous allusions to French and Indian hostilities during that second Bainbridge cycle meant to suggest the unlikely time frame of the War of 1812, when France was actually an ally of America, this would have placed Bainbridge's age at a highly improbable seventy—on the assumption, of course, that the given date of 1742 was his year of birth rather than the year of his arrival on the American plane, or scene. So we revert to our original, and far more likely, set of speculations.)

Considering, then, that Bainbridge and Mrs. [1523]—then known as Mae Umbor—began their liaison, as stated in the readings, some few years before the French and Indian attack upon the fort, which may be estimated to have occurred in 1754 or thereabouts, a thread of logic can now be established to link events, dates, and ages in a common frame of reference without straining credulity. If we take 1742 as the year of Bainbridge's arrival in America, where he came as a soldier in the forces of King George II at the outset, initially arriving on Canadian shores, we might reasonably estimate that he was a young man in his early twenties at the time. Thus, his frontier encounter with his final mistress, Mrs. [1523], probably occurred in the vicinity of his thirtieth year, in 1751. His death from drowning, in a subsequent escape from the besieged fort in 1754, would have taken place when he was probably thirty-three or thirty-four.

But we are getting ahead of our story . . .

It starts, as noted, with Bainbridge arriving in the New World as "the soldier in the British forces" on Canadian assignment and proceeding some while later from the Canadian frontiers, coming into what is now the United States, presumably as the ex-soldier and adventurer. We are told that he was connected with a seafaring group that landed on the east coast of America "near where is now the resort known as Virginia Beach."[23] (Already, we see, he was subconsciously retracing his steps during that former Bainbridge cycle.)

Yet the landing party was apparently attacked in a raid by hostile Indians, for, "When the raid was made, this John Bainbridge was carried in this raid to the Southern coasts of the country; escaped, and with the forces then going in the inland way," over a period of time made his way "to the fort then on the Great Lakes, now in place known as Chicago" (an apparent reference to the predecessor of Fort Dearborn, later destroyed; Reading 5070–1 refers to "what is now Chicago, then known as Dearborn" [sic]). The account continues, in a time frame several years later. Following an attack upon the fort that could not be repulsed by the available forces, Bainbridge apparently led the scattered remnants in a hasty retreat, "in which the crossing was later attempted in the Ohio River, and there [he] met death, as known in the earth plane."[24]

Omitted from this skeletal telling of an all-too-colorful tale, however, is any account of those "many escapades that have to do with those of the nature of the relations with the opposite sex,"[25] which occurred along the way, or the gambling and other vices, by means of which "many peoples suffered in the wake of the individual."[26] We are told that the entity lost itself and its development in the earth's plane, becoming a wanderer in the land, yet, from that experience, the soul-entity gained one virtue, which the entity Edgar Cayce was able to put to good use, namely, "the ability to take cognizance of detail, especially in following instructions as given from other minds or sources of information."[27]

Before moving on, let me pause to relate an anecdote pertaining to Bainbridge's negative impact on Edgar Cayce's life. His son, Hugh Lynn, once remarked to me that his father always regarded his chronic financial problems in the present lifetime as a direct karmic result of his gambling activities as Bainbridge, who was able to use his innate psychic abilities to cheat the other players at the table. Once, in fact, in a dramatic illustration of this point, Edgar responded to Hugh Lynn's insistent demand that he join them in a game of cards by tersely ordering his son to deal out the various hands. Then, going mentally around the table, he called out the cards in every hand but his own. This last, he slapped down, face up, on the table. 'Now you know why I never play cards,' he said, unsmiling, as he pushed back his chair and stalked away from the astounded players.

So numerous were the people who were to learn through their life readings that they had karmic involvement with Edgar Cayce in that second Bainbridge period that I will not attempt to cover them all.

Instead, let us touch upon but a few, choosing those from whose perspective we may hope to gain some larger insights into that downward-gravitating cycle and better understand the workings of both individual and group karma.

First, we encounter another male Bainbridge, who may have been the descendant of one of John's several illegitimate offspring in that incarnation, and cut from the same cloth. We deduce this from the fact that his early peregrinations, as he moved westward, appear to have followed an identical path, although rather than stopping in Illinois, he pushed farther west, eventually "taking up the fighting spirit in the defense of then Fort Dodge,"[28] founded in 1851. It says of his experience that he gained "in the latter days"; in the earlier period, following in John's footloose ways, he lost "in that gratifying of the desires of the flesh without respect to place or person." In seeking karmic ties between the two, we find that this same entity, Mr. [427], had been "the companion [Timothy?] of the teacher [Paul] who came to Rome as the prisoner bound to Caesar," and he was probably acquainted with Lucius in that experience, through their joint spiritual travels.

Meanwhile, back in Cornwall, England, there was yet another old associate of Cayce's, Mrs. [1472], who may have known John Bainbridge in her childhood, or been acquainted with his family, and had heard reports of the promising new life in that land of religious and political liberties—matters of special concern to her. At any rate, in 1750, at the age of twenty-two, she arrived with a rather distinguished group, including the Boyntons (later to be known as the Byrds), and settled in the area of Williamsburg and Jamestown. Known as Clementine, she was active in teaching, ministering, and lecturing, particularly in spiritual affairs, even as she had done as the entity Judy, in the Holy Land, and as a Carpathian princess in the days of Ra. But although her entry into the earth-plane may have been timed to coincide with Bainbridge's to be a constructive force, joining hands with him to serve the common good, this never came about; for Bainbridge had chosen an opposite course, and it is doubtful that their paths ever crossed after Clementine's arrival in Virginia in 1750.

Mae Umbor—currently known as Mrs. [1523]—appears to have been the only one of John Bainbridge's many female companions with whom he managed to maintain a relatively stable relationship. They apparently met at the Dearborn inn where "most of those stayed who were a part of the dance hall activities."[29] (The inn was operated by one Grace Winslow, whose karmic role this time around was to be the mother of Mrs. [1523] as well as a channel for the entering of several other souls involved in that Dearborn experience.)

However, while enjoying a close sexual liaison for some three years before the fatal attack upon the fort in 1754, neither Bainbridge nor his companion, Mae Umbor, were "exclusive" in their love-making. With Mae, it was a matter of necessity: her livelihood depended upon her position as an entertainer, a waitress, and "the activity in the inn there that was known as 'You Know'—*you know!*"[30] In fact, she had been brought there at the age of seventeen by her ne'er-do-well companion (now Mr. [4930]) and was obliged to support a daughter, Azilee, from that union, since her companion spent most of his time gambling and drinking. The inn was frequented by transient frontiersmen, traders, groups of pioneers pushing farther west, and a motley assemblage of local hangers-on. Mae's duty was to induce them to spend their money.

With the sacking and burning of the fort by French troops and hostile Indians, however, Mae and other survivors, under the leadership of Bainbridge, fled to the south and east, with the Tidewater area of Virginia as their ultimate goal. Their escape route, however, was blocked by the raging currents of the Ohio River; it was necessary to attempt a crossing or be killed by their pursuers. Mae Umbor was carried to the opposite bank of the river by Bainbridge, but he himself perished:

The entity was a companion with Bainbridge at the crossing of the Ohio; though the entity succeeded in escaping—through the efforts of Bainbridge, who lost his life there. (1523-11)

Mae was to spend the remainder of her days in "those acitivites of the colonizations about what is now Williamsburg, Jamestown, Norfolk, and Yorktown," but in a reversal of her former loose life-style, she "became rather as one to whom many came for counsel and advice." (It was an interesting parallel with her final years as Vesta, in the Laodicean experience recounted in a previous chapter, when she became a deaconess in the church.) Yet, as the turbulent days of the American Revolution came about, the entity made its exit from the earth-plane at age forty-eight. Here is our closing excerpt from that life reading:

The entity lived then to be only forty-eight—when the disturbing forces by raids from the warring forces cut or brought that experience to a close. (1523–11)

This, plus an earlier reference to the fact that Mae Umbor had initially gone to the so-called Dearborn area at the age of seventeen, aids us greatly in establishing a fairly accurate time frame for Bainbridge's second incarnation, lest any doubts persist in the mind of the reader. If we deduct forty-eight years from 1775 (the probable date of Mae Umbor's demise at the onset of the revolutionary struggle), we arrive at 1727 as her likely year of birth. We have already noted a three-year liaison between Bainbridge and Umbor preceding the 1754 outbreak of the French and Indian War, and although that conflict did not actually terminate until 1763, the raid upon the fort is believed to have occurred in the initial phase of hostilities, taking the occupants totally by surprise. Thus, we may deduce that Bainbridge's liaison with the seductive Umbor began in 1751, or thereabouts. Having already speculated that his 1742 arrival in America probably occurred during his early twenties, when he would have been a freshly trained soldier-recruit, his death from drowning in 1754 places his demise, as given earlier, at thirty-three or -four by the most logical estimate.

A brief word about [1523]'s little daughter in that incarnation, Azilee: she had carried a rather similar name, Euzela, in the Persian experience, where she contributed much to the healing and ministering activities at Is-Shlan-doen.[31] As Azilee, however, her unhappy life was a short one, we are told without further detail.

Another among the many sexual companions of Bainbridge in that turbulent life was Mrs. [369], who had been his first wife in the Ra Ta period. She was one of those who lost her life in the attempted crossing of the Ohio; she lost, too, in a spiritual sense "through holding of malice and of the determination to get even." On this point, her life reading admonished her, "Can't be done!"[32]

Yet another companion, Miss [243], had been an Indian, whose husband, Ouiw, was among those Indians who stormed the fort with the attacking French troops. She fled in company with Bainbridge, losing her life in the jagged ice of the flooding river. Of her relationship with Bainbridge, she was told that the companionship had been "beautiful"—but "not always moral."[33] The karmic links were interesting: she had been a sister of the priest in the Ra Ta period. (Her Indian husband, Ouiw, had been one of those guards at the gates of Troy who lost his life.)

In addition to a trail of broken hearts, Bainbridge apparently left in his wake a number of illegitimate offspring, as well. Two of these—daughters by different companions—had readings from Mr. Cayce, in a clear demonstration of one's karmic ties with the past. One of them was named Mary Bainbridge [259], the other Clara Page Bainbridge [3635], the latter being told that she was "the child of one of the many companions of Bainbridge in what a life!"[34]

From the common perspective, as we close this chapter, the two lives of John Bainbridge might well appear to have been "wasted." Indeed, as already noted, the readings have referred to him as a "wastrel." But there is more to a man than the appearance of things; we see that there was an underlying purpose being served, after all, throughout those incarnations:

As Bainbridge, the entity in the material sojourn was a wastrel, one who considered only self; *having to know the extremes in the own experience as well as of others.* Hence the entity was drawn to that environ. Or, how did the Master put it? 'As the tree falls, so does it lie.' (5755–1, italics added)

Many were the turmoils he created for himself and others along the way, this tragic Bainbridge, throughout both cycles. Yet he had great courage and on occasion could display an innate nobility: in the end, he gave his life to save another.

The entity gained in that.

14. The Love Child

Louis XIV, the Sun King, ruled France like a god. This was not surprising. After all, he was born in an age that fostered a belief in the "divine right" of kings, and Louis was a monarch who enjoyed exercising his prerogatives, divine or otherwise.

Although the king was invariably polite, underneath the *politesse* lay an acute sensitivity to criticism. At the least offense, he was apt to mete out stiff retribution to the hapless offender. Consequently, during his long and powerful reign as Europe's greatest monarch (1643–1715), any grave scandal that might have involved the king personally, or the immediate members of his household, was sure to have been suppressed. Indeed, most court gossip affecting the king was (wisely) confined to carefully guarded whispers behind closed doors, under penalty of excommunication from the court— or worse. It was an effective form of censorship throughout his lifetime, and since Louis outlasted most of his contemporaries, history has had very little of a genuinely wicked nature to record concerning him. One might conclude that this simply confirms the essential virtue of modern history's most famous monarch. And this might be largely true. Louis XIV was a superb statesman, a firm defender of the Catholic faith, and a zealous reformer to the end, despite his succession of mistresses and illegitimate offspring (some of whom were legitimized at his command).

And so, if one had reason to search out dark secrets of his reign, one could not find them in the pages of a history book. One would have to rely, instead, upon rumors extant in the posthumously published writings of such contemporaries as the Marquis de Dangeau (whose diary of the period is considered "the dullest but most reliable") or the Duc de Saint-Simon, whose voluminous memoirs are colored somewhat by his prejudices. Finally, there are the personal papers of numerous other chroniclers of the era, varying in their degree of importance and interest.

In researching these unofficial sources, Nancy Mitford, in her splendid biography of the Sun King, has unearthed what appears to be a royal scandal of truly shocking dimensions. It merits our examination. This is not because I wish to focus on its sensational aspects but because it contains profound implications for a French incarnation of Edgar Cayce, an incarnation as a love child born to a virtually unknown daughter of the Sun King, whose given name was apparently Gracia, in a secret liaison with James, the Duke of York.

The reported scandal, one suspects, may be exaggerated in some of its details, considering the prejudices of the times, as well as the setting. Certain embellishments of the bare facts were probably an aspect of all court rumors. Even so, if only the essential elements of the report are true, it excites us. For it may serve to clarify and corroborate a number of heretofore unauthenticated historical references contained in the life readings given by Edgar Cayce for several individuals who were reportedly direct descendants of the Sun King or actively associated with his court; this included Cayce himself, of course, as the illegitimate offspring of that liaison already mentioned.

Some historical background, though, must precede our revelations. We draw on the official records for this data.

When Marie Thérèse married King Louis XIV in 1660, her rather pretty childlike face and blond tresses bespoke the Hapsburg side of her heritage. But her more immediate bloodlines included Latin roots as well. For she was the eldest daughter of King Philip IV of Spain and Maria of Portugal (who were cousins) and the granddaughter of Isabella of Portugal; somewhere in the genetic background of this royal admixture lay the likelihood of traces of Moorish blood, attributable to the Muslim domination of Spain and Portugal for many centuries. Even after the Spanish conquest of the last Moorish stronghold, at Granada, in 1492, the genetic influence of the Moors (not to mention the cultural) persisted. It is strongly visible even today in the swarthy complexions of many Spaniards,

Portuguese, and southern Italians, whose forebears commingled freely with the dark-skinned conquerors from Arabia, particularly those from the nearby North African bastions across the Mediterranean.

It is doubtful that any French-born member of the haughty Bourbon court of Louis XIV, most notably the king himself, would have been at all receptive to the notion of an olive-skinned heir to the throne. In fact, Saint-Simon gives an account of the tragic suicide of the Comte de la Vauguyon, an impoverished member of the court at Versailles who "had a superb figure, but was very dark and Spanish-looking"; his swarthy appearance seems to have hindered his due recognition by the king or by his fellow courtiers.

Moreover, it is quite conceivable that the king's apparent intolerance in such matters had deep psychological roots: it is generally believed that he had both Jewish and Moorish blood, inherited through the Aragons. As a reaction, he may have felt an unreasonable compulsion to remove from his presence any reminder of a part of his own genetic heritage that he personally disliked and dreaded in the bigoted fasion of his era, with its strong racial and religious prejudices. This would explain, in part, the tragic story that follows. For we find him projecting hs own secret guilt about mixed bloodlines upon others, including his legitimate queen and certain of their offspring, if the scandal as related by Mitford is accurate.

Fortunately, the first offspring of Louis and his Spanish-born queen, though somewhat dark-complexioned, according to Saint-Simon's description of him, was blessed with a luxuriant growth of chestnut-colored hair. The proud father named him Louis, after himself, and the boy became known as the Grand Dauphin, heir apparent to the throne. However, Louis XIV outlived his son by several years, so that the actual successor was the dauphin's little grandson, the Duke of Anjou—a pale-faced child, according to his portrait, with raven black locks. He was only five years old at the time of his succession, having been born in 1710. He became Louis XV, of course.

Let it be noted here, as an aside, that both of these former French rulers followed a karmic path to Edgar Cayce in their twentieth-century return to the flesh. The one who had been the great-grandson of the Sun King was now a realtor; and in a life reading, he learned that he had "lost" during his rulership due to a "mighty manner" and "the gratification of many of selfish desires."[1] As for the former Sun King himself, his only reading was a "physical" one, relating to a temporary ailment. It is a pity he did not seek a life reading instead; for he was told: *"Much* might be given as to latent abilities."[2] (His true identity only came out through a subsequent "check" life reading for Mrs. [1523], a former mistress of the Sun King, who was briefly and unhappily married to him in the present incarnation.)

In addition to the Grand Dauphin, history records five other infants born to Louis XIV and Queen Marie Thérèse (although Saint-Simon names only four—a second son and three daughters), of whom two supposedly died in infancy, while the remaining three are said to have died at a few years of age. *All* were reportedly dead by 1672.

The historical record is contradicted, however, by the Edgar Cayce readings, as already noted. It is *also* contradicted by Miss Mitford's findings, which we shall review further on.

First, the readings: We are told that the entity [288] was the second daughter of King Louis XIV and Queen Marie Thérèse. At seventeen, she had become involved with the exiled Duke of York, who apparently made a commitment of marriage (pending a church-ordained annulment of his existing Catholic marriage, presumably), seduced her, and then abandoned her. Yet a love child, as noted, was born of this blissful but deceptive union.

Here is how we find the matter initially stated (including a couple of psychic gaffes that were subsequently corrected) in one of the life readings for Miss [288]:

At this time, we find this entity's earthly sojourn was in the court of Louis 15th *[sic],* and this one as then shown was in the household, and the second daughter of the king, born in the palace of the then legal wife of the monarch, raised and educated in the monastery or in the school of the monasteries in the courts of the country, yet not in the walls of same.

At the age of seventeen we find the body first makes the acquaintance and meets the Duke of York, son *[sic]* of the monarch [Charles II] then ruling in adjoining country. The seduction of this maiden followed, and with the birth of the son [294] the [French] ruler has the ejection [of the daughter] from the court, as the mother [of 288] had then lost favor with the monarch, and amid these surroundings this brings a great distrust of all men, as has been given. Yet, when the body finds the Duke has been unfaithful, the love does not cease in the heart but all is centered in the offspring of that love, as has been given. (288–5)

In view of the fact that King James II (formerly the Duke of York) died in 1701, a full fourteen years before Louis XV ascended the throne of France, it becomes obvious that the information in this reading contains a discrepancy or has not been properly understood. Moreover, James, the Duke of York, was not the "son" of Charles II, the monarch then ruling in England ("the adjoining country"), but was his younger brother. In a subsequent reading, answers to the following questions cleared up the confusion:

Q–12. *What was my full name in the French period, and whose daughter was I?*

A–12. Louis the 14th. Full name, Agatha Beille. *[Note: Name elsewhere given as "Gracia"; this seeming inconsistency will be explained.]*

Q–13. *Was James, the brother of Charles the 2nd, the one to whom I became betrothed?*

A–13. The Duke of York, James.

Q–14. *Why was this not consummated?*

A–14. Political influences and conditions. (288–27)

Interestingly enough, Louis XIV and the Duke of York were first cousins. When the latter was nineteen, and the Sun King only fourteen, James joined the French army and fought valiantly for his adoptive land in four campaigns. But when France allied itself with Cromwell against Spain in 1655, James very reluctantly moved to the Spanish Netherlands and joined the Spanish army there, before finally returning to England. He was then twenty-three. It was somewhat ironic, perhaps, that Louis XIV, who later made peace with the Spanish throne and married the king's daughter to cement the alliance, did not see his English cousin again until 1679, when James—now forty-six—was once again in exile on the Continent. And it was during this brief period of exile, from March until August of 1679, apparently, that the duke must have met and fallen in love with the Sun King's own daughter by that "marriage of convenience" with the daughter of the Spanish ruler, Philip IV.

At the time, James, whose first wife had died in 1671, was already married—this time to Mary of Modena, a devout Catholic like himself. In fact, it was his secret conversion to Catholicism and his subsequent marriage to a Catholic that had finally roused the ire of Protestant England; his supporters were charged with a "popish plot," and James was forced to flee into temporary exile until his brother, Charles II, could restore Parliament's confidence in his closest successor. In the light of this background, it is doubtful that the Duke of York could ever have entertained any serious intentions toward Agatha Beille, the beautiful young lady whose warm affections he betrayed; yet he may have "half meant" his false promises at the time. That he genuinely loved her, however, seems obvious from the readings, and his sudden departure, in all likelihood, was triggered by "political influences and conditions," as stated. For it is known that Charles II signaled for his brother's surreptitious return to England, and eventually Scotland, in August of 1679. But the honor of the Sun King's daughter had nevertheless been defiled.

Yet a highly curious aspect of the whole affair, as already noted in the preceding excerpt from Reading 288-5, is that Louis XIV cruelly ejected his own daughter from the court (meaning, apparently, the queen's palace or affiliated cloister, inasmuch as there is no evidence that this daughter was ever introduced among the courtiers at the Versailles palace, and in fact, her initial meeting with the Duke of York must have been a chance encounter during one of the latter's courtesy calls upon the queen). The Sun King took this harsh action upon receiving word of the birth of a love child from his daughter's illicit union with his cousin James, although we have already observed that he acted partially out of spite toward the queen, who had fallen out of favor. Yet he appeared to hold no rancor whatever toward his philandering cousin. This was proven some ten years later, when James was once again in trouble at home and forced into exile—this time as King of England, rather than Duke of York. History relates that Louis welcomed him to the court at Saint-Germain with open arms. There he was permitted to remain with his queen and family, including the young Prince of Wales, living a devout and quiet life until his death on the afternoon of September 16, 1701. During this period, the former lover and beloved were never reunited, for Agatha had taken the veil some three years after being forsaken by James, and she died in the convent in 1693, at the age of thirty.

This unsettling chain of events must raise in our minds some probing questions. Yet these will be answered as the narrative proceeds.

In Mitford's biography, the first revelation we encounter concerning the possible fate of the five "missing" infants born to Louis XIV and Marie-Thérèse following the birth of the dauphin in 1661 is this chilling statement, based on extant rumors that cannot be historically confirmed, of course, but that gain some degree of credibility from the fact that an air of total mystery surrounds the death of the children: "The Queen was far from sterile," writes Mitford; "she had six children, but all except the Dauphin were dead by 1672, two as infants and the other three at a few years old. *They were murdered,* not by Madame de Montespan's spells but by the Court doctors"[3] *(italics added).*

In the court of the Sun King, nothing of consequence happened without his personal knowledge or direction. Even the court physicians were under his direct command. Therefore, if any of the king's offspring were murdered, it was undoubtedly at his bidding. Yet Louis XIV was not ostensibly an evil man; such a heinous crime as the murder of his own children, though accomplished at the hands of the court doctors, must have been somehow justifiable in his eyes. The inevitable question, then, is *why?* Were they deformed? mentally retarded? diseased? A full range of possible explanations comes to mind. Certainly these later offspring of the king were not put on display at his court as the infant dauphin frequently was; there had to be some reason for their concealment. (In an allegorical and idealized painting of the royal family by Jean Nocret, dubbed "Apollo's Family," we find in the foreground a winged pair of infants, and adjoining them is a propped-up "painting within a painting," apparently intended to depict two deceased offspring. This totally undependable and flattering rendition—including ten adult figures, plus several older children, of whom only the dauphin is clearly identifiable as Louis's direct offspring by Marie Thérèse—is posterity's only pictorial record of those "lost" children to whom Mitford alludes.)

Somewhat further on in her biography, though, in reporting yet another scandal of a related nature, Miss Mitford provides us with a plausible clue to the whole clandestine affair. Furthermore, this additional rumor suggests that at least one of the five hapless infants—a daughter—was spared an untimely death at the hands of the court physicians. The fact that she was apparently "kept in a convent" bears a close parallel to Cayce's account of Agatha's monastic existence. Here is the revealing quotation from Miss Mitford's intriguing book, *The Sun King*: "According to various contemporaries, the King and Queen had a black daughter who was kept in a convent near Melun. Certainly a little 'Moor' existed there and was regularly visited by the Queen and women of the royal family when the Court was at Fontainebleau. Whether she was really the daughter of Marie Thérèse and Louis XIV will probably never be known."[4]

Whatever truth may underlie this rather shocking story, I think we can almost surely discount the reference to a "black" daughter as hyperbole born of malicious rumors. Among the aristocracy of Europe in those elegantly pretentious times, anything other than a pale of rouged complexion would have been distastefully regarded; we may surmise that an olive-skinned offspring of royalty would have been looked upon with genuine horror by most of those within the sophisticated Bourbon milieu. The king, in all probability, would have been the most horrified of all and would have wanted such a social stigma forever removed from his sight or conscience. Yet the queen, whose Spanish roots had always made her seem alien and provincial to the French nobility, would not have shared the prejudices common to them. The same would have been largely true, in all probability, of those chosen women who surrounded her in her own private court.

Although the given name for the Sun King's daughter is "Agatha Beille" in Reading 288–27, previously cited, an earlier reading[5] refers to "this body, Gracia [288]"; and we find this latter name confirmed in one of Edgar Cayce's life readings on that French incarnation, in which the entity [294], who was the love child born of the union between [288] and the Duke of York, is told that he was "born of Gracia, the beloved of the court, and of the ruler's son [sic] of the territory just across the waters."[6] Presumably the "court" in reference here was the private court of the queen, the intimate circle where Gracia was familiar and cherished.

We are told that this entity, Gracia, "was of beautiful figure and loving in every manner."[7] No further description of her appearance is given; but if it is fair to speculate, she probably had the dark, lovely eyes and hair and olive complexion that are the hallmark of the Mediterranean peoples. And if so, it is easy to see why James, who did not share the narrow prejudices of the Bourbon court in such matters, was smitten by her wholly natural and innocent charms.

As for the two names given in the readings for the entity [288] as the Sun King's daughter, we need not be confused. It would appear that she was christened "Gracia," in view of the Latin connotations of that name, while "Agatha Beille" would have been a name assumed later on to disguise her identity as the king's daughter.

Meanwhile, in the limited roster of names provided by Saint-Simon, who has identified only four out of the five infants reportedly born to Louis XIV and his queen following the dauphin's birth in 1661, we find three daughters, identified as Anne-Elisabeth (b. 1662), Marie-Anne (b. 1664), and Marie-Thérèse (b. 1667). A brother, Philippe, born 1668, is also listed. But there is no "Gracia," and certainly no "Agatha"! However, we can gain some assistance in our search. Reading 288–5 should help us to establish just where this "missing" daughter probably fits into the lineup of the five children, for that reading sets her age at seventeen when she met the Duke of York—a meeting that we have already ascertained must have taken place between March and August of 1679. This means that Gracia (alias Agatha) was apparently born in the latter part of 1662 or the first part of 1663. However, 1663 is the more likely date, inasmuch as she is referred to as "the second daughter of the King"—and Anne-Elisabeth, born sometime in 1662, had to be the first; for the initial offspring was the dauphin, born the previous year, in 1661. But was this "second daughter" the only child, after the dauphin, to escape elimination at the hands of the court doctors? Apparently not; for, according to Reading 288–5, a friend of the entity [288] in her present lifetime had been "that one close in the household and a sister in the flesh then." So it would seem that at least one other daughter survived, if only for a relatively limited span of years.

At this point, we must pay close heed to the given dates.

Those daughters born in the early years of the Sun King's marriage to Marie Thérèse had a much better chance of survival than those born after the king's liaison with Louise de La Vallière became "official," with the passing of his mother, Queen Anne, in 1666. The queen mother was a close ally always of Marie Thérèse, frequently taking her side in disputes with her son, the king. Thus, if Louis might have had it in mind to dispatch any olive-hued heirs by Marie Thérèse, such a plan would probably have been adamantly vetoed by Anne, in compassionate support of her poor, aggrieved daughter-in-law (as well as in defense of her own natural instincts in the matter). For, however he overrode others, the Sun King always had an inordinate respect for his mother's wishes. This fact might account for the first two daughters having been sent off to a convent instead of being placed at the mercy of the court doctors. The third daughter, Marie-Anne, born in 1664, may also have survived, but the readings do not make any reference to yet another "sister in the flesh" being with Agatha Beille in the days of her childhood or at the convent or monastery school where she was raised. Perhaps, like the last two children of that ill-starred marriage, she was less fortunate? It is doubtful, in any case, that Louis XIV felt any strong paternal affection toward any of his legitimate offspring after his first, the Grand Dauphin. His fickle ways were already off to a secret start before his wife's second pregnancy.

We come, now, to the concluding portion of our story. It concerns a mother-and-son relationship, tragically brief in its life span, yet infinite in the scope of its tenderness and love. Its meanings are universal.

In a special reading on her past associations with [294] (Edgar Cayce), the entity [288] was told that they had had "many experiences together, and their soul and spirit are well knit."[8] As revealed in earlier chapters, it was noted that they had been as one in the beginning, entering in at least two androgynous projections; in Egypt, during the Ra Ta period, they had been father and daughter and in Persia, lifelong mates, as was presumably repeated during the Pythagorean cycle and perhaps in other cycles not given. Now, in France, the relationship was as mother and son:

In the courts again [France], when they were mother and son, the greater portions of the body beautiful [in the female] became the system of one and the life of the other. (288-6)

Is it any wonder, then, that Edgar Cayce, in that abortive and seemingly purposeless incarnation in which his life was cut short through a king's cruel orders, was nevertheless considered fortunate to have had the experience of being "a child of love"?

He had entered the earth-plane from the forces of Venus:

We find that the activity of the same entity [Edgar Cayce] in the earthly experience before that, in a French sojourn, followed the entrance into Venus.

What was the life there? How the application?

A child of love! A child of love—the most hopeful of all experiences of any that may come into a material existence; and to some in the earth that most dreaded, that most feared! (5755-1)

The boy was given the name of Ralph Dahl (or Dale, in an alternate spelling), presumably as a cover-up of his true identity as son of the Duke of York and grandson of Louis XIV. His illegitimacy and the French rule of direct male succession to the throne were mere legal limitations that any Machiavellian schemer could overturn, so the lad's royal parentage made him a potential threat to the thrones of both England and France—a fact of which the Sun King, who had more than once changed a law to his own advantage, would have been most acutely aware. For three happy but uneasy years, the mother protected and cared for her child, but at the age of twenty, she entered a convent—apparently under some duress—and turned the child's care and safekeeping over to those she felt were her most trusted friends in the household of the king:

> With the ejection from the courts the girl, [288], becomes then a sister in one of the near convents, and enters there at the age of twenty, having had three years of the mother love for the boy, Dale. In this meeting at the last we find much affection shown, and the promises of those of the monarch's household. We find the monarch had given in to a great deal of the distrust to exercising of the vengeance as wreaked on the mother of the mother [288] of the offspring [294]. Hence it [the child] is left in the care of those whom this body [288] felt were the closest friends in the household of the king when she takes the veil. (288–5)

At least two of those into whose care the child was entrusted, apparently, were Mrs. [1523] and Mr. [4121]. The former, in her life reading touching upon that period, learned that she had been a mistress of Louis XIV—probably Louise de La Vallière, from various indications, although her origins appeared to have been under a different name—who had taken up convent life in 1674, after a final break with the king, ironically, because of his infidelity. It was at the same convent, presumably, that she met the Sun King's daughter when the latter entered as a novitiate; and [1523] then began caring for the child, toward whom she felt an innate affection (quite naturally, considering their prior-life relationships).[9] As for [4121], who had been in the Trojan experience with Cayce, he now was to serve as a guard, later losing his life in defense of the hapless youngster.[10]

It was but two years later, at the age of five, that the child met his death, apparently murdered on orders from the king:

> In the sojourn here [in the convent] we find soon after this body [288] has entered this home, from which she cannot return under three years, that with the return to see the offspring [294], and when first being told of his death, without knowing the cause thereof, there is brought the great dread and the inability of any to satisfy that desire of the heart and life, or to fill the longing for that one who has become dearer than life itself to this body, Gracia [288]. Then we find the body gradually gives way to the physical defects and goes to the resting place at the age of thirty. (288–5)

All told, it is a tale of tragic dimensions for both mother and child, but particularly grievous for the heartbroken mother.

We now glimpse it from the child's perspective, as drawn from two separate life readings of Edgar Cayce's. In the first, 294–8, we are told that the child was placed in the care of certain elements of the royal guard after the separation from its mother, specifically that attendant, [4121], who "lost the elements of life" in its defense of the one placed in its care. Cayce was told that his life "was of short duration" in that experience, but that from that particular sojourn he had gained a strong sense of the "defense of those principles that to the entity's inmost soul or force is the right." The name is given as Ralph Dahl. In the next reading, 294–9, we learn of "the change necessary in court proceedings" that apparently "prevented the culmination" of James's "recognizing the earthly fatherhood of Dahl [Dale]." (So apparently the Duke of York was not altogether without honor, since he seems to have tried to legitimize his son born out of wedlock.) But, finally, the reading continues with an imputation of murder at the command of King Louis XIV, following a heart-wrenching description of the lad's separation from his mother:

> The life that was lived in this court we find the first years in the heart and affection of the mother, who was of beautiful figure and loving in every manner. The great trials came to the entity (speaking from earth's

plane view) when the separation was effected between mother and son, when there was the great yearning in the days when the young life was gradually taken out on account of the jealousy arising in the court. *For the king became fully aware of the lad's appearance,* and the possibility of it becoming the ruler forces others to play the traitor to the mother, who loved the entity so well. (294-9, italics added)

In that final sentence, it would seem that we have struck upon the underlying motivation for the boy's murder—and the probable murder, years earlier, of several of the king's own children, as reported by Mitford. For there was something in the lad's "appearance," which must have been concealed initially from the king's attention, that in light of "the possibility of it becoming the ruler" somehow forced the hand of somebody close to the child— possibly the entity [1523]?—to divulge the secret to jealous elements in the court, so that the king learned about it.

What could the secret have been? It does not seem too presumptuous on our part, in light of the revelations reported earlier, to speculate that the boy was "too Spanish-looking"! That is to say, like the king's own children before him, he had inherited the olive complexion and other quasi-Moorish Mediterranean features that were so offensive to the king and, presumably, most of the Bourbon court. Thus, he had to go.

It is a depressing story.

But wait. One wonders if it may not contain an important lesson if we analyze it closely. For it is a story told in dark, karmic brush strokes, suggesting that the entity [294] may conceivably have been meeting self in that harsh experience. Indeed, from what we have already seen of his former lives, how could we conclude otherwise? And it is an established dictum of the readings that *every* entity is ever meeting self throughout its experiences in the earth-plane.

His murder quite aside, there is another, subtler aspect of Cayce's French incarnation to be considered. It relates to his life in ancient Egypt, where the entity as Ra had accomplished much in cleansing the early human form, eliminating those animalistic elements that hindered, and establishing certain standards of perfection for the new root race. The priest himself, it will be remembered, embodied that example of "the first *pure* white in the experience then of the earth."[11] Yet the readings suggest that Ra, in his overeagerness to regenerate the human form and hasten the numbers of those acquiring the pure white pigmentation similar to his own, was apparently misinterpreting the laws of spiritual evolution:

For, the Priest had not interpreted in himself that even that being attempted was a matter of spiritual evolution. Thus, as many an individual, the Priest had attempted to hurry the process, or to placate God's purposes with individuals. (2390–7)

For there was the attempt to placate the law of evolution. While those activities brought within themselves conditions that greatly improved the situations, they left in the mental self the applying of spiritual law to attain material desires—without the mental concepts being in accord. (2823–3)

For, few of those had arisen to that state in which there were the preparations so as to produce the alabaster or all white. (2329–3)

Finally, we come to these specific comments from one of Cayce's own life readings, which are very much to the point:

As to race, color or sex—this depends upon that experience necessary for the completion, for the building up of the purposes for which each and every soul manifests in the material experience. (294–189)

And the same reading adds: "For if there has been the error in that phase, in that expression, the error must be met. For indeed . . . whatsoever ye sow, so shall ye reap."

May we not conclude, then, if our speculations concerning the matter have been correct, that Cayce's French incarnation under disturbing genetic forces presented him with an opportunity to meet in self that which he had sown as the high priest Ra? The fact that his dark pigmentation was apparently "unacceptable" to the one in power reveals, I think, the karmic nature of his fate.

Yet, how does this account for his childhood separation from his mother or his premature death at the command of the king? Here, too, we can see the karmic wheel in motion if we go back to that same Egyptian cycle. Just as Ra Ta's illicit union with Isris had led to his banishment and enforced separation from his infant daughter, who was left as a hostage in the hands of the king and died in desolation, now he himself was the desolate child, unwanted and destined to meet an early death.

Ah, the karmic webs we weave are sometimes intricate indeed! And those who hope to escape one jot or tittle of the law are only deceiving themselves.

At the same time, the law of grace is ever accessible to us, we are told. And it must have been that law at work that brought Edgar's twin soul, [288], into the picture in that incarnation as his self-sacrificing mother. As his other self, she apparently chose in advance to enter into that role, taking upon herself a seeming "stigma" in the flesh that would later be transmitted to her little love child, Ralph Dahl. It was an act of supreme self-sacrifice on her part, as well as an act of great love. And in that latter sense, both entities surely gained.

How clearly, then, being the offspring of such unselfish love must indeed represent "the most hopeful of all experiences," regardless of its brevity. Yet, to some, "that most dreaded, that most feared," we are told. Why so? Presumably because of the inherent responsibility to fulfill whatever promise is embodied in such a unique opportunity—even to the meeting of self.

Yet in the deprivation of mother love and the early loss of life in that incarnation, one can perhaps more readily understand the entity's subsequent urge to rub out the past and enter the flesh again as the hedonistic Bainbridge.

Alas, poor Bainbridge! He came, that second time around, even as in the first, as one who was unwilling to give of self, hoping thereby to fill his unsatisfied longings for life and love without paying a price. Yet the price he was required to pay was the loss of everything dear to his soul-self.

And that was the needed lesson he learned from that experience.

15. A Civil War Vignette

"Next I came into the earth as a man, still in America, at the time of the Civil War."[1]

So begins the final segment of Edgar Cayce's long allegorical dream of September 19, 1933, in which actual incarnations in the flesh were interspersed with purely emblematic representations in creaturely form. After several flashbacks too fleeting to fix upon, there had been his vivid recall (while in the flesh as Xenon) of Hector's horrible death at the hand of Achilles and, subsequently, a life in the days of Columbus, apparently among the Arawak Indians inhabiting Hispaniola and neighboring islands in the West Indies (the subject of a previous chapter). Now, in this final portion of the dream, there appears to be a sudden drawing together of all of the allegorical depictions in creaturely form—snails, fishes, cows, cats, dogs, and sheep and such—to suggest the broad range of character development or expression a soul-entity may undergo within the "one force, or one source, from which all manifested forms may take their activity." In the varied cycles, there is that ever-growing association with a great diversity of souls, whose kindred thoughts in the individual expressions now lead them to seek each other out anew for further development and understanding. (Underlying the symbolism, there was an obvious parallel with the dreamer's real-life experience as Edgar Cayce, in which the entity attracted to himself an incredible variety of fellow souls with whom he had been previously associated in the flesh, for weal or woe, down through the ages.)

Here, then, viewed without reference to the allegorical trappings of creaturely symbolism (which were already given a detailed explanation in Chapter 12, "Among the Arawaks"), is the conclusion of Mr. Cayce's enigmatic dream; these brief lines provide us with all that's available concerning an apparent incarnation during the dark and bloody days of the War Between the States (1861–1865):

> I knew there was a war going on between the north and south country, and that I was in or about the place where I was born in the present. I noticed the home where I was born this time, and the changes—there were more woods then. . . . I started off to see one of the armies where many soldiers were gathered, to find someone I had known before in the various manifestations. . . . I met some of all these, . . . and I recognized them as being individuals whom I know today. Here I awoke. (294–161)

Despite the paucity of detail, one or two interesting clues have been provided. First, the fact that the entity recognizes the home in Christian County, Kentucky, outside of Hopkinsville, were he was later to be born as Edgar Cayce, suggests the obvious likelihood that he was even then a member of the Cayce clan, if not of the same immediate household. (The number of Cayces in Christian County, Kentucky, this writer has been told, is legion.) Also, one gets the feeling, from the wording of that dream-experience, that this is a very young man—perhaps still a teenager—who is excited by a gathering of troops nearby and goes to investigate.

At this point, we can even hazard a guess that the year was 1862 and the month October. This is because the only major encounter of the war on Kentucky soil occurred in that month and year, when General Bragg with his Confederate Army of Tennessee engaged the Union forces under General Buell at Perryville in an attempt to wrest Kentucky from the Union. He won a tactical victory at that site in central Kentucky, but then withdrew. (Though Kentucky was known as a slave state, it had carefully weighed the alternatives and sided with the Union.)

What happened to the young man? Did he decide to join the fray, and did he therein lose his life? In any event, since he was to be born again as Edgar Cayce in 1877, he had to have departed the earth-plane sometime between 1862 and that date.

Whatever his fate was, we bid him a gentle adieu. To die young is always sad—from our mortal perspective.

At this writing, we have no record of those Cayce men who may have lost their lives in the American Civil War. Agewise, it could have been one of Edgar's uncles.

In an interesting digression, however, we find that the entity [2390], who was born in Georgia on August 24, 1910, had been an older sister of Edgar's, named Leila, who had died some seven months prior to his birth. In one of her life readings, it stated that "the entity's departure and entrance in the present covered an earthly cycle, according to that accounted by those of Holy Writ. The entity departed on the 24th of August 1876. It entered again the 24th of August 1910. Thus a cycle."[2]

Although the entry into the earth-plane as Leila Cayce had been prompted by "the greater hope and desire of the mother," said her reading, "the activity upon the part of the earthly parent, the father, brought that disappointment" which led to the entity's "decision *not* to live."

Kentucky is still famous, even as then, for its bluegrass, its horses, and its bourbon. An excessive intake of the latter, it seems, was the offending act on the part of the male parent, which caused [2390] to seek a premature exit from the flesh that time around; yet she was forced to meet a similar situation in her next entry—so perhaps she should have stuck it out!

We trust, though, that it was not an excess of bourbon that caused the youthful demise of [294] in that earlier Kentucky incarnation. My own great-great-grandfather, Lazarus Powell, a governor and later a senator of Kentucky in that era, once chided his fellow Kentuckians for their laggard agricultural efforts with these words: "There is too much corn in the colonels, and not enough kernels in the corn!"

16. The First Return of Edgar Cayce

My rendezvous is appointed, it is certain;
The Lord will be there and wait till I come . . .

—WALT WHITMAN

The Year of Our Lord 1998, if the Edgar Cayce readings are to be relied upon in the matter, is to be a highly significant one.

First, we are told that it is to be the year of that long-awaited religious event, the Second Coming, or "the entrance of the Messiah in this period—1998."[1] (In this respect, Edgar Cayce's twentieth-century role was once described as that of a forerunner,[2] or one who aided in preparing the way; the readings indicated that another will follow him as the event draws closer, and "his name shall be John"—John Peniel. A reincarnation of John the Beloved, he will come, not as a forerunner, which was Cayce's role, but as a messenger,[3] proclaiming the Messiah's imminent arrival.) As to the nature of that arrival, one of the readings states: "He will come in the flesh, in the earth, to call His own by name."[4] Yet it will apparently be in a resurrected body that is free from death or birth or any of the customary mortal limitations: "For He shall come as ye have seen Him go, in the body He occupied in Galilee. The body that He formed, that was crucified on the cross, that appeared to Philip, that appeared to John."[5]

The mystical nature and purpose of the Second Coming are dealt with more fully in the following excerpt, in which Cayce confirms the biblical prophecy of a millennium of peace under the spiritual rulership of the Christ:

He will not tarry, for having overcome He shall appear even as the Lord and Master. Not as one born, but as one that returneth to His own, for He will walk and talk with men of every clime, and those that are faithful and just in their reckoning shall be caught up with Him to rule and to do *judgment* for a thousand years! (364–7)

But if 1998 is to be the year of the Messiah's return, the Cayce readings indicate that it will also be a time of great strife and turmoil, marked simultaneously by the purging and regeneration of mankind and by the swift culmination of a series of catastrophic earth changes. This coincidence of events, the readings suggest, is a natural consequence of the overlapping influence of the closing Piscean era and the opening of the Aquarian Age, which "we will begin to understand fully in '98."[6]

The trumpet of prophecy will undoubtedly sound anew as the awestruck children of men witness the millennium being ushered in, whether or not they are ready for it. It will signal the dayspring of a bright New Order taking hold and the arrival of a new root race. Some, however, will not yet have their eyes fully open. They will be among the long-oppressed and downtrodden of the planet or those still caught in the net of their own iniquities. To awaken them to the releasing power of the Christ activity, which is a universal force that lies as a seed within all of us, if Cayce was right, they will require a "liberator" who can unseal their blocked vision. Such a role, say the readings, will be filled by that soul-entity we know today as Edgar Cayce, who will be reborn into the earth-plane in that year of momentous events, 1998, apparently accompanied by many helpers who served with him initially in the Egyptian cycle, where they received "the mark":

> Is it not fitting, then, that these [a reference to the former priest, Ra, and his band of exiled followers in the Egyptian cycle] must return? as this priest may develop himself to be in that position, to be in that capacity of a *liberator* of the world in its relationships to individuals in those periods to come; for he must enter again at that period, or in 1998. (294–151)

That psychic reading, in which Edgar Cayce prophesied his own return to earth in 1998 as a "liberator," was followed some five years later by one of the most mind-boggling dreams imaginable. In his dream he "saw" himself back at Virginia Beach in what was apparently a New Age continuation of his present psychic role, surrounded by many of those who had been with him in the furtherance of the work at that earlier time. One may readily conclude that an A.R.E.-sponsored archaeological mission, headed by Mr. [378] and his two fellow initiates, as related in an earlier chapter, had succeeded in gaining entrance to the concealed Pyramid of Records, bringing back with them certain precious artifacts —most notably, a sealed sacrcophagus containing the mummified remains of one of those buried there under the direction of Ra and Hermes some 12,500 years earlier, as well as a great stack of clay tablets containing undecipherable hieroglyphics.

The dream, although a fairly long one, deserves to be presented here in its entirety:

[Background: Dream narrated by Edgar Cayce on awaking from night's sleep at the home of David and Lucille Kahn, in New York, early on Thursday morning, December 2, 1937.]

I was at home in Virginia Beach, but there had been a *strong room* built to the side and in the rear of the front of the house. In it there were great stacks of tablets, about 11″ × 14″, about an inch thick—clay tablets, all written in hieroglyphics. I especially noted that they were numbered from one to three in what appeared to be Roman characters but the rest were something different. There was also a mummy. All of these [artifacts] had been allowed to be brought back here by an expedition that had been sent out by our Association. I remained with these findings and could hardly be persuaded to go away even to eat or do anything else but study them.

The members of the Board of the Association were arriving at the Beach. I saw Mr. Harrison with several men, most of them scientists or archaeologists; Mr. Parker with several; Mr. Johnston had only two but they were very dark men and seemed to be in oriental costume. When Lucille and Dave came with the others, Lucille had two East Indians with her; one was very smooth-faced, inclined to be rather fleshy, very smiling and very pleasant, but wore a turban which was white and gold; and the other was a very thin, very old man, with a long white beard, inclined to be stooped, and rather tall—his turban was black and gold, with seemingly moon stars or star and crescent, but a very flat turban. Mr. Goetz had a lot of them but all seemed to be executives of some large group. Miss

Wynne was very busy with a whole lot of people and was keeping them away from me. Alf Butler seemed to be acting as a guard, as was Mr. Poole. Florence and Edith Edmonds were dressed in very old costumes but were sitting in the room where I was, but seemed to be very quiet—just meditating. These people who had come to try to interpret were only let in one at a time, and were allowed to remain five days—with one. Many houses were built on all the land close by, little places for people to live in—and people were coming by the thousands. Then Mr. and Mrs. Zentgraf and Margaret and Lillian came. Apparently it was Mr. Zentgraf who had headed the expedition to look for these tablets. It was through Mr. Harrison and Mr. Goetz and their associates that he had been allowed to bring them back to this country. It was decided that they would allow Mr. Zentgraf to lecture or tell the story of how the tablets and the body (mummy) were found. So a very large building was put up, similar to the one Mr. Whitehead has at the Beach but a good deal larger—on the point right above our house. Dave Kahn and Edgar Evans had charge of the doors letting people in, and they decided they would charge them to come to the lecture. I seemed to recognize these things going on about me but still remained with the tablets and the mummy. On one side to the east was a table on which the tablets were piled. It was a stack at least five feet high. The mummy in a very beautiful casket or sarcophagus was on the west side but facing the door, but was set up on a stand like a coffin. Mr. Zentgraf started and the crowds were going in to the lecture. That's where I woke up.

Then I commenced [dreaming] again. It seems there had been a reading to try to interpret the first tablet, that seemed to be the key that no one had been able to interpret. And there were such crowds they had been insistent that Hugh Lynn tell the crowd what had been said. I was alone in this place with the tablets and the figure, when I realized the figure was beginning to come to life. The figure had been dark and apparently painted over; this began to crack off like a shell, and I saw the upper left side of the face and left eye break first, and it was perfectly white—very dark hair, and very blue eyes. Gradually then I began to see—as I took the top off—that the paint was cracking off all over. I wondered how it could possibly come to life, as I thought within myself that all of the organs had been removed when it was embalmed. But it was very apparent that they had not been. It gradually kept moving and moving, until there was something like a convulsion; and the figure sat up. It spoke but I couldn't understand the language. Apparently, then, from just under its arms to the knees, as it climbed out of the box, it was wrapped in very fine linen—and I understood from its motions that it wanted water; and I gave it a sip of water. Then it made a motion that I was to throw a quantity of water upon it. I drew a bucket of water and dashed it over the whole body; and it became clear, clean-looking—and began to make motions and signs to me until I could understand what it was saying, or interpret the language, or [it was able] to speak in a language I could understand. It asked for food, and it told me, "I must have ground figs, dates, with corn meal, cooked in it with milk," which I prepared and gave him—a little bit at the time. I knew that Hugh Lynn was talking over in the large building, and I told this person (didn't know whether it was male or female) he must remain there and I would get someone else. I went out and closed the door, and walked over to the building—which was not far away. There appeared to be at least twelve or fourteen hundred people in the building, and Hugh Lynn was talking. Everybody seemed to be amazed when I walked in, and Hugh Lynn was telling of what was in the reading —which had said we would only get the interpretation by the figure coming to life, which everybody knew was impossible as it had been dead at least fourteen [sic] thousand years. And I held up my *left* hand, didn't approach the platform very close, and called Hugh Lynn to come at once, that the figure was alive. *Hundreds* of the people in the building fainted, others fell back away from me as Hugh Lynn came down and joined me. And we walked over to the place. That's where I woke up.

[12/2/37—During A.M. Reading 1434-2, a life reading, the dream continued.]

I had remained it seemed for days and days in the strong room, with no one except this person—whom now I knew to be a woman. There were cries and demands, and they outside were apparently unable to keep the throngs back—there were literally *thousands* of people; newspaper people, cameramen, people from all over the world had come to get a glimpse, even, of the person who had come to life after being dead so long. Finally Gertrude came to the door and insisted on speaking to me, saying that it was out of the question for me to stay in a room alone with a woman—or someone she didn't know as to whether she was a man or woman, and it wasn't right. And when I told her it was a woman, she was all the more determined I was not to stay there alone—for I now had been there for *weeks*. And I didn't even go out to eat or anything; ate only this ground figs, ground dates, and corn meal cooked together with milk—which apparently was some other kind than cow's milk; neither did I know from where the supply came. And when I told Gertrude that she (the person) was translating the tablet[s], and I was writing it on a typewriter, she insisted that I should let Miss Gladys come and do the writing; and I said she couldn't interpret the tablets if there was anyone else there but me, that she had assured me she was the favorite daughter of Ra Ta [2329?] and that I *was* Ra Ta. We had about five of the tablets translated, which were giving a history of the period, and she insisted she must see every person first who had been in the Egyptian period as the life reading had given—and then we would talk to picture people and the newspaper people.

[12/5/37, P.M.—During check physical reading 275–44, Edgar Cayce had continuation of dream.]

I was with this "risen" lady, or one that had come to life, in this strong room, reading the tablets; and we had come to where she had said, "I want all of those who feel they were in Egypt, from what you have given, and we will see how well the actual record here tallies with their interpretation from what you gave." Outside there were more and more throngs of people, and as they kept insisting upon entrance, Hugh Lynn, Miss Gladys and Gertrude, Mr. Poole and Alf, were having a harder time keeping the people back; and they even had policemen. And as she saw the policemen pass she asked if some of them weren't old Egyptians. Dave and Edgar Evans were making arrangements with reporters and newspaper people for interviews and making contracts for the moving picture people, some very high figures, and were very insistent—to all of those that were standing guard, as it were, at the door—that we must begin to give interviews and pictures. This girl or figure couldn't understand why she was unusual. They began to clamor from the outside that they had not even examined the casket or sarcophagus, and were questioning Hugh Lynn and Edith and Florence especially.

That's where I woke up. (294–189)

Before examining certain aspects of this strange, prophetic dream, here is a fascinating excerpt from Reading 2329–3, dated May 1, 1941—some three-and-a-half years later—which was a "check" life reading on [2329]'s Egyptian incarnation as Aris-Hobeth, Ra Ta's favorite daughter:

It was this entity, this body, that was visioned in this present experience by that entity who was the Priest, as being that channel through which much of the tenets of that particular period might be made known to people in the present [i.e., in the time frame envisioned in Cayce's dream]. (294-189)

In giving a quite literal interpretation to Mr. Cayce's highly unusual dream, we are obliged to make some logical assumptions.

The scene is Virginia Beach, and various references—particularly as they relate to the social structure of the times, such as the presence of policemen, cameramen, newspaper reporters, and motion-picture representatives—clearly suggest a period in the future not too far removed from the present. In fact, we might reasonably speculate that the scene takes place in the early part of the next century, within the cycle of Edgar Cayce's 1998 return, as this present century draws to its close.

We find, in this dream, that the association founded by Edgar in 1931 is still very much alive. Moreover, the original cast of characters appears to have reincarnated in the central roles they formerly occupied. But while it is quite conceivable that Edgar Cayce will have reincarnated under the same familial name and again head up the organization he had founded, even giving psychic readings again as he did in his life as Edgar Cayce, the names and specific relationships of the various "members of the cast" would undoubtedly have altered considerably. Yet this is not to say that "Miss Gladys" would not have re-entered, though under a different identity, as Edgar's secretary once more, or Gertrude (with another name than formerly) as his wife. In short, Edgar's dream identification of these various people gave them their existing names in the present, not the names by which they will be known in that future period covered by the dream—a time during the first half of the twenty-first century, well over the cusp of the incoming Aquarian Age.

The dream's reference to the mummified figure as having been dead "at least fourteen thousand years" is, we may logically assume, another of those curious psychic gaffes with respect to ancient dates that we have found to be a not uncommon occurrence (although here we are dealing with a dream, of course, and not a reading). As of A.D. 2130 or so, the mummified figure of Aris-Hobeth would have lain in its tomb for twelve and a half millennia.

Probably the most "suspect" feature of the dream, from a strictly scientific perspective, is the return to life of a body that had been interred under some mode of special preservation about 12,-500 years earlier, in the days of Ra and Hermes. But if we will recall that Hermes was an incarnation of the Master—that same Great Initiate who reappeared as Jesus, and called Lazarus forth from his tomb—much of our natural skepticism is laid to rest. By what spiritual alchemy the Master of masters, probably officiating at the burial process for Aris-Hobeth with Ra, was able to preserve the physical form of the deceased so that it might be resuscitated in a far-distant age coincidental with His own Second Coming as the resurrected Christ, we shall never know, of course. But can we label such a seeming miracle as "impossible"?

Most intriguing, perhaps, is that the soul-entity known as both Aris-Hobeth and Mrs. [2329] had been able to continue its soul development down through the ages, reincarnating again and again, and only resuming its former identity as the long-comatose Aris-Hobeth in time for its twenty-first-century role!

A remarkable dream. Some of those in the earth-plane today, among the younger generation, may still be around in half a century or so to see whether or not it was truly prophetic of things to come—others of us, if destiny permits, may reincarnate in time to be New Age witnesses of either a "nonevent" or one of the most spectacular chapters in human history.

17. The Second Return of Edgar Cayce

This concluding chapter of our story of the lives of Edgar Cayce is singularly brief. It relates to a dream he experienced on March 3, 1936:

I had been born again in 2100 A.D. in Nebraska. The sea apparently covered all of the western part of the country, as the city where I lived was on the coast. The family name was a strange one. At an early age as a child I declared myself to be Edgar Cayce who had lived 200 years before.

Scientists, men with long beards, little hair, and thick glasses, were called in to observe me. They decided to visit the places where I said I had been born, lived, and worked, in Kentucky, Alabama, New York, Michigan, and Virginia. Taking me with them, the group of scientists visited these places in a long, cigar-shaped, metal flying ship which moved at high speed.

Water covered part of Alabama. Norfolk, Virginia, had become an immense seaport. New York had been destroyed either by war or an earthquake and was being rebuilt. Industries were scattered over the countryside. Most of the houses were of glass.

Many records of my work as Edgar Cayce were discovered and collected. The group returned to Nebraska, taking the records with them to study.

In an interpretation of the dream, Cayce was told, in part:

That the periods from the material angle as visioned are to come to pass matters not to the soul, but do thy duty *today! Tomorrow* will take care for itself.

These changes in the earth will come to pass, for the time and times and half times are at an end, and there begin those periods for the readjust-

ments. For how hath He given? "The righteous shall inherit the earth."
(294–185)

And so, on a note of inevitable wonderment at what may still lie
ahead, we must bring to a close this unfinished record of the journey of a soul. Yet there can be no doubt in our minds, really, that
the soul in question will find its way back to its Maker. The event
is certain, and the compass is set to a homeward course. The soul
will keep its appointed rendezvous.

Notes

CHAPTER 2

1. Page 299, *The Secret Life of Plants*, by Peter Tompkins and Christopher Bird (Harper & Row: New York, 1973).
2. Ibid.
3. Page 9, *Cayce, Karma, and Reincarnation*, by I. C. Sharma (Harper & Row: New York, 1975).
4. Supplement, Edgar Cayce Reading 507-1.
5. Ibid.
6. Pages 21–22, *What I Believe*, by Edgar Cayce (A.R.E. Press: Virginia Beach, Va., 1946).
7. Reading 254-2, Q&A-1.
8. Reading 254-67, Q&A-4.
9. Reading 254-67.
10. Ref. article, "The Life Readings: A Look at Some Puzzling Cases," by Hugh Lynn Cayce with W. H. Church, The *A.R.E. Journal*, vol. XIV, no. 3 (May 1979).
11. Page 69, *Twelve World Teachers: A Summary of Their Lives and Teachings,* by Manly Palmer Hall (Philosophical Research Society: Los Angeles, 1947).
12. Supplement, Reading 507-1.
13. Ref. article, "The Case of the Wrong Richelieu," by W. H. Church, The *A.R.E. Journal*, vol. XVI, no. 5 (Sept. 1981).

CHAPTER 3

1. Reading 5748-2 set an apparently flawed date of ten-and-a-half million years before the present in pinpointing an ancient conclave, but this date underwent a drastic correction in a later reading (262-39). (See Chapter 4 for details.)

CHAPTER 4

1. *Dictionary of All Scriptures and Myths*, by G. A. Gaskell (The Julian Press: New York, 1969).
2. *The Witness of the Stars*, by E. W. Bullinger (Kregel Publications: Grand Rapids, Mich., 1981, repro. of 1893 ed).
3. *The Forgotten Books of Eden*, chap. 67, "The Secrets of Enoch" (Alpha House: New York, 1927).

CHAPTER 5

1. Reading 294-151 refers to "Ra Ta's coming in the experience from the gods in the Caspian and the Caucasian mountains," and 294-147 says he was "the son of a daughter of Zu that was *not* begotten of man."

2. Ref. 294–147.
3. An approximation, in the absence of a given date for Ra Ta's birth. It coincides, however, with other dates and facts given in the readings covering the Ra Ta era, such as the information that the priest was over one hundred years old when his rejuvenation commenced, approximately a decade before construction on the Great Pyramid began in 10,490 B.C.
4. Reading 3976–26.
5. Reading 900–277.
6. Readings 281–43, 281–44.
7. Reading 900–277.
8. Reading 136–1
9. Reading 1734–3.
10. See GDT note, Reading 900–6, suggesting a possible correlation with Uranus.
11. Reading 900–275.
12. Reading 900–275 gives a nebulous dating for the invasion battle—"ten thousand and fifty-six years before the Prince of Peace"—which GDT interpreted to mean, possibly, 10,506 B.C., knowing that it had to be an earlier date than 10,056 B.C., which would have postdated the Great Pyramid's construction (10,490–10,390 B.C.), years after the invasion occurred. However, it is my interpretation of Cayce's rather nebulous phrasing that he may have meant 10,-560 B.C., which would coincide with other chronological aspects of the era.
13. Of the twelve councillors, seven are known to have reincarnated in the twentieth century, having been intuitively directed to Edgar Cayce for life readings. (See 294–153 supplement, Millicent Horton's history of Ra Ta era, p. 6.)
14. Reading 5750–1.
15. Reading 294–148.
16. Genesis 5:24, KJV.
17. See article, "As Above, So Below," by W. H. Church, *The A.R.E. Journal,* vol. IX, nos. 3 and 4 (May and July 1974).
18. Reading 311–2
19. Ref. footnote, Reading 538–59.
20. Vol. I, p. 407, *The Gods of the Egyptians,* by E. A. Wallis Budge (Dover: New York, 1969).
21. Reading 294–151. (Note: 167 souls returned with Ra Ta from Nubia. This number may have represented "the faithful" who received the mark.)
22. Reading 991–1 (cf. 294–151).
23. Reading 294–141.
24. Reading 294–151.
25. Reading 1472–10.
26. Reading 900–275.
27. Reading 866–1.
28. Reading 440–5.
29. Reading 5749–2.
30. Reading 378–14.
31. Reading 341–9.
32. Reading 5748–5.
33. Reading 3976–15.
34. Reading 294–151.

35. Reading 378–16. (Also see Q&A–5, Reading 3976–15.)
36. Page 87, *Earth Changes Update,* by Hugh Lynn Cayce (A.R.E. Press: Virginia Beach, Va., 1980.)
37. Reading 275–33.

CHAPTER 6

1. Genesis 18:22, KJV.
2. Hebrews 7:3, KJV.
3. Reading 5749–14.
4. Reading 5023–2.
5. Reading 262–119.
6. Genesis 12:7, KJV.
7. Page 17, *An Introduction to the Cabala,* by Z'ev ben Shimon Halevi (Samuel Weiser: New York, 1972).
8. Ref. article, "Sea Shell Evidence of an Old Flood," *San Francisco Chronicle,* September 22, 1975. See also report by Cesare Emiliani, prof. of marine geology in *Science,* September 22, 1975.
9. Reading 5755–1.
10. Reading 827–1.
11. Reading 5749–14.
12. Reading 900–10.
13. Reading 1152–11.
14. Genesis 19:27, 28, KJV.
15. Reading 294–136.
16. Reading 1616–1.
17. Reading 1859–1.
18. Ezekiel 1:4, 5, 18, and 19, KJV.

CHAPTER 7

1. Reading 3976–15. (See GDT footnote, Reading 870–1, for further explanation of 8058 B.C., dating.)
2. Reading 288–48.
3. Reading 507–1, Supplement.
4. Reading 5001–1.
5. Reading 1265–1.
6. Reading 993–1.
7. Reading 294–174.
8. Reading 2091–2.
9. Reading 2072–8.
10. Reading 538–32.
11. Reading 333–2.
12. Reading 288–1.
13. Reading 2709–1.
14. Reading 294–138.
15. Reading 294–142.
16. Ibid.

CHAPTER 8

1. Reading 262–9.
2. Reading 2886–1.
3. Reading 900–63.
4. Reading 900–38.
5. Reading 692–1.
6. Reading 470–2.
7. Reading 5717–5.
8. Reading 281–8.
9. Reading 262–24.
10. Reading 294–8.
11. Reading 900–63.

CHAPTER 9

1. Page 70, *Twelve World Teachers: A Summary of Their Lives and Teachings,* by Manly Palmer Hall (Philosophical Research Society: Los Angeles, 1947).
2. Ref. chap. 2, part 9, "Pythagoras," in *The History of Philosophy,* by Thomas Stanley (facsimile of 1687 ed. reproduced by Philosophical Research Society: Los Angeles, 1970). Hereafter referred to as Stanley.
3. Page 159, *City of Revelation,* by John Michell (David McKay: New York, 1972).
4. Page 329, *Age of Fable* by Bulfinch (New American Library edition: New York, 1962).
5. Ref. "Pythagoras and Pythagoreanism," *Encyclopaedia Britannica.*
6. Page 674, vol. 18, *The Symbolic Life,* The Collected Works, Bollingen Series XX (Princeton University Press: Princeton, N.J., 1976).
7. Page vii, "Introductory Essay," Stanley.
8. "The Edgar Cayce Readings," Library Series, vols. 4 and 5, *Dreams and Dreaming* (Association for Research and Enlightenment: Virginia Beach, Va., 1976).
9. Page 98, *The Phoenix,* by Manly P. Hall. (Philosophical Research Society: Los Angeles, 1971).
10. Reading 275–43.
11. Pages 565–66, Stanley.
12. Reading 699–1.
13. Page 114, *Astrology,* by Louis MacNeice (Doubleday: New York, 1964).
14. Page 184, edited by Frank Gaynor (Citadel Press: Secaucus, N.J., 1973).
15. Reading 1472–12 (also see 1472–13).

CHAPTER 10

1. Reading 6717–5.
2. Reading 2903–1.
3. Reading 538–59.
4. Reading 760–4.
5. Reading 5249–1.
6. Reading 1208–1.
7. Reading 3657–1.
8. Reading 2698–1.

CHAPTER 11

1. Reading 294–192.
2. Luke 10:1, KJV.
3. Reading 254–83.
4. Revelation 3:15, 16, KJV.
5. Reading 1598–2.
6. Reading 816–4.
7. Reading 294–192.
8. Reading 2310–2.
9. Reading 866–1.
10. Reading 294–192.
11. Reading 538–59.
12. Reading 2390–1.
13. Reading 2390–3.
14. See Readings 2390–3 and 1523–16.
15. Reading 2390–1.
16. Ibid.
17. Reading 1523–16.
18. Reading 1990–3.
19. Reading 3685–1.
20. Reading 2574–1.
21. Reading 1468–1.
22. Reading 5755–1.

CHAPTER 12

1. Reading 294–161.
2. Reading 2464–2.
3. Ibid.
4. Reading 294–161.
5. Reading 5717–5.

CHAPTER 13

1. Reading 3660–1.
2. Reading 294–19.
3. Reading 2753–2.
4. Reading 3416–1.
5. Readings 3027–2 and 1771–2.
6. Reading 2072–1.
7. Reading 1097–2.
8. Reading 866–1.
9. Reading 5281–1.
10. Reading 69–1.
11. Reading 415–1.
12. Reading 543–11.
13. Reading 415–1.
14. Reading 543–11.

15. Reading 500–1.
16. Reading 289–9.
17. Reading 405–1.
18. Reading 264–31.
19. Reading 294–8.
20. Reading 2390–1.
21. Reading 900–25.
22. Reading 5755–1.
23. Reading 294–8.
24. Ibid.
25. Ibid.
26. Reading 294–19.
27. Reading 294–8.
28. Reading 427–3.
29. Reading 1541–11.
30. Reading 1523–11.
31. Reading 2778–2.
32. Reading 369–3.
33. Reading 243–10.
34. Reading 3635–1.

CHAPTER 14

1. Reading 1001–7.
2. Reading 2508–1.
3. Page 47, *The Sun King,* by Nancy Mitford (Harper & Row: New York, 1966).
4. Ibid., p. 54.
5. Reading 288–5.
6. Reading 294–9.
7. Ibid.
8. Reading 288–6.
9. Reading 1523–13.
10. Reading 4121–2.
11. Reading 294–147.

CHAPTER 15

1. Reading 294–161.
2. Reading 2390–2.

CHAPTER 16

1. Reading 5748–5.
2. Reading 5749–5.
3. Reading 3976–15.
4. Reading 5749–5.
5. Reading 5749–4. (For a detailed account of the Second Coming, as presented in the Edgar Cayce readings, see *Gods in the Making,* by W. H. Church [A.R.E. Press: Virginia Beach, Va., 1983].)
6. Reading 1602–3.